Postcard History Series

Along Chautauqua Lake

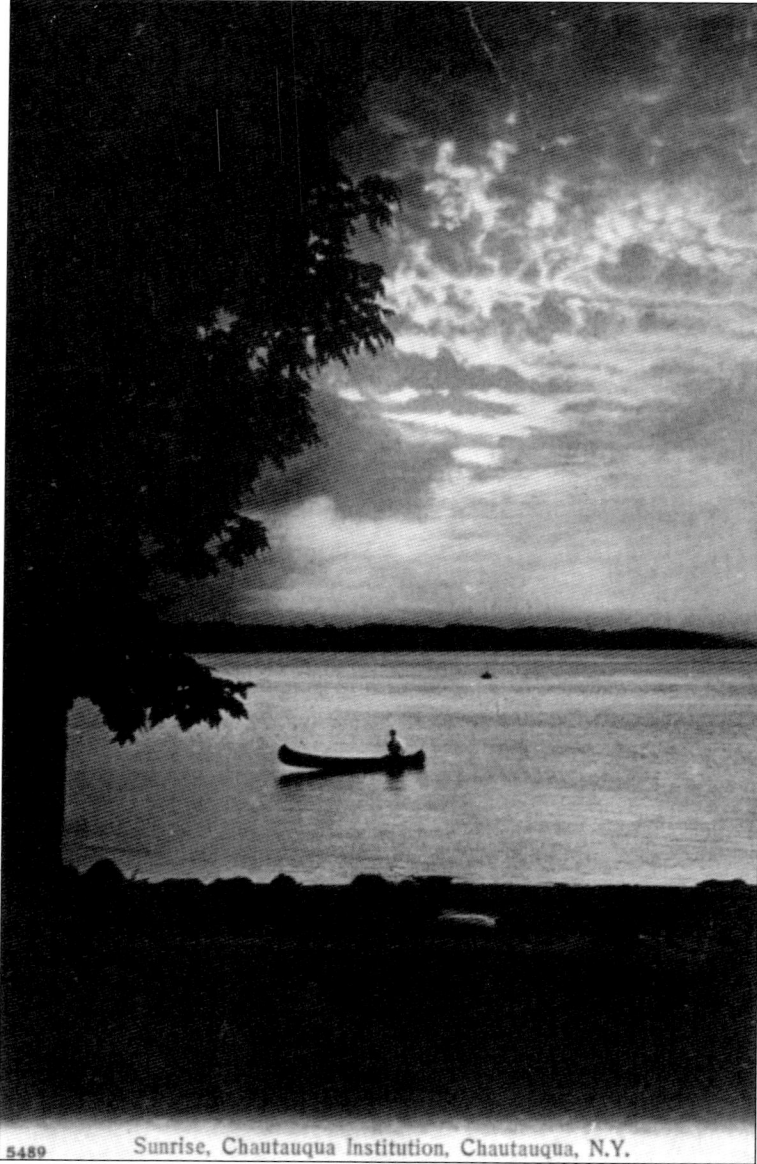

Chautauqua Lake drew thousands to its shores during the summer season. Celoron Park had as many as 40,000 people one Fourth of July. The steamboats carried hundreds of people at a time. Trolleys could speed fewer riders per car but make many trips in the same time. Yet the lake could give the individual a quiet solitude for relaxation and contemplation. (Courtesy of the author's collection.)

ON THE FRONT COVER: The dock at Celoron Park was very long because of the shallow depths of the lower lake. This dock was the first stop for steamboats leaving from the Jamestown Boatlanding. Trolleys went to the end of the dock for passengers to transfer from one mode of transportation to the other. Small boats were rented at the park and elsewhere for pleasure or fishing. (Courtesy of the author's collection.)

ON THE BACK COVER: Rowboats could be rented all along the lake, and the many inlets to the lake offered secluded spots that became destinations for rowers. This family at the Dewittville Inlet may have rowed in from close-by Point Chautauqua. Rowboats rented by fishermen came equipped with fishing gear as part of the rental. Rowing was a leisure activity during the resort era. (Courtesy of the author's collection.)

POSTCARD HISTORY SERIES

Ch

Karen E. Livsey and Dorothy E. Levin

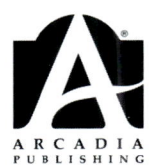

Copyright © 2010 by Karen E. Livsey and Dorothy E. Levin
ISBN 978-0-7385-7289-5

Published by Arcadia Publishing
Charleston SC, Chicago IL, Portsmouth NH, San Francisco CA

Printed in the United States of America

Library of Congress Control Number: 2009939869

For all general information contact Arcadia Publishing at:
Telephone 843-853-2070
Fax 843-853-0044
E-mail sales@arcadiapublishing.com
For customer service and orders:
Toll-Free 1-888-313-2665

Visit us on the Internet at www.arcadiapublishing.com

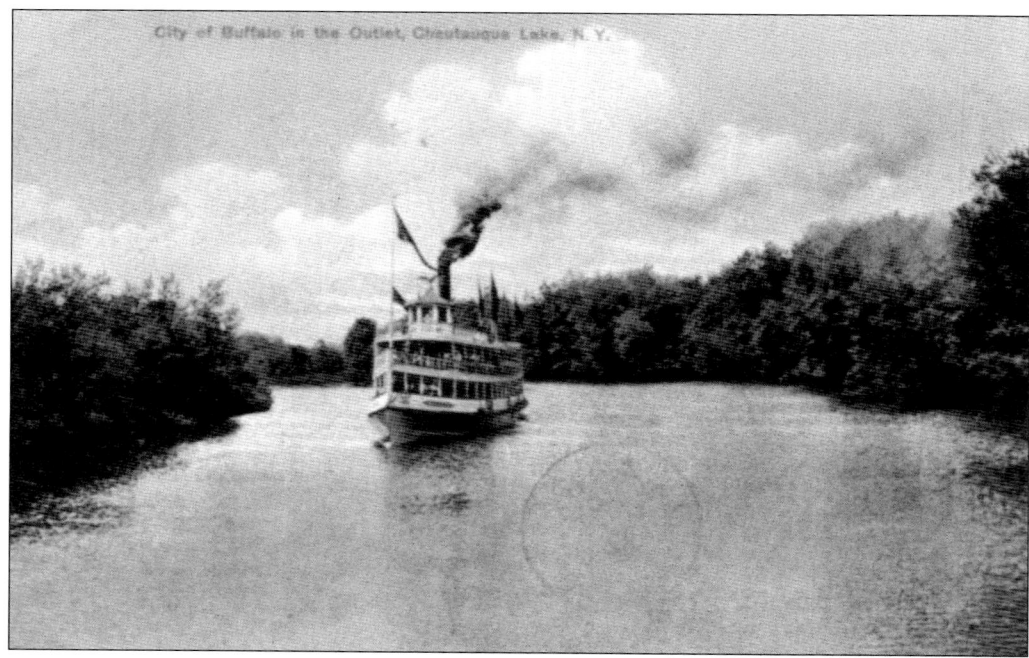

It took about 30 minutes for the large steamers to negotiate the nine bends of the Chadakoin River, the outlet of the Chautauqua Lake, between Celoron and the boat landing in Jamestown. This steamer, the *City of Buffalo*, plied these waters from 1890 to 1929. For more than 100 years, steamers transported people and supplies along Chautauqua Lake. (Courtesy of the author's collection.)

Contents

Acknowledgments		6
Introduction		7
1.	Jamestown and the Town of Ellicott	9
2.	Town of Busti	37
3.	Town of North Harmony	47
4.	Town of Chautauqua	57
5.	Town of Ellery	85
6.	Town of Ellicott and Jamestown	113
7.	The Steamboats	117

Acknowledgments

First we must express our thanks for Dottie's mother, Alice Levin, who collected many of these postcards during her lifetime. They are now part of the family's extensive collection of postcards. It is to Alice that we dedicate this book. Dottie has spent many hours (and dollars) in the pursuit of a very enjoyable hobby. It all started because she found a postcard and wondered just where the picture had been taken.

There are many others who have gone before us and recorded history—as stories, reminiscences, and published books and photographs. The details visible in the many photographs turned into postcards can sometimes only be identified after reading many accounts or even letters and diaries. The pieces are there and have to be put together just like a jigsaw puzzle. This is the fun part for Karen, who "always liked history." It was through genealogy that she realized that history did not happen somewhere else, as it did in history classes, but happened in the hometown and local area, making the research even more fun and challenging.

We thank all the recorders of local Chautauqua County history who have gone before and our colleagues who continue the study of the area's history. Jamestown's Fenton History Center-Museum and Research Center, where Karen is the librarian/archivist, holds many printed books and booklets, along with manuscript material, that were consulted for this project. We thank the research center and all of the staff for their support and cooperation during the creation of this volume.

We want to thank a fellow postcard collector, Marlin Casker, who lent some cards to help fill gaps in telling the story of Chautauqua Lake's Golden Age, from the late Victorian era into the 20th century. Cards from his collection are indicated by MC. The Fenton History Center also lent some cards to add more stories to the mix. These are indicated by FHC.

We hope that you enjoy this selection of postcards about the many places and activities along Chautauqua Lake from the 1880s through the 1920s. Unless otherwise noted, all images come from the collections of the authors.

—Karen E. Livsey and Dorothy E. Levin

INTRODUCTION

Early settlers in Chautauqua County chose land near the water. The McMahons favored the lake plain along Lake Erie. Alexander Findley settled on what was to be called Findley's Lake. The Prendergasts, Cheneys, Griffiths, and Bemuses chose to settle on Chautauqua Lake. Creeks and streams provided water for the settlers, and civilization moved away from the lakes. The hills surrounding the lake were covered with huge trees, and lumbering was an activity for the farmer and the lumberman from the beginning. Logs or sawn lumber were rafted down the lake in the spring through the connecting river system and sold along the way in the growing settlements of Pittsburgh and Cincinnati and even as far as New Orleans.

Chautauqua Lake, approximately 18 miles long and from 1,000 feet to 2 miles wide, is the largest lake in Chautauqua County. Running from the northwest to the southeast near the middle of the county, much of the county's watershed east of the escarpment flows into Chautauqua Lake. At the head of the lake, the Holland Land Company platted a village that became Mayville, the county seat. Along the lakeshore and its larger tributaries, families of farmers and lumbermen took up residence. James Prendergast realized the rapids in the outlet of Chautauqua Lake could provide waterpower for mills and purchased land, which became part of the present city of Jamestown. This all happened in the first decade of the 1800s.

Chautauqua Lake was the transportation route linking the settlements along the shore by boat and by ice in the winter. Keelboats and canoes provided a supply line in the early decades. Rough roads were the alternative routes. The first steamboat on Chautauqua Lake was the *Chautauque*, launched in 1828. The route of the *Chautauque* was from Mayville to Jamestown and back. Stops could be made along the lake to pick up or deliver people and goods. It was in the 1870s that business had increased enough for additional steamboats to be added to the lake. By then, a few people were able to just enjoy a ride on the steamboat.

There was good fishing and hunting along the lake that first provided sustenance for the early settlers and later food and recreation for residents and visitors. By 1836, Samuel Whittemore had built a hotel in Fluvanna, up the lake from Jamestown, to accommodate hunters, fishermen, and travelers. As urban life became crowded and hot in the summer, Whittemore's hotel became an escape for urban families. Chautauqua Lake was praised for its healthful climate and scenic beauty. More hotels appeared, and activities and pastimes were provided to entertain the guests. Soon development of resort areas began along Chautauqua Lake. Long docks and dredging enabled steamboats to stop at many of these places.

Long Point, a favored hunting spot, became a picnic grove after the Civil War, with steamboats stopping to disembark picnickers and later picking them up on a return run. Other areas became picnic groves, more hotels appeared, the railroads expanded, and travelers from the urban centers of Pittsburgh, Cleveland, Buffalo, Cincinnati, New York City, and spots in between came for a few weeks or for the summer. Local residents sought a respite by the lake.

The mid-1880s found horse-drawn trolleys in the city of Jamestown. The trolley company electrified the lines in 1891, and the expansion of the lines began. The trolley line went to Celoron, and another branch went to Lakewood. At Celoron, the trolley company opened a trolley park, which provided entertainment and a destination to entice more riders for the trolleys. A succession of railroad companies operated trains along the east side of the lake, while the trolley company expanded its line along the west side all the way to Mayville. Extensions over the hill to Westfield made connections to more rail lines available.

Railroads began offering special excursion rates for a day trip to the Chautauqua Lake area. These excursion trains coordinated with the trolleys and steamboats spreading the day-trippers along Chautauqua Lake to enjoy a pleasant day "in the country" and be entertained.

As these picnic groves, hotels, and amusements were developing, postcards and photography were also developing. Photographers were looking for images, and the views of Chautauqua Lake and its resort areas were readily captured by the camera. These photographs could then be printed on the new postcards that were capturing the imagination of the visitor. Government-issued postcards entered the communication scene in the early 1870s. Postage was a penny, delivery was speedy, and they were a hit with the public. The *Jamestown Evening Journal* in 1876 carried the comment that because of postcards, mail delivery would be slower, and the postmen would still only be able to read half of the postcards they had to deliver.

Private mailing cards were allowed beginning on May 19, 1898. Still only the address was allowed on the back and the picture on the front often had a short message scrawled over or around the image. In 1901, the designation "post card" was allowed to be used by private publishers but the undivided back was still only for the address. The date March 1, 1907, marked the change to a divided back, allowing writing on part of the back along with the address. These restrictions help date the cards today if there is no postmark. These cards, besides being mailed to family and friends, were highly collectible as mementos of a person's trip. Albums in which to keep and display postcards were popular. These albums, when found today, may have postcards of the original owner's trips or the postcards may be of the many places visited by friends and relatives.

Photographs of any picnic grove, scenic landscape, or activity that people visited appeared on postcards. Today these postcards are still collected by later generations to enjoy a bygone era. Some places on the cards still exist; others have disappeared or changed greatly. Family historians like to find postcards or photographs of the places that were part of their family's history.

The images chosen for this book are postcards depicting the activity and places enjoyed in the 1880s through the 1920s by year-round residents, summer residents, and visitors along Chautauqua Lake. Cars have replaced the trolleys and passenger railroads. Pleasure boats, jet skis, and one replica steamboat now ply the waters of Chautauqua Lake. Today bathers bare more of their bodies, and rowing a boat is considered work. Fishing is still a prime activity year-round, and hunting is limited by the settled areas, but game still occupies the wooded areas and the farm fields. Picnics are still enjoyed. Tourists still spend days, weeks, or a few months along Chautauqua Lake and its rolling hills, with creeks and streams. A rural county, Chautauqua is still easily reached by a large portion of the population. New York City, Chicago, Cincinnati, Pittsburgh, Toronto, and Washington, D.C., are all within 500 miles of Chautauqua County.

Please enjoy these postcards as you travel along Chautauqua Lake to see the sights enjoyed by your parents, grandparents, or great-grandparents. The journey begins in the present city of Jamestown, going up the west side of the lake and following the trolley lines and steamboat stops. From the village of Mayville at the head of the lake, we will continue down the east side of the lake, returning to Jamestown and following the outlet out of the county.

One

Jamestown and the Town of Ellicott

The city of Jamestown and the town of Ellicott are both divided by the Chadakoin River, Chautauqua Lake's outlet. The Chadakoin flows through the city into the village of Falconer in the town of Ellicott. When Jamestown was incorporated as a city in 1886 and no longer under the jurisdiction of the Town of Ellicott, the town was split into two parts. Traveling from one part to the other involves going through the city of Jamestown or crossing the lake or outlet.

James Prendergast realized the outlet's waterpower potential and purchased acreage, which is now the west part of Jamestown. He built a sawmill and a gristmill, and he encouraged others to settle nearby. Originally called "The Rapids," the name was changed to Jamestown in honor of its founder and incorporated as a village in 1827. The first business district of the village developed along the Chadakoin as it flowed beyond the rapids.

Activity around the lake increased. In 1828, the first steamboat began its run between Mayville, the county seat at the head of the lake, and Jamestown, the industrial center on the outlet. The first lakeside hotel opened in Fluvanna, in the northern part of the town of Ellicott, in 1836. Popular with hunters and fishermen, the reputation of the hotel and the lake was carried back to urban centers and remembered when the same families wished to leave the unhealthy cities in the summer. Chautauqua Lake, 700 feet higher than nearby Lake Erie, was considered to be a healthy climate.

By the end of the Civil War, the railroads crossing the county gave a large segment of the population access to the Chautauqua Lake region. Steamboats and trains made timely connections to enable passengers to transfer and continue their journey to and from lakeside resorts. The boat landing became a busy place. Trolley lines expanded from Jamestown.

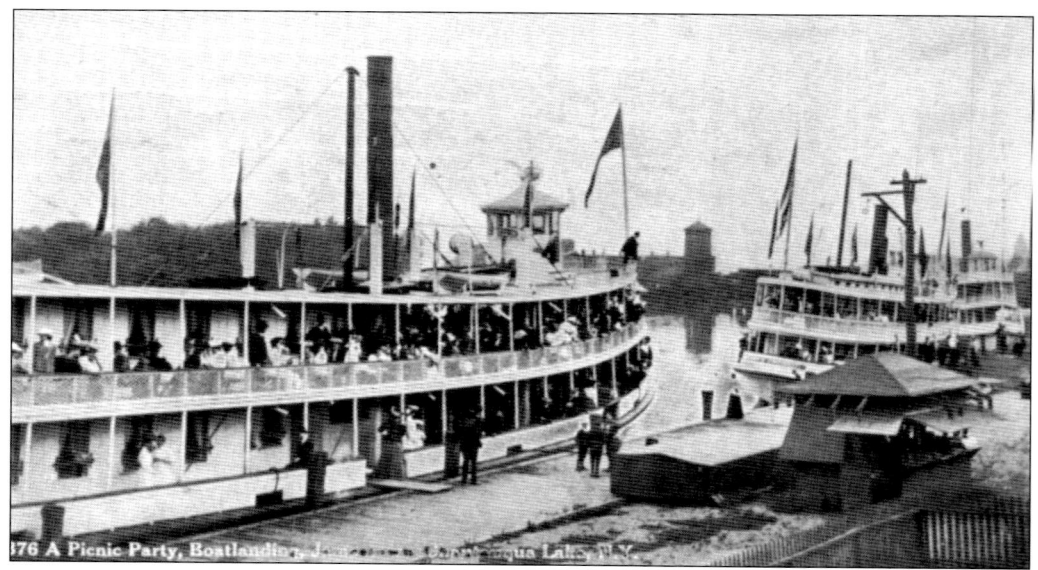

In 1828, a steamboat began plying the waters of Chautauqua Lake, providing transportation for people and supplies. The number of small steamboats grew, and soon more and larger steamboats transported picnickers to picnic groves and summer visitors to destinations along Chautauqua Lake. The Jamestown Boatlanding was the starting point for most of the trips on the lake. Here at the boat landing are two steamboats ready to transport picnickers. (Courtesy of MC.)

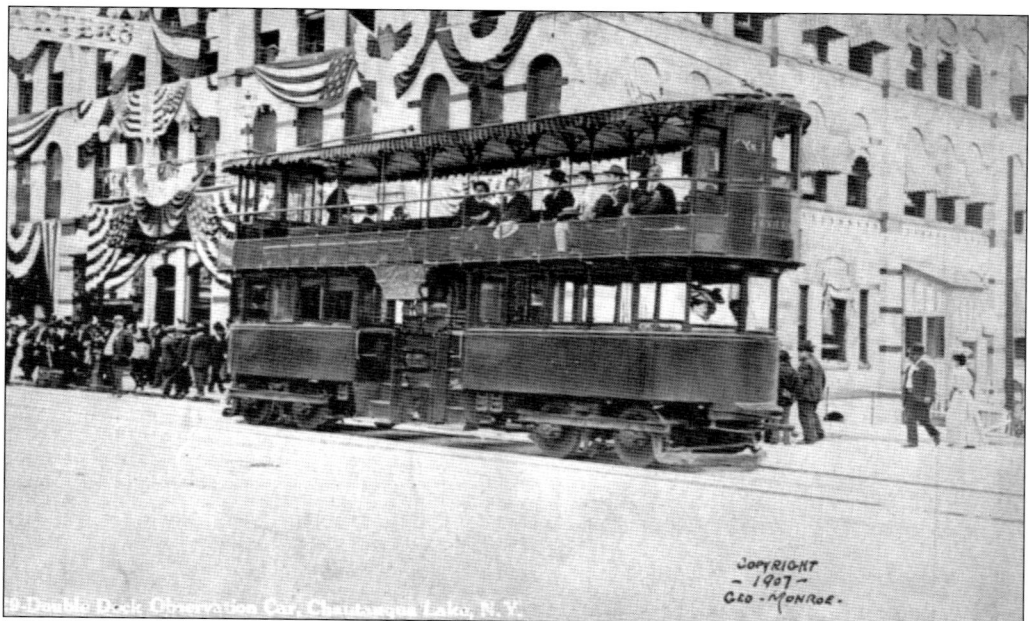

Later transportation along the lake included trolley lines. This is the *Columbia*, the showpiece car of the Jamestown Street Railway, in front of the Sherman House in Jamestown. The trolley line ran "around the hill" from Jamestown to the boat landing so passengers could transfer between trolleys and steamboats. Passengers could choose their transportation depending on the need for speed or which stopped at their destination.

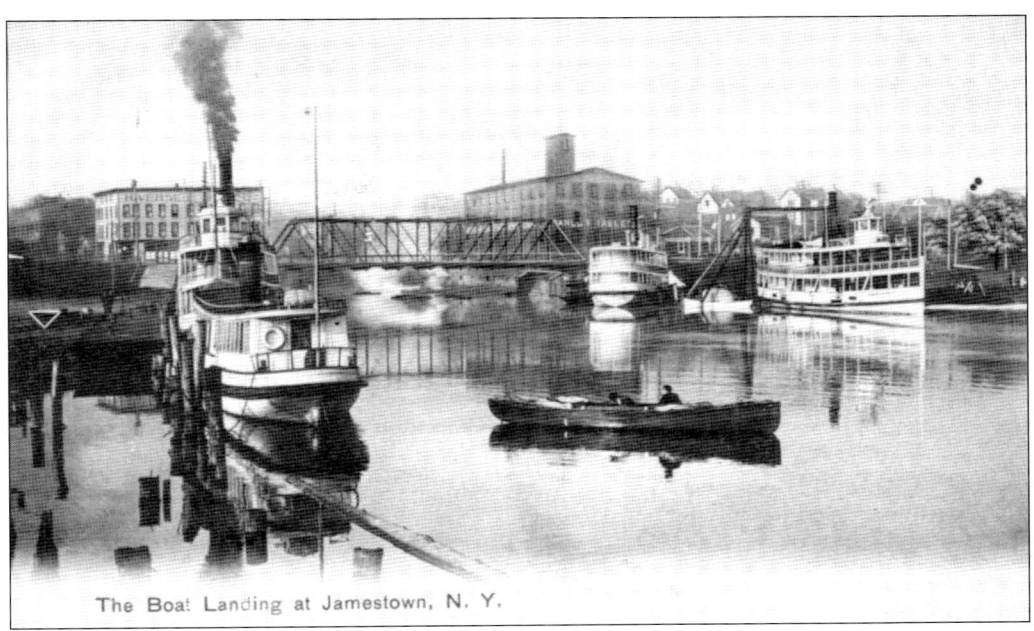

The Boat Landing at Jamestown, N. Y.

The boat landing in Jamestown provided anchorages for the large and small steamboats, with enough room to turn the boats. The iron bridge spanning the Chadakoin River connected Jamestown with the western shore of the lake. The trolley line eventually expanded over the bridge and along the shore to Celoron Park. The large building at the right end of the bridge is the Jamestown Table Company.

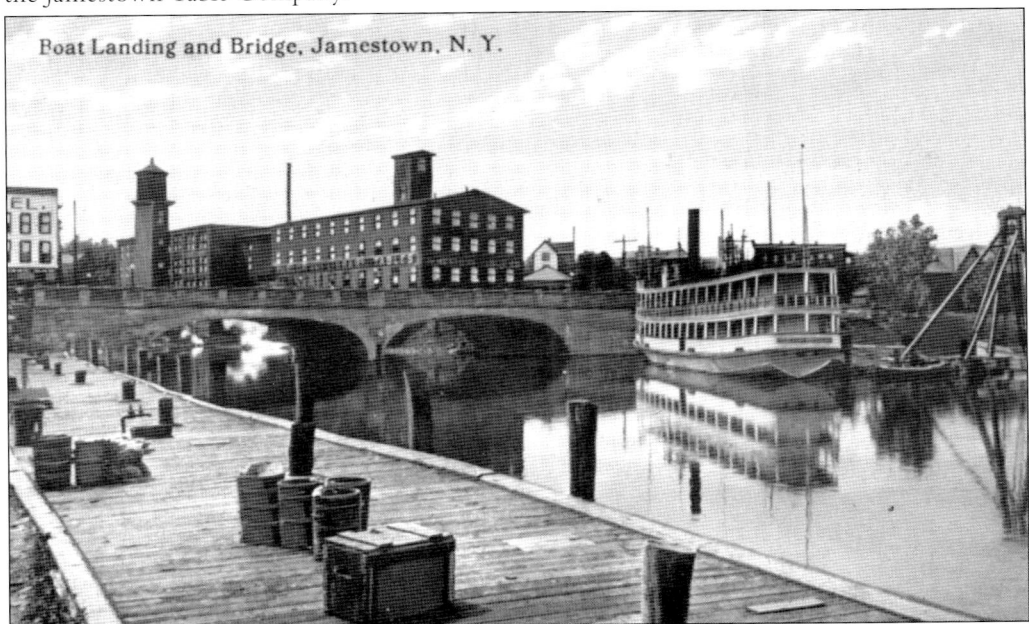

Boat Landing and Bridge, Jamestown, N. Y.

This picture, taken after September 1911, shows the completed concrete bridge, which replaced the iron one. This may have been taken shortly after its completion in September, when most of the steamboats would have been moved to winter quarters up the outlet at Clifton. The Jamestown Table Company factory has expanded with an addition.

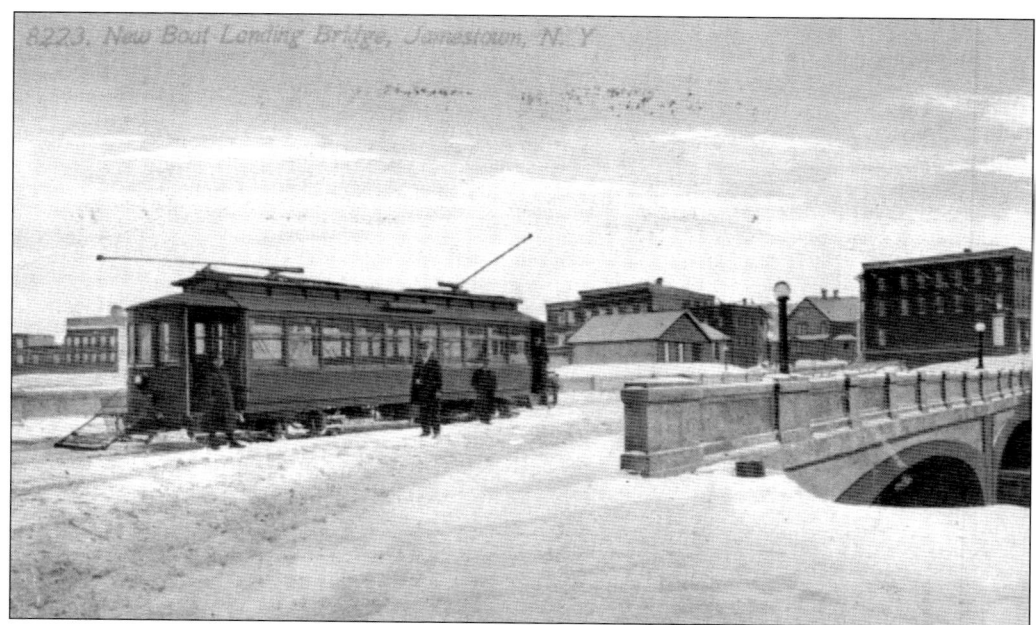

This is one of the 10 "Third Avenue Cars" purchased in 1909 from the Third Avenue Railway in New York City. These cars were used on the Lakewood and Falconer lines of the Jamestown Street Railway. This car is shown on the south end of the 1911 concrete bridge at the boat landing, ready for a run to Lakewood. The buildings in the background are along Eighth Street.

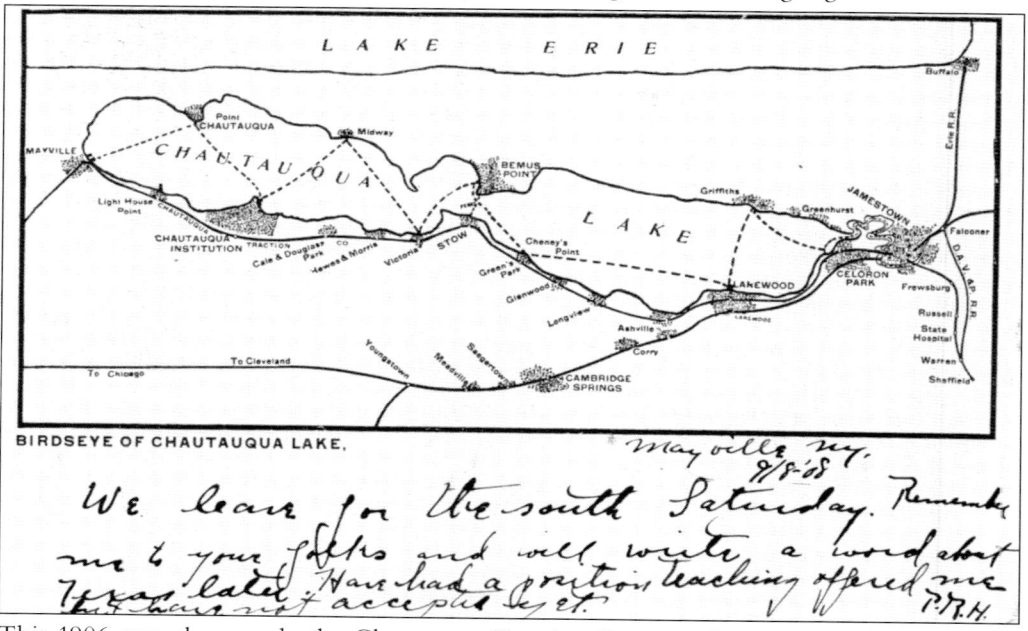

This 1906 map shows only the Chautauqua Traction Company line on the west side of the lake and the steamboat stops. The line was constructed in 1903–1904 and reached the Mayville Courthouse on September 1. This card could have been distributed by the Erie Railroad, which did extensive marketing, producing many brochures and offering excursion rates to Chautauqua Lake resorts. The trolley line connected with the Erie at Lakewood.

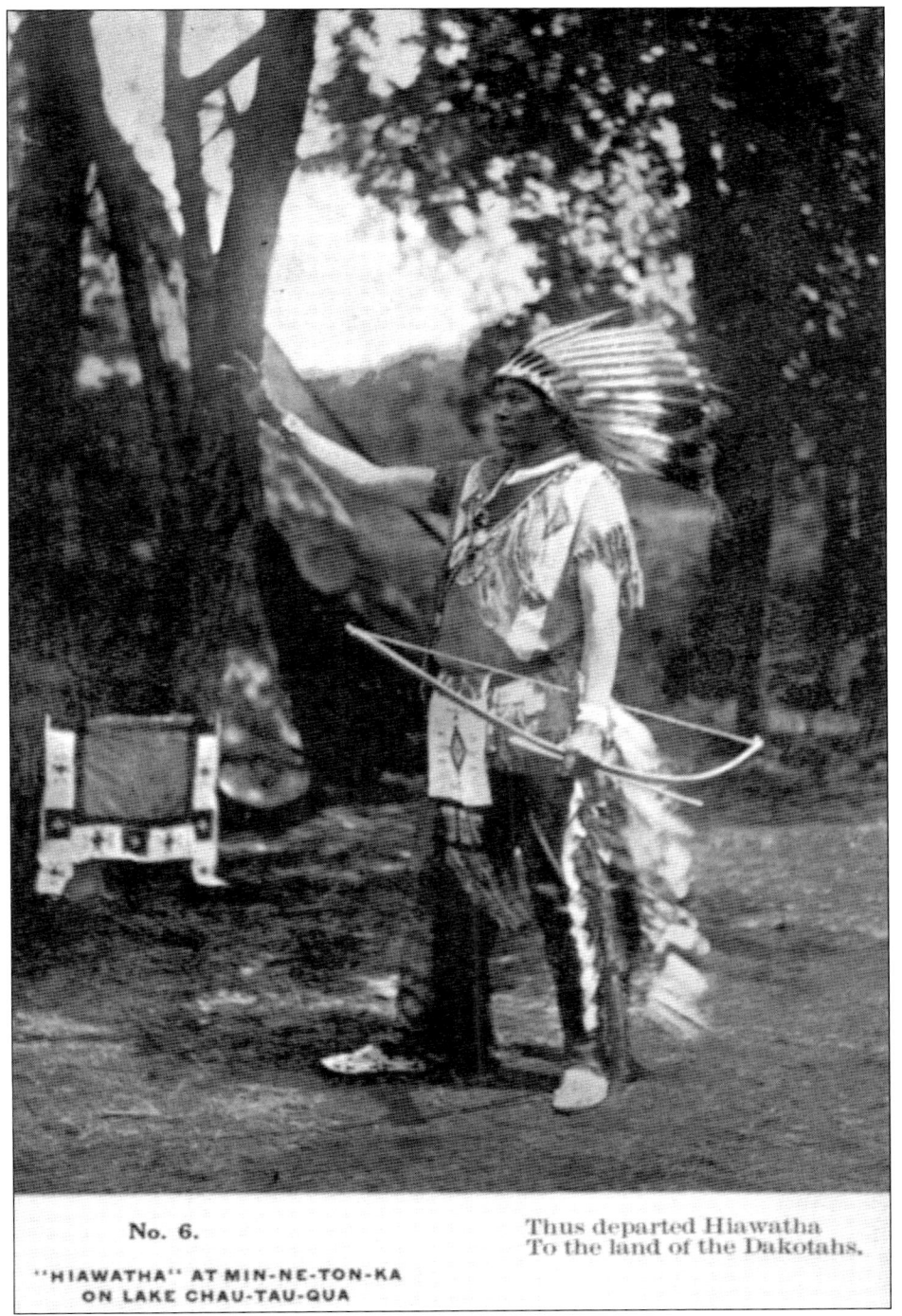

In 1906, the *Indian Passion Play* was produced at the Native American village Min-ne-ton-ka, set up in Jones Memorial Park between Celoron and the boat landing in Jamestown. When the play was not in progress, visitors could observe the Native Americans engaged in various lines of work. "Hiawatha ready to depart" was one of several cards produced.

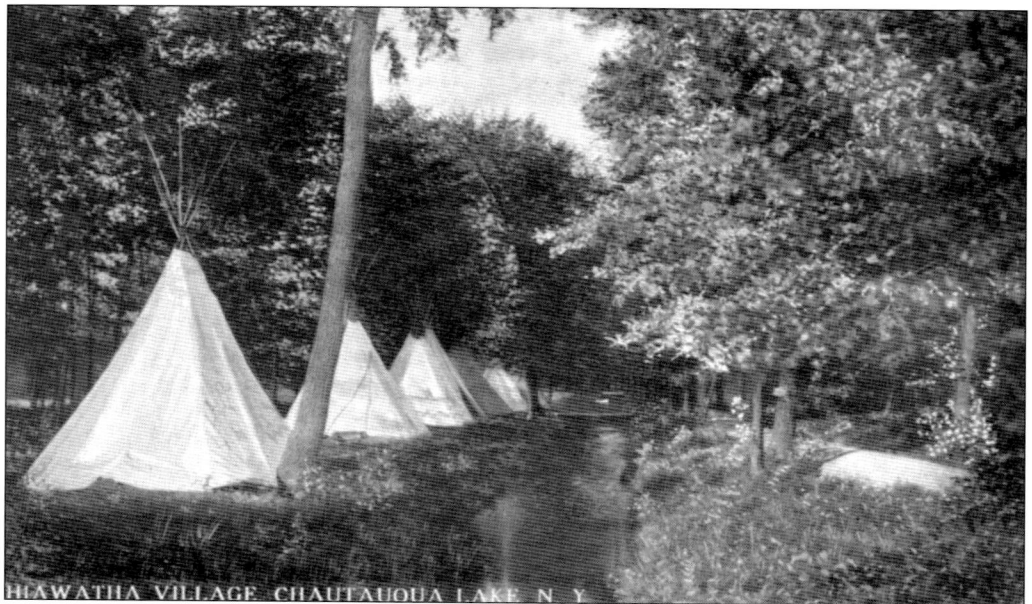

Another card shows the wigwams of the Native American village Min-ne-ton-ka, which were set up during the summers for the *Indian Passion Play*. A newspaper article mentioned that the wigwams had many examples of Native American picture writing on them that told of historical events of Native American legends. Some of those drawings are visible on these wigwams.

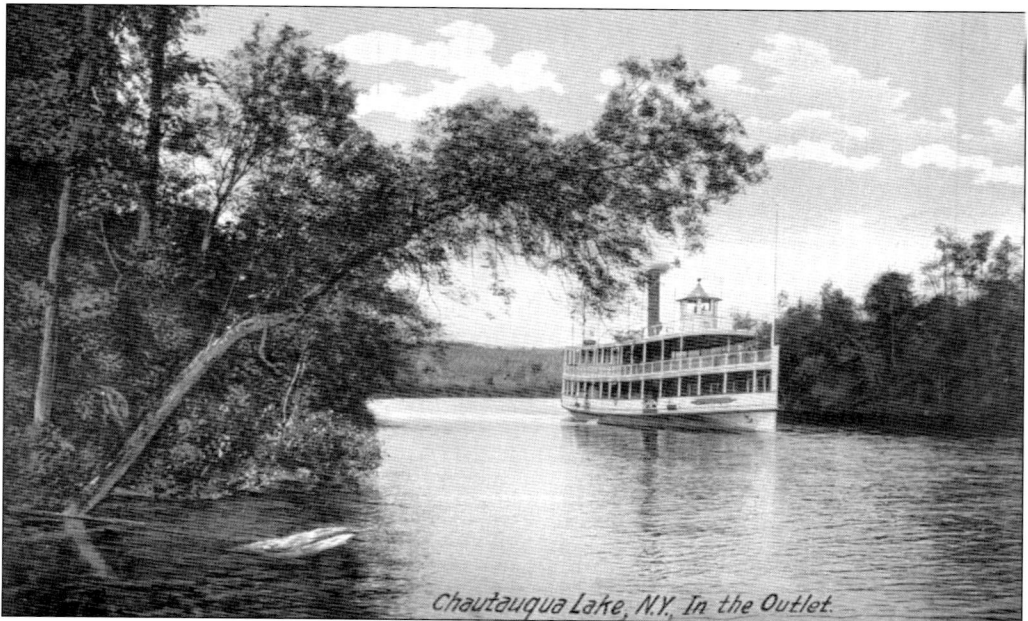

This classic postcard shows one of the fleet of large steamboats making its way along the winding outlet. Each day, all steamers had to make at least one trip through the outlet for another supply of coal. When the trolley line ran to the end of the steamboat dock at Celoron, passengers often preferred the 10-minute trolley ride to Jamestown over the half-hour steamboat cruise.

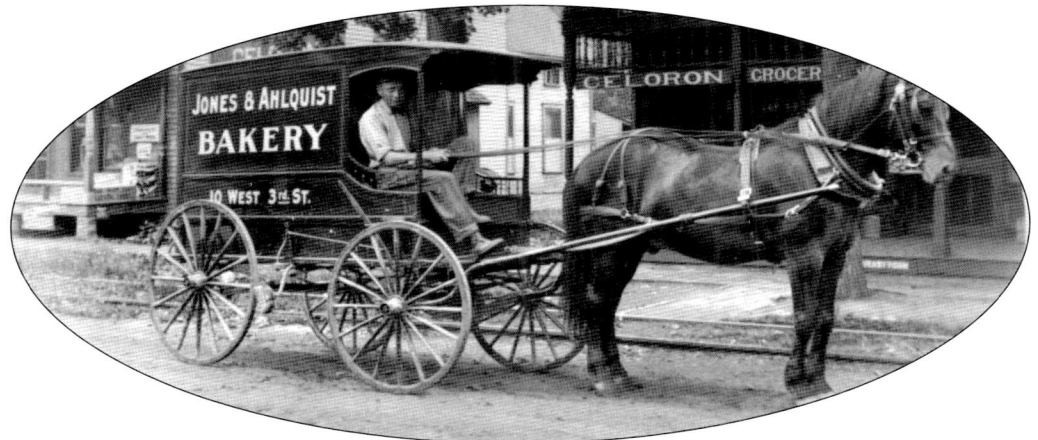

Started in 1907, this commercial bakery delivered baked goods to nearby communities. This delivery wagon is in front of the Celoron Grocery outside Celoron Park. Loaves of bread were loaded onto the steamboats for the many eating establishments along the lake. The Jones family continued the business until 2004, and now another generation has started a restaurant with a small bakery in Jamestown.

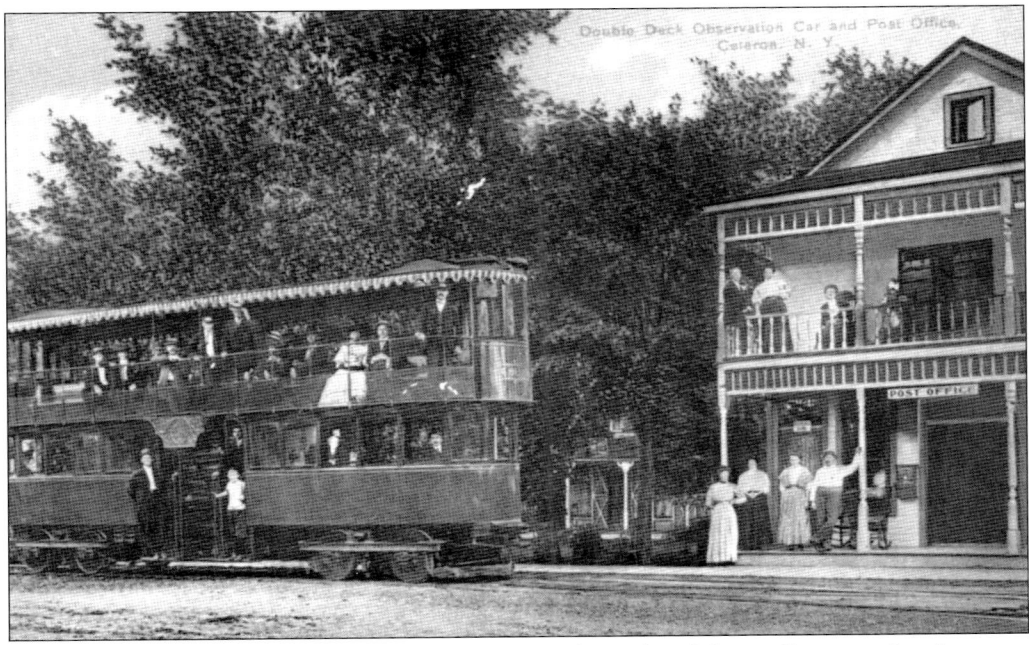

The *Columbia*, a double-decker streetcar, was used on the Celoron line running between Jamestown and Celoron Park. Here the *Columbia* is stopped in front of the post office in the village of Celoron, which was near the entrance to Celoron Park. The *Columbia*, brought many visitors to Celoron Park, a trolley park developed by the Jamestown Street Railway Company, the owner of the car.

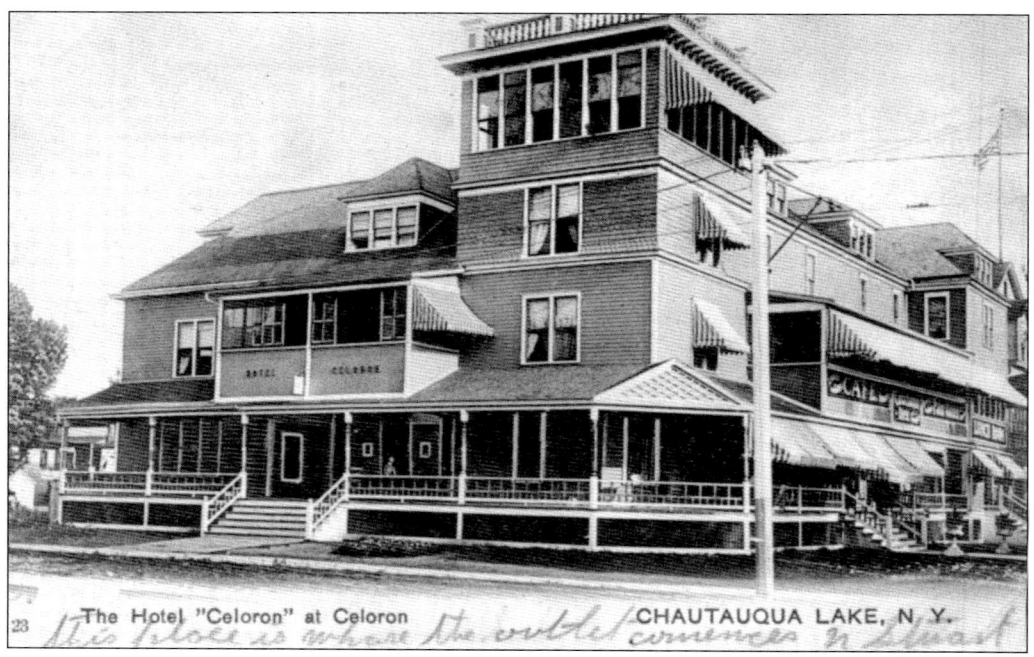

The Hotel de Celoron, built in 1892 on Dunham Avenue, benefitted from the next year's development of Celoron Park. The hotel served the many summer visitors to the park either by renting rooms or by providing lunches and dinners in its dining room. A 1902 fire damaged the pointed roofline of the tower section, which became a flat roof until the hotel was destroyed by fire in 1914.

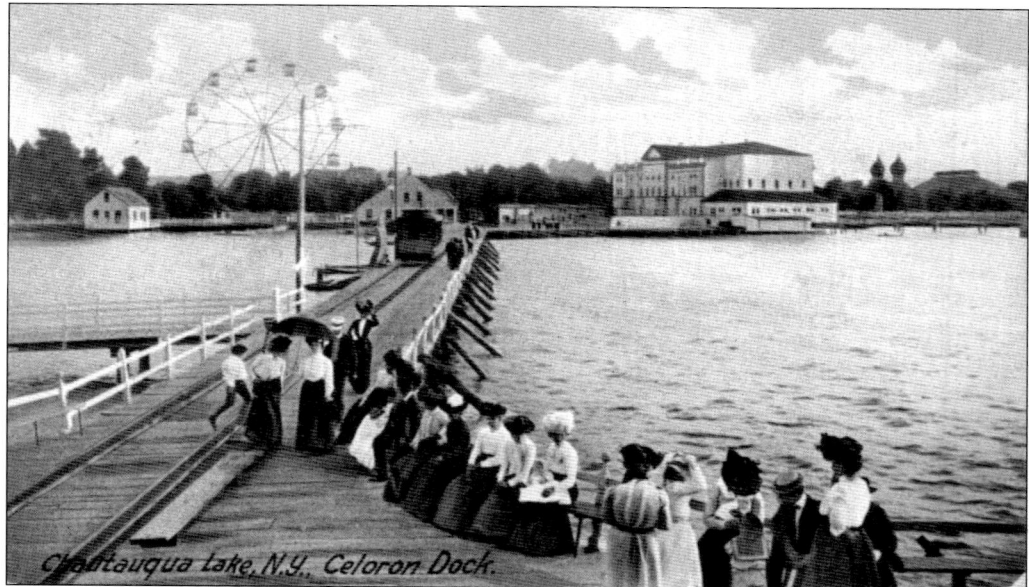

The long dock at Celoron Park carried the trolleys right out to the steamers, which docked at the end. This photograph shows people waiting for the next scheduled boat or trolley, and a trolley car is coming or going along the tracks laid on the dock. The skyline, from left to right, includes the Phoenix Wheel, the Richmond Hotel, the Celoron Theater, and the auditorium.

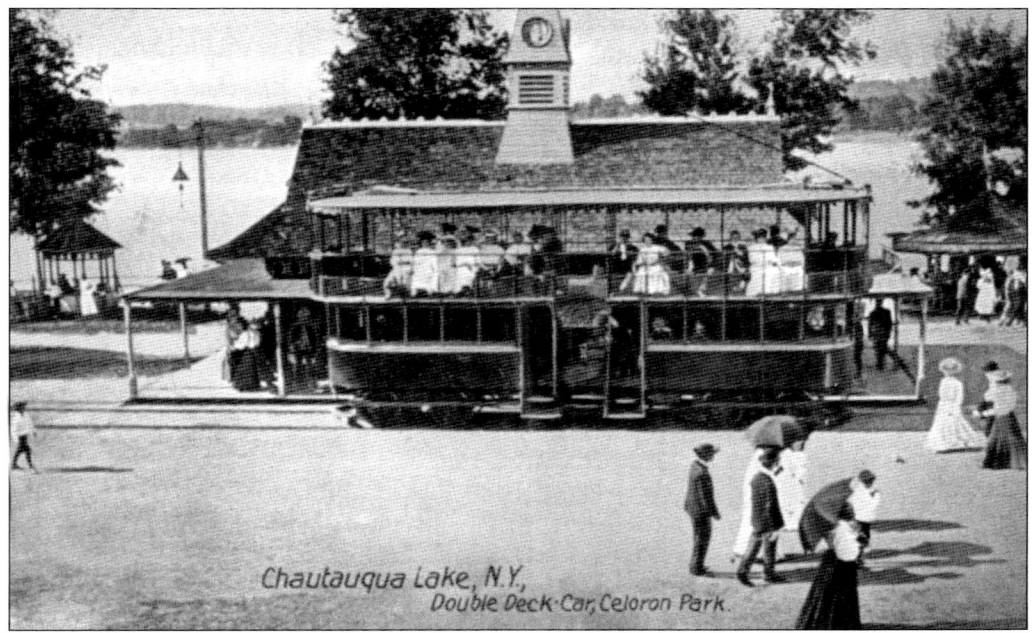

Purchased by the Jamestown Street Railway from the Pullman Palace Car Company, the double-decker car, seen here in front of the Penny Arcade at Celoron Park, was 35 feet long and 17 feet high. On the first level, the woman's compartment, finished in blue upholstery with carpets and curtains, was similar to the smoking compartment at the other end, which had light garnet plush upholstery and rubber matting.

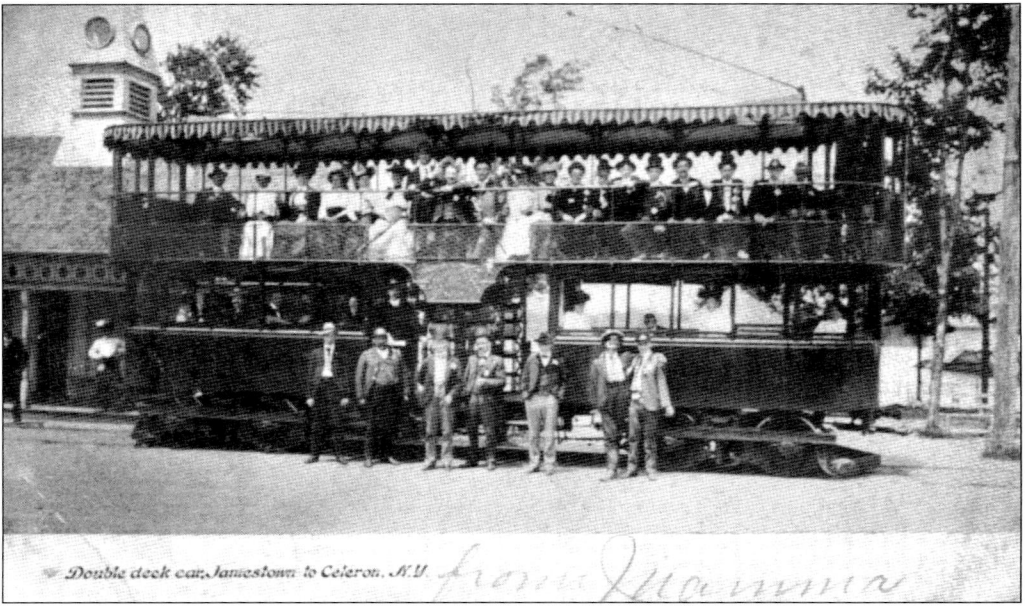

The outside, finished in dark blue with gilt stripes and bronze trimmings, had iron folding gates placed at each vestibule that looked similar to a Pullman sleeping car. The car weighed 16 tons, had a seating capacity of 72, and cost about $7,000. Each semicircle of seats afforded a view through the 12 plate-glass windows, while the upper deck was open with benches facing out.

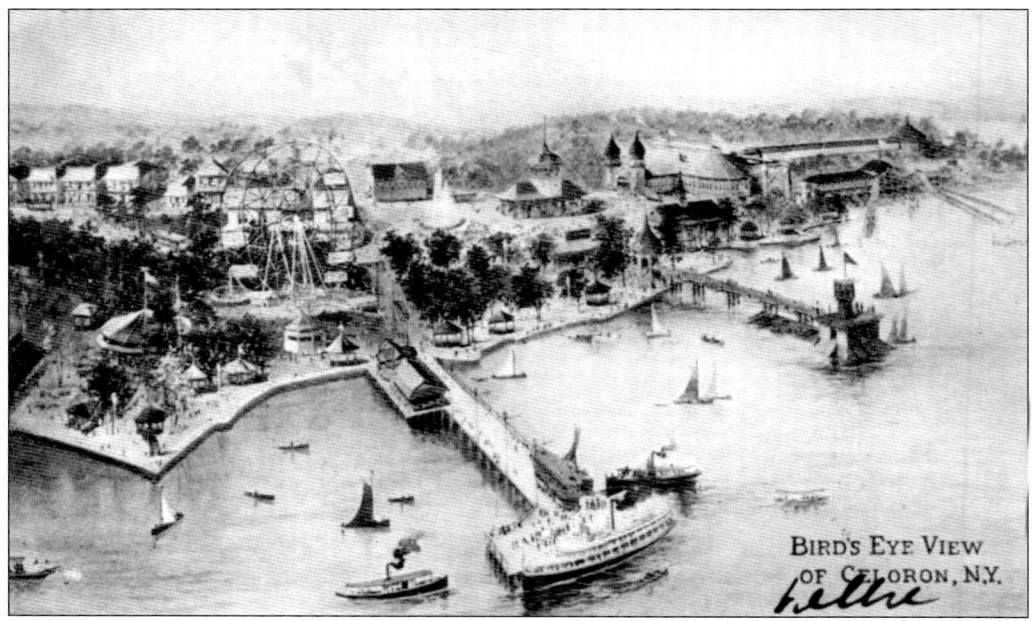

Celoron Park, the "Coney Island of the West," was developed beginning in 1893 by the Broadheads and the Jamestown Street Railway Company. It became a trolley park, providing a destination that encouraged people to ride the trolleys. Steamboats were an alternative transportation to the park. The Phoenix Wheel, a theater, a band shell, an auditorium, a baseball field, a zoo, and many rides and amusements awaited the summer visitor.

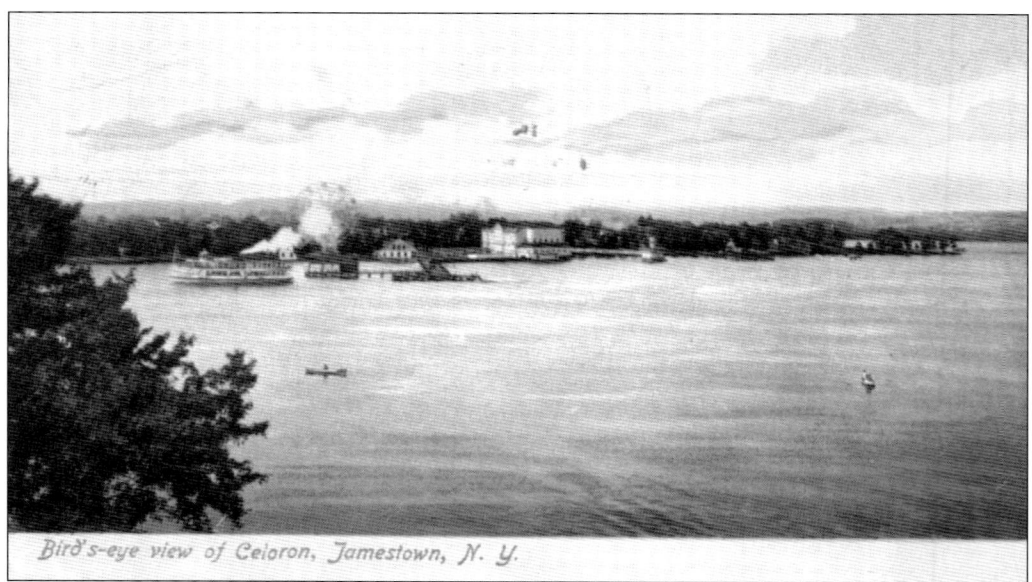

This Celoron Park view shows a steamboat leaving the dock, the Phoenix Wheel to the left of the dock, and the theater in the large building to the right. To the right of the theater in the water is the searchlight tower, while a bathhouse and its toboggan slides are farther to the right. The Hotel de Celoron can be seen behind the Richmond Hotel at the end of the dock.

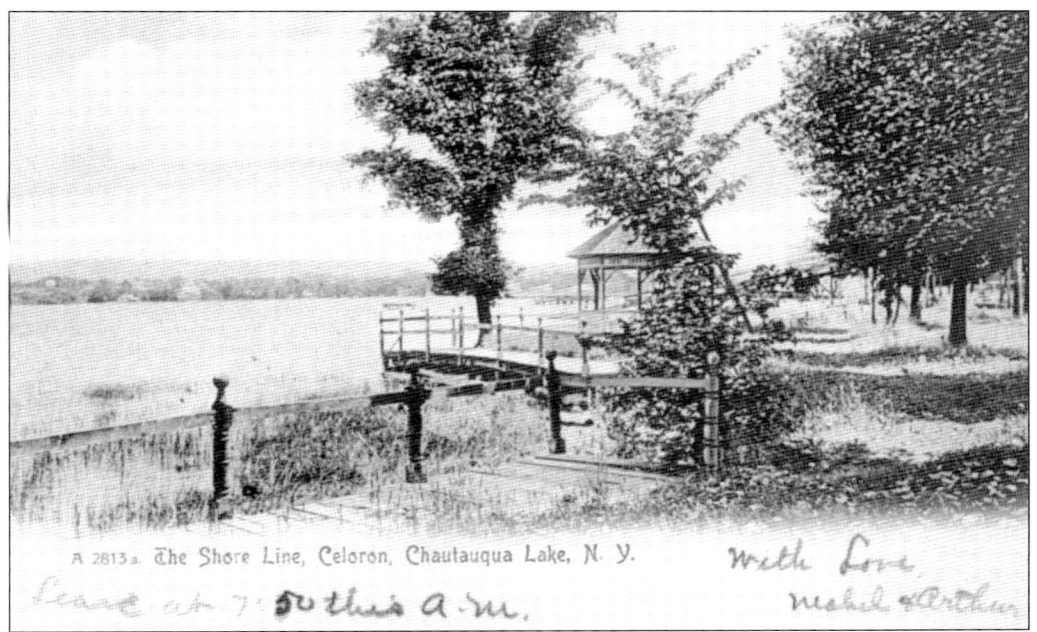

A gracefully curving boardwalk, with railings and alcoves providing seats, skirted the shore of Celoron Park. There were summerhouses to provide shade. Numerous stands for the sale of ice cream, popcorn, and other refreshments were scattered along the 3,500-foot boardwalk, which extended from one end of the park to the other. (Courtesy of FHC.)

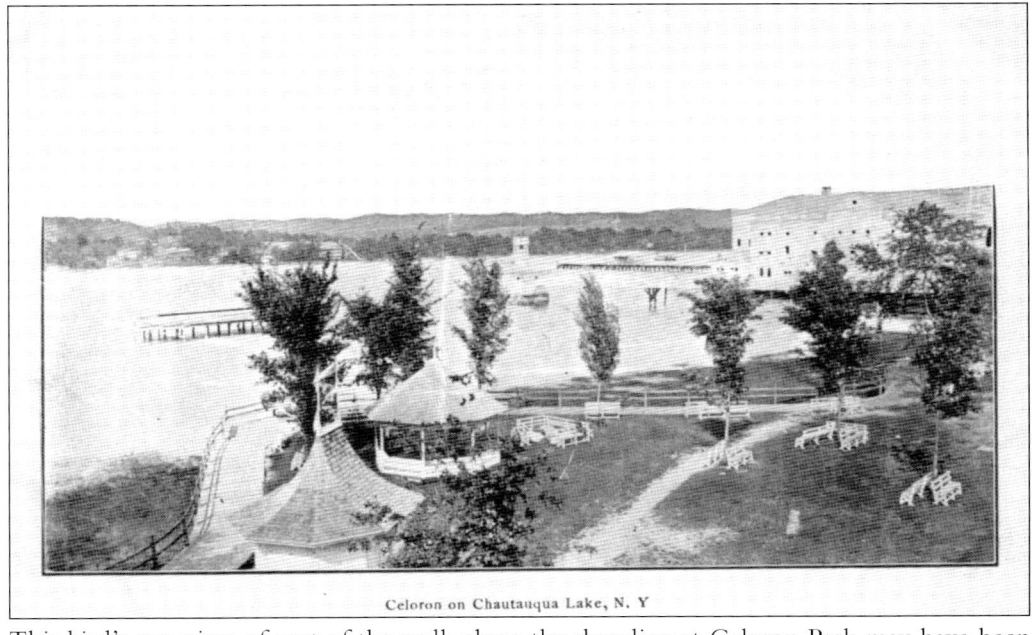

This bird's-eye view of part of the walk along the shoreline at Celoron Park may have been taken after the cement wall and walk were constructed in 1908. The searchlight tower can be seen in the center of the picture, and the large Celoron Theater is at right. More benches, pathways, and landscaping are evident compared to the earlier view above.

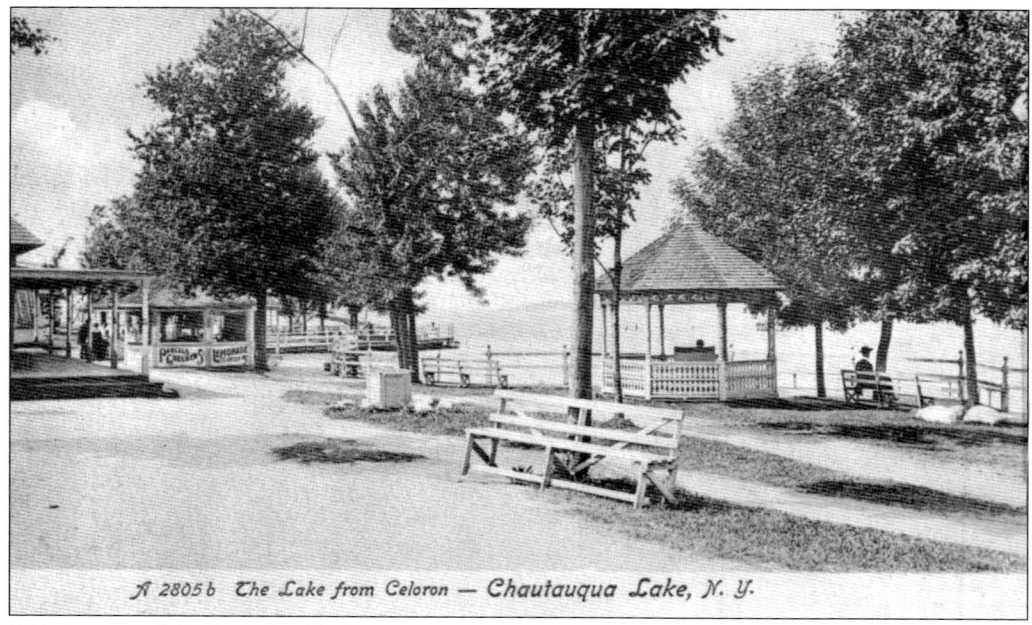

A 2805b The Lake from Celoron — Chautauqua Lake, N. Y.

This is part of the boardwalk that extended the length of the park. There are summerhouses, benches, and railings. On the left is part of the Penny Arcade, where the trolleys stopped. The other side of the Penny Arcade was the main open area where people could view the band shell, the open-air theater, the electric fountain, and other daily attractions. (Courtesy of FHC.)

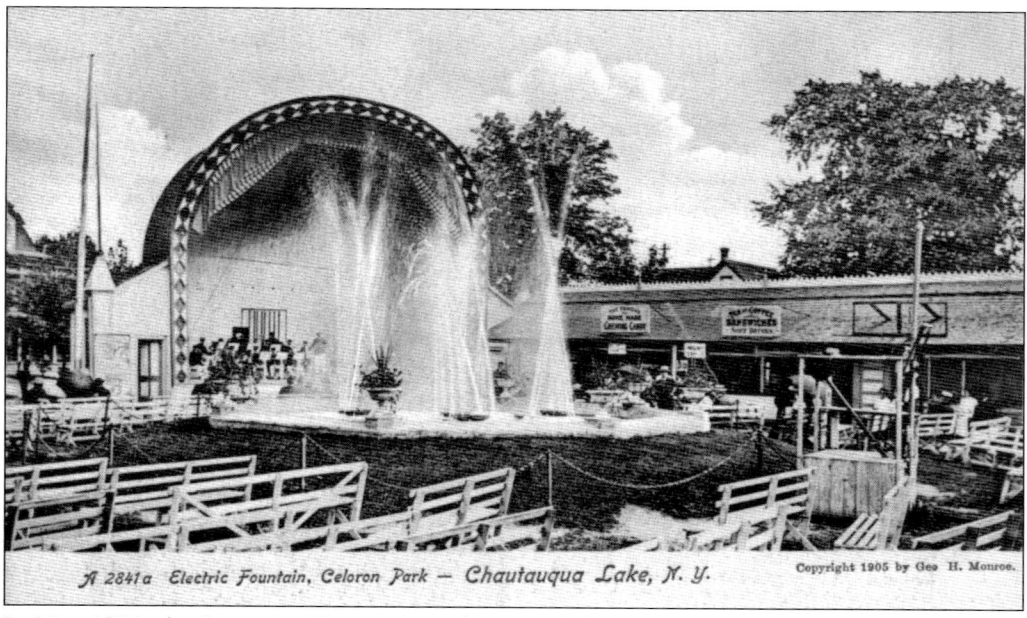

A 2841a Electric Fountain, Celoron Park — Chautauqua Lake, N. Y. Copyright 1905 by Geo H. Monroe.

In May 1894, the *Jamestown Evening Journal* reported that the electric fountain at Celoron Park was an exact duplicate of the ones at the Chicago World's Fair. The operator was concealed underground, and by means of a complicated system of valves and switches, he produced the most exquisite figures and colors in water and lights. It played most nights. (Courtesy of FHC.)

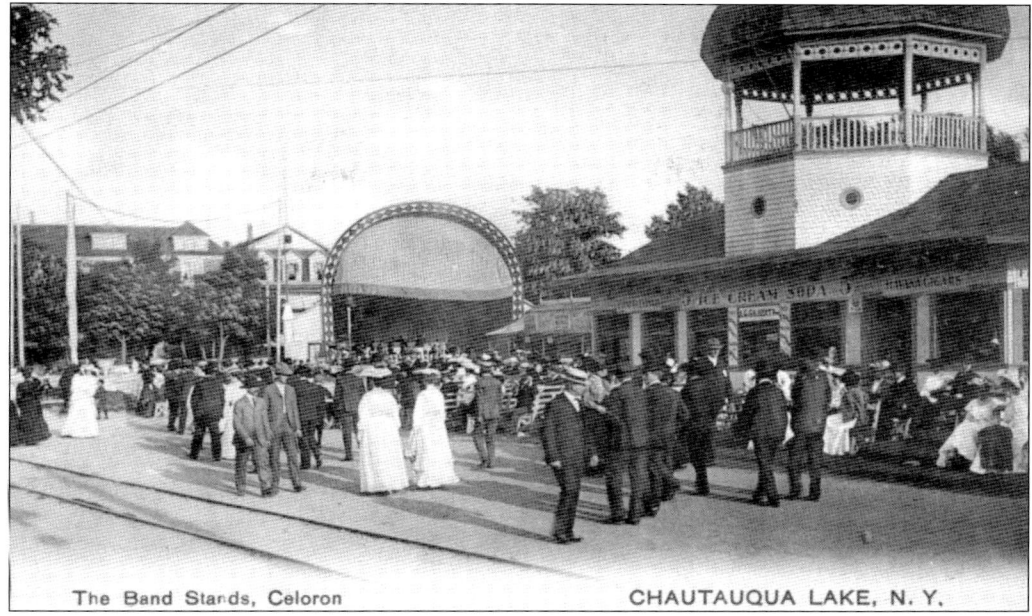

The building to the right was the pavilion, which had an ice cream stand on the first floor and a bandstand on the second level. The end of the long refreshment stand can be seen between the pavilion and the large band shell, with its striped awning. The trolley tracks can be seen in the foreground as the crowd looks for the next activity to attract their attention. (Courtesy of FHC.)

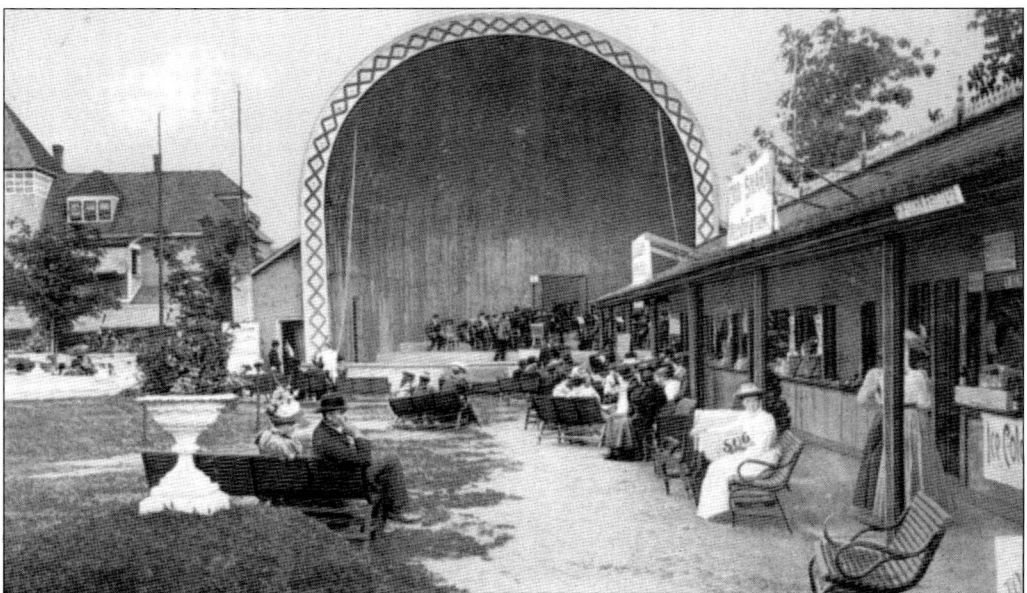

The large band shell, originally a theater on piles over the lake, is prominent in this picture. The half-dome structure became a band shell when it was moved inland so the water site could be used for the new Celoron Theater. The long building on the right housed refreshment and concession stands. The Hotel de Celoron's pointed roof indicates this photograph was taken before the hotel's 1902 fire. (Courtesy of FHC.)

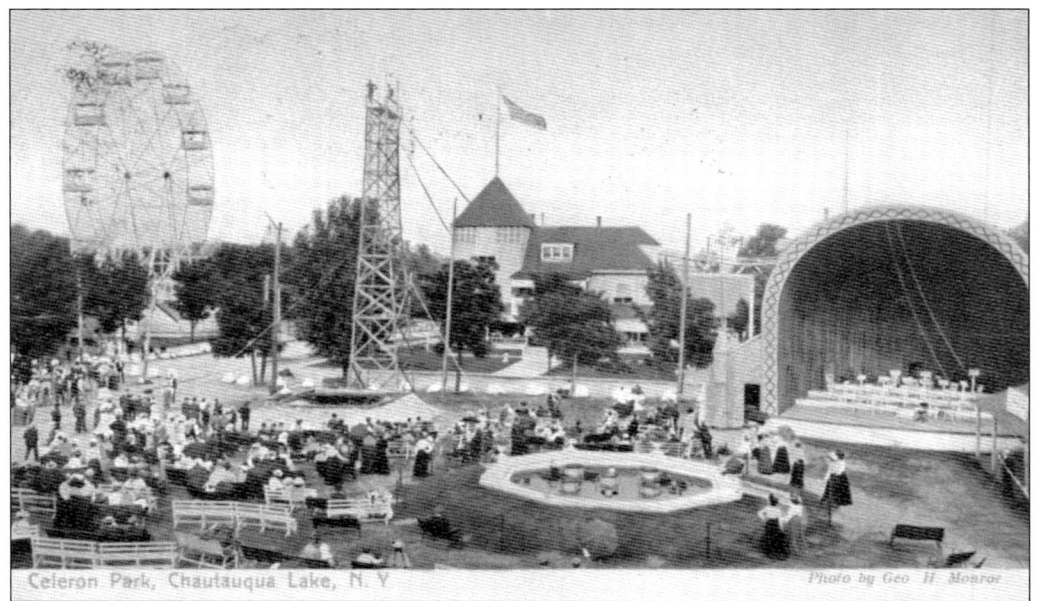

The Phoenix Wheel is to the left in this photograph. The tower was probably used for high diving, slack-rope walking, or some of the other performances at the park. The Hotel de Celoron is in the center background. On the right is the band shell. The stilled electric fountain is in the right foreground. Crowds are beginning to gather to enjoy the next scheduled attraction at the park.

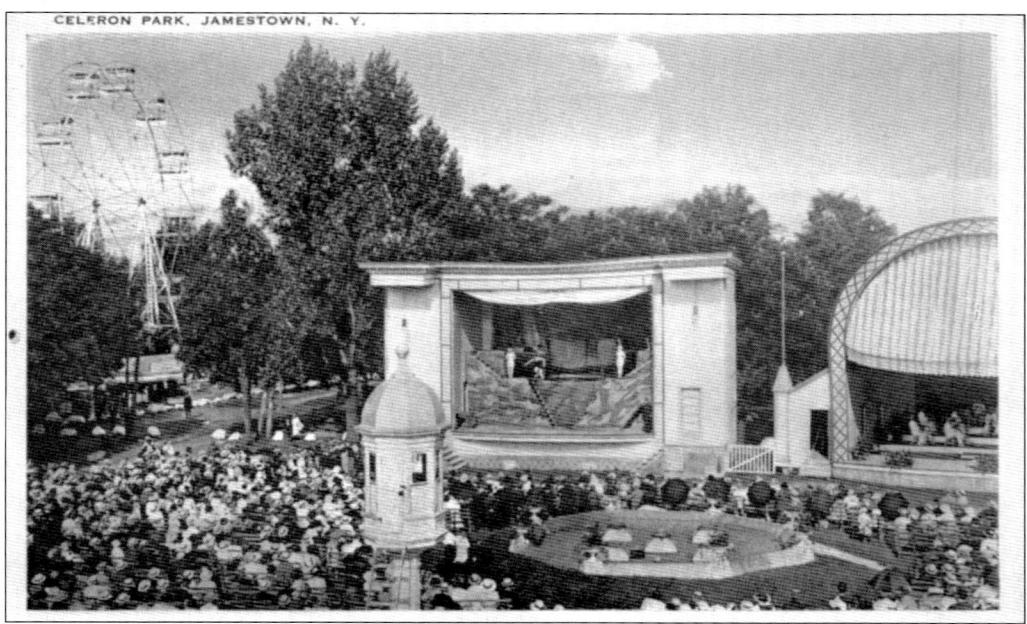

The center structure is the outdoor theater, built in 1909. The performances could be presented outdoors, and at night movies were shown on a large screen. The projection booth is in the center foreground. The movies were free for anyone in the park. After 1927, a sound system was hung on the side of the booth so the crowds could enjoy the "talkies."

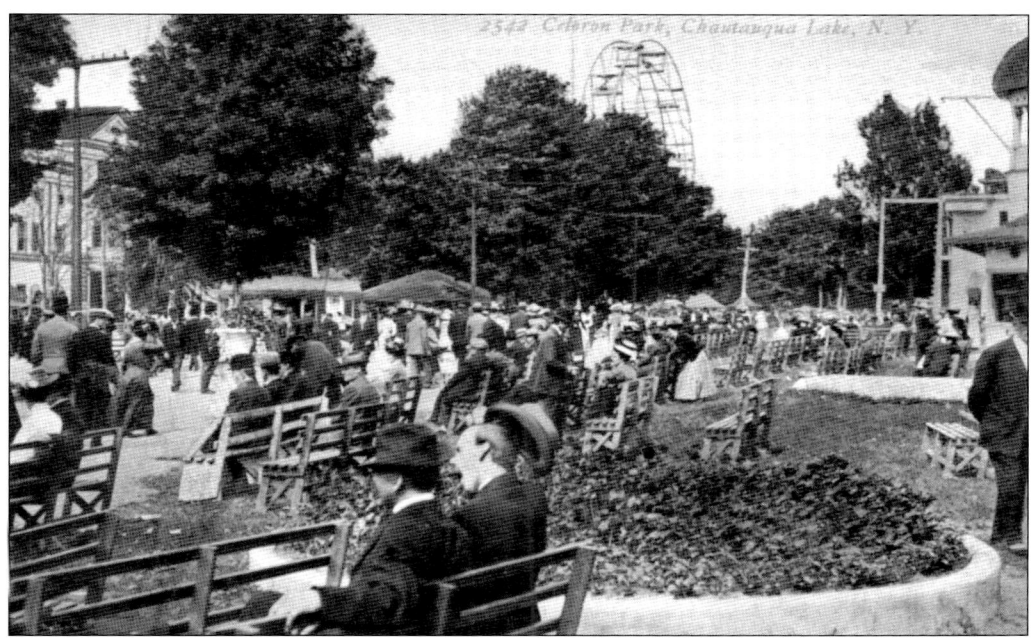

An afternoon crowd at Celoron Park is enjoying the good weather. Some are relaxing on the many benches that are facing the area where the trolleys arrive. The park was decorated with flower beds, as seen in the foreground. The Phoenix Wheel is in the background. The theater is to the left, and the pavilion, with the outdoor theater behind it, is just at the right edge.

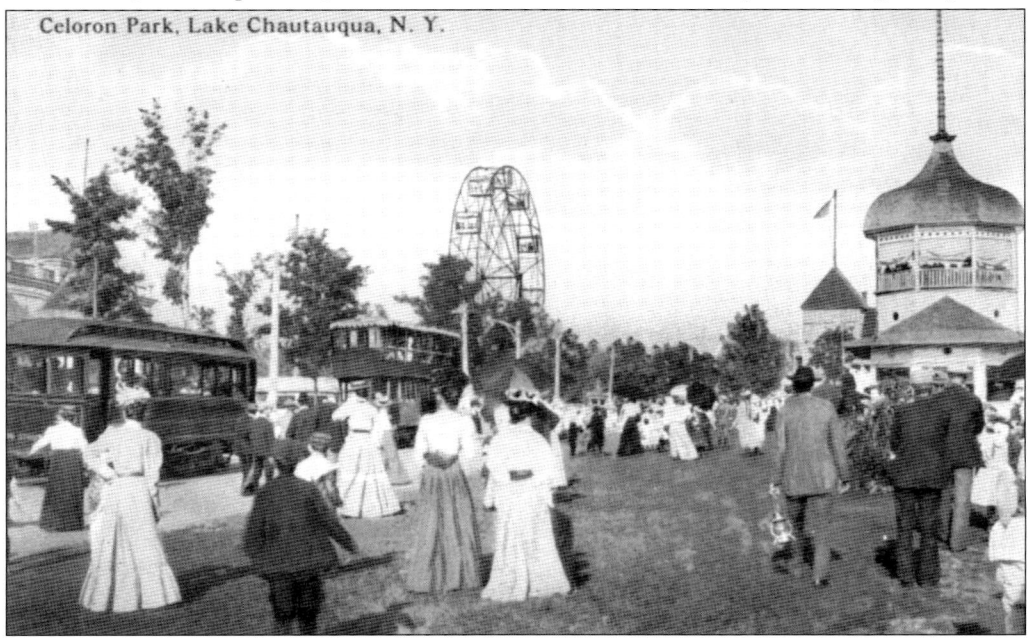

Another crowd is heading toward the entrance for an activity. The double-decker streetcar and another streetcar are in the park. The pointed roof on the Hotel de Celoron shows that this was before the August 1902 fire. One man seems to plan to stay after dark, as he is carrying a lantern.

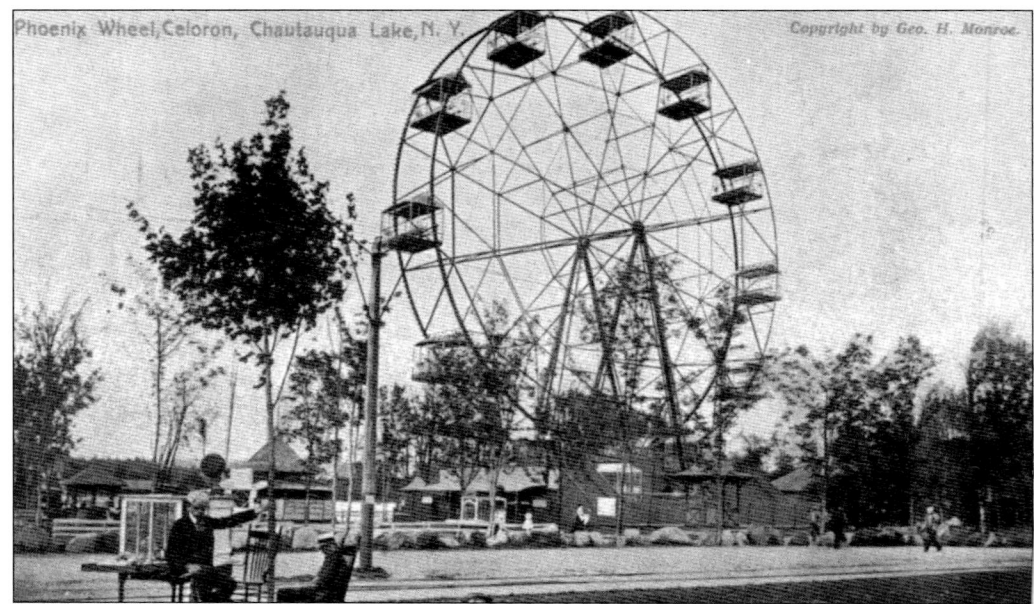

The Phoenix Wheel, at 125 feet high with 12 cars able to carry 12 to 14 passengers each, welcomed visitors to the park in 1896. It took 10 freight cars and $18,000 to bring it from Atlanta's Cotton States Exposition. At night, it was outlined with 300 electric lamps. Sixty thousand bricks were used for its foundation. Moved to Pomona, California, in 1952, it reached the scrap pile in 1982. (Courtesy of MC.)

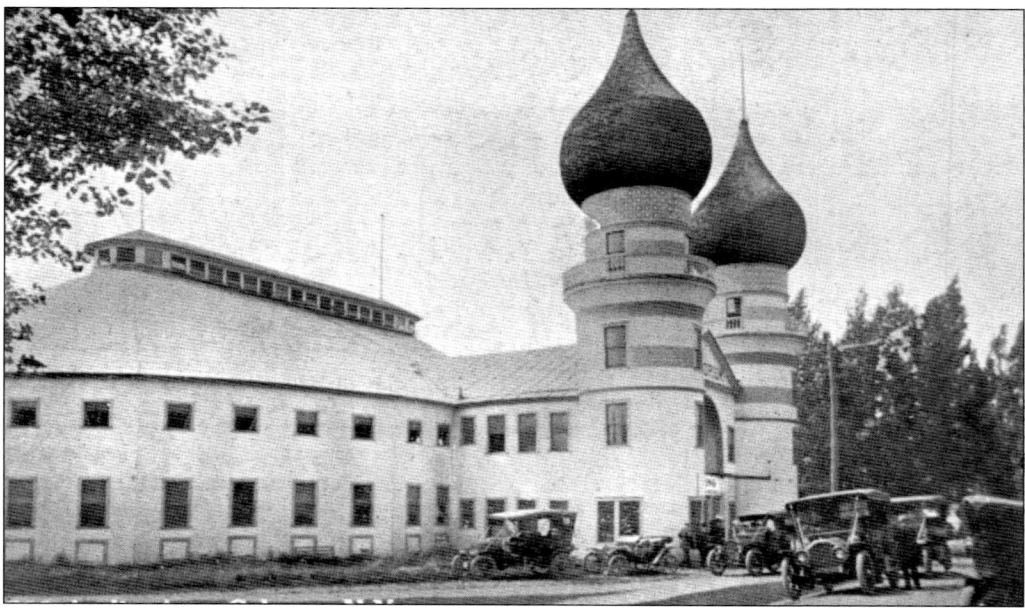

The auditorium/skating rink opened in January 1895. During the summer, it was an assembly hall that could accommodate 8,400 people, and many conventions used the large hall. William Jennings Bryan and many others spoke here. A bandstand at one end was for the band that provided music for the skaters, and balconies provided seating for those who only wanted to observe the skating. (Courtesy of MC.)

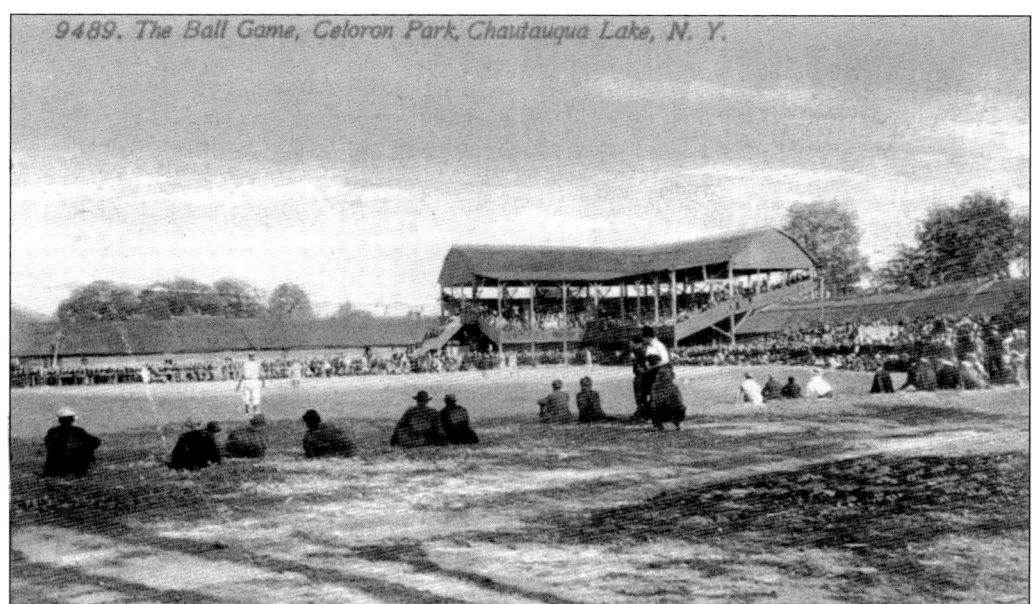

Local and professional teams played at the ballpark and grandstand. Barnstorming major-league players, including George Herman "Babe" Ruth, played here. Football and baseball games, cricket matches, and even Wild West shows were performed here. The roofed area behind the bleachers is the annex of the auditorium, which was used as part of the skating rink in the winter and as a covered promenade and extra exhibit space in the summer.

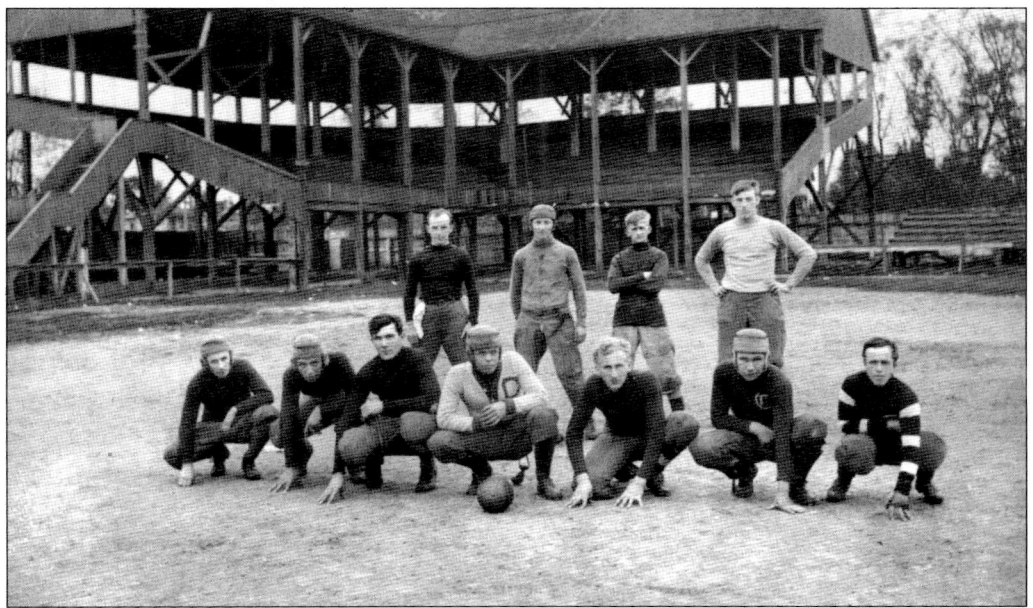

Since the area behind the bleachers is open, this picture was taken after 1909, when the auditorium annex was dismantled. In the early days of the park, any team was invited to use the field for free. Baseball games played here between Jamestown and other local teams against teams from other areas familiarized out-of-towners with the park. These football players are unidentified. (Courtesy of FHC.)

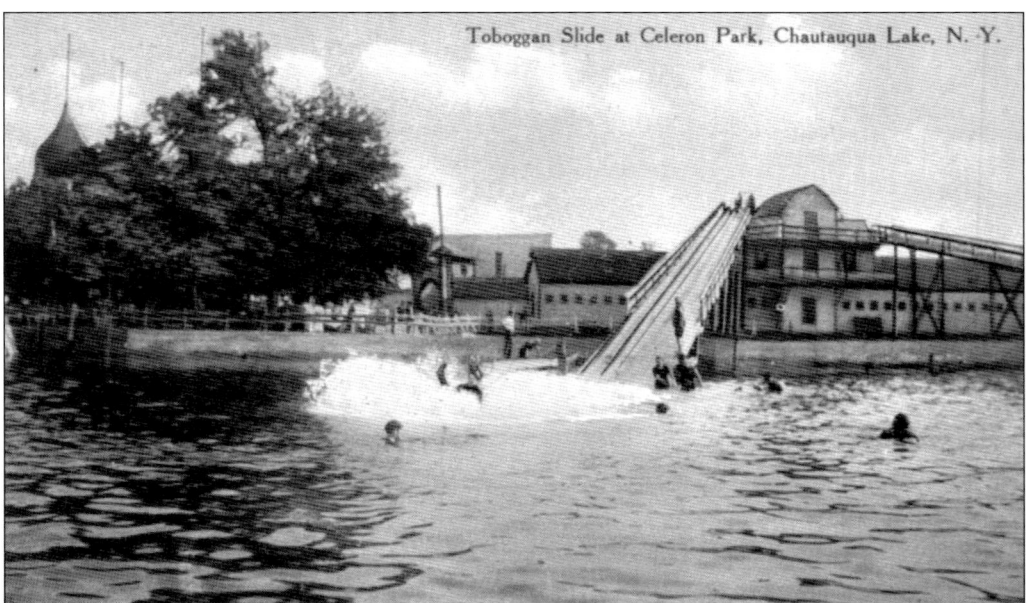

Toboggan slides were popular attractions at waterfronts. Celoron had one as early as 1893. A larger bathhouse was built in 1894 and had three slides from the third story. After the May 1900 fire, the bathhouse was quickly rebuilt for the season, but only two slides were constructed, both coming from the third story.

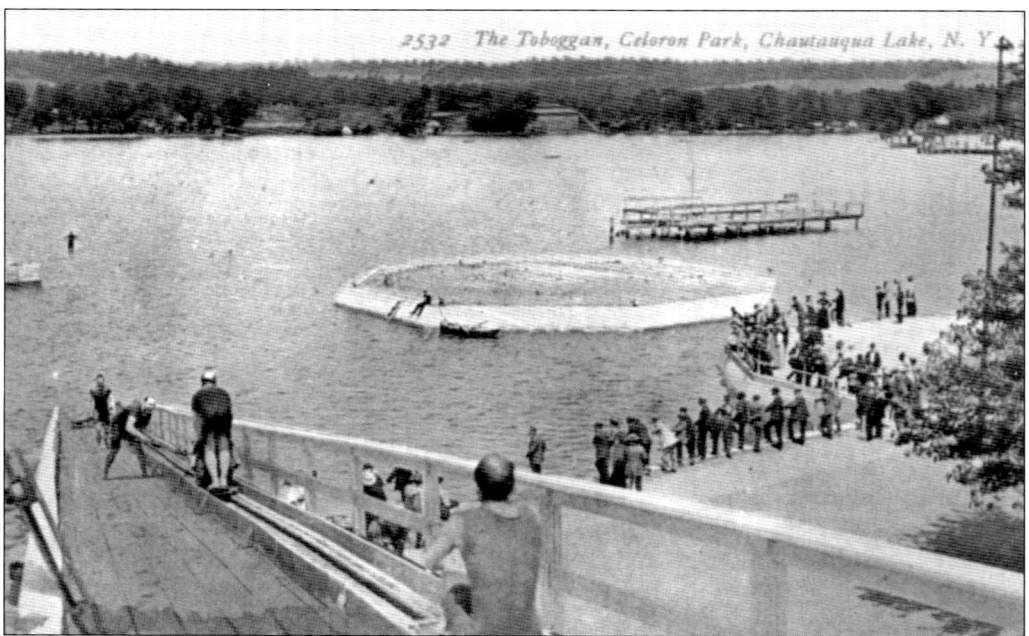

This is a close-up of the toboggans and the rail they followed to the water. The other side of the slide allowed the riders to walk back up for another ride. The "island" in the water was later used for the airplane swings. The railed structure in the water was used for fireworks. The shoreline seems to have a cement wall and walk, so this image was taken after 1908.

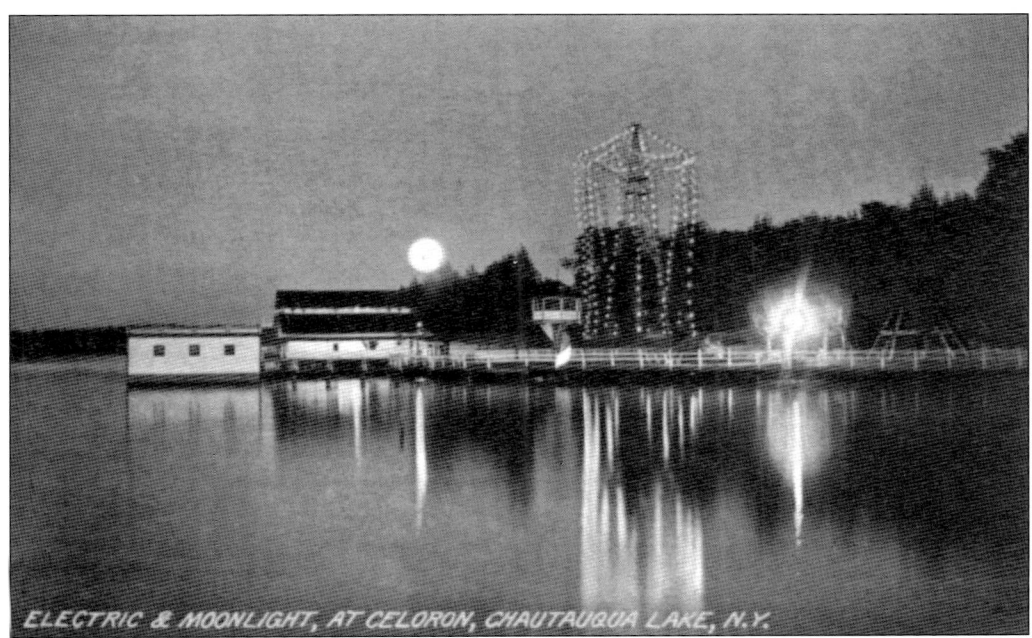

In 1905, another ride was added to the park. The Circle Swing was located near the dance hall and the Phoenix Wheel in the east end. Wicker gondolas held the riders, and as the rotating ride sped up, the centrifugal force swung them out from the ride. Electric lights outlined the ride. The observation tower with the spiral staircase can be seen in the foreground.

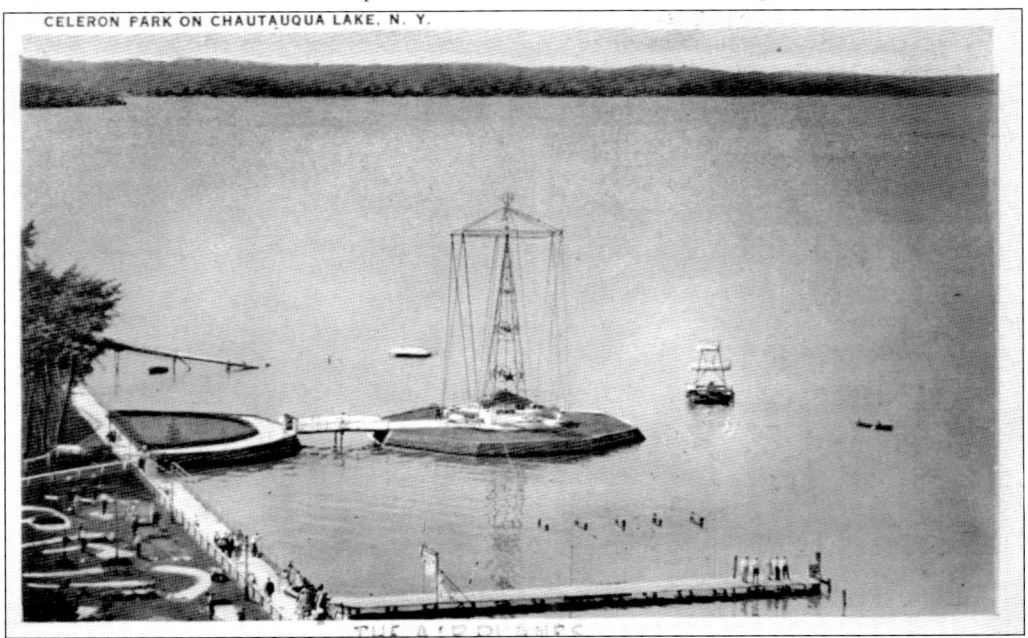

In the mid-1920s, the Circle Swing was moved to the island between the toboggan slide and the theater. The wicker gondolas were replaced with wooden airplanes so one had the sensation of flying over the water. The searchlight and the bridge were gone by then, and there is a dock in the picture, probably for small boats arriving at the park.

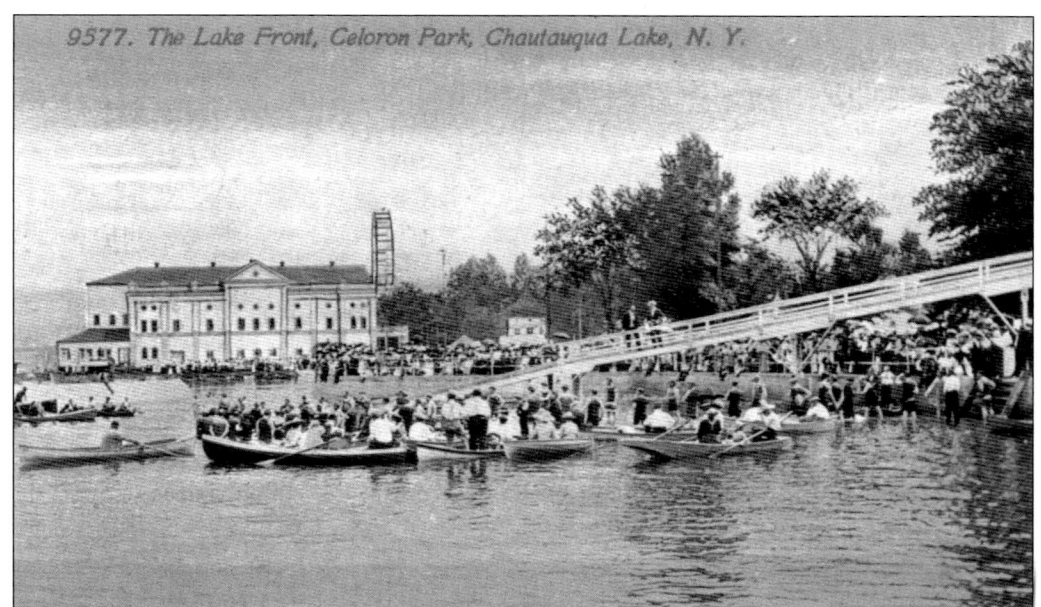

There are a large number of small boats and people around the toboggan slide and many people along the shoreline. This is probably the 1910 mass baptism that took place during a convention of Pastor C. T. Russell's Bible students. Other photographs of that event look similar to this scene. The photograph of the large crowd was a good marketing ploy without stating the nature of the event.

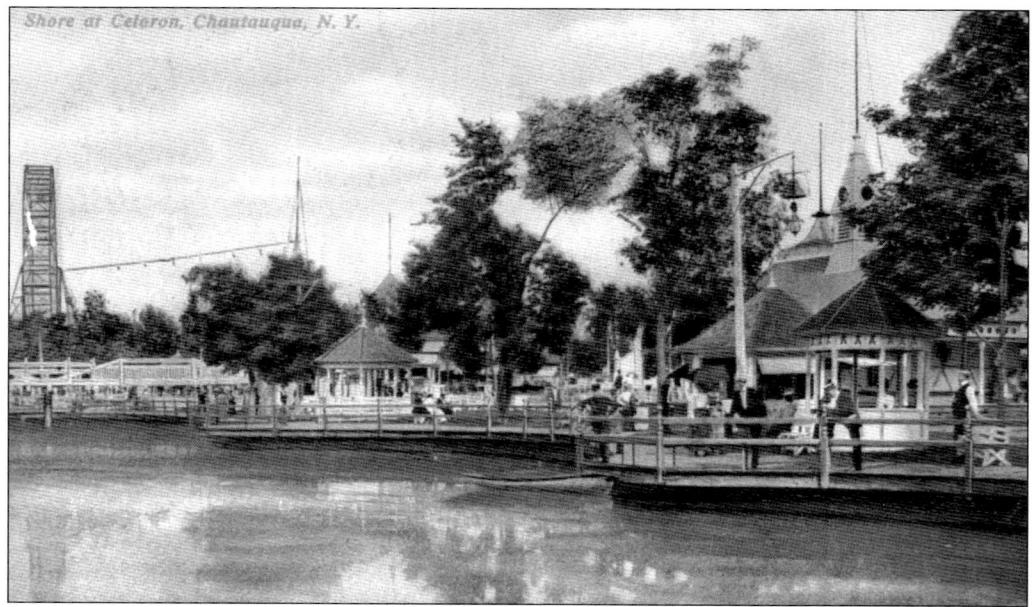

This scene, looking east from near the toboggan slide, shows the curving shoreline; this image was obviously taken before the shoreline was straightened. The straightening may have occurred in 1908 when a concrete seawall and walk were installed through the west end of the park. The boardwalk provided a pleasant promenade with cooling breezes by the lake and access to summerhouses and refreshment stands.

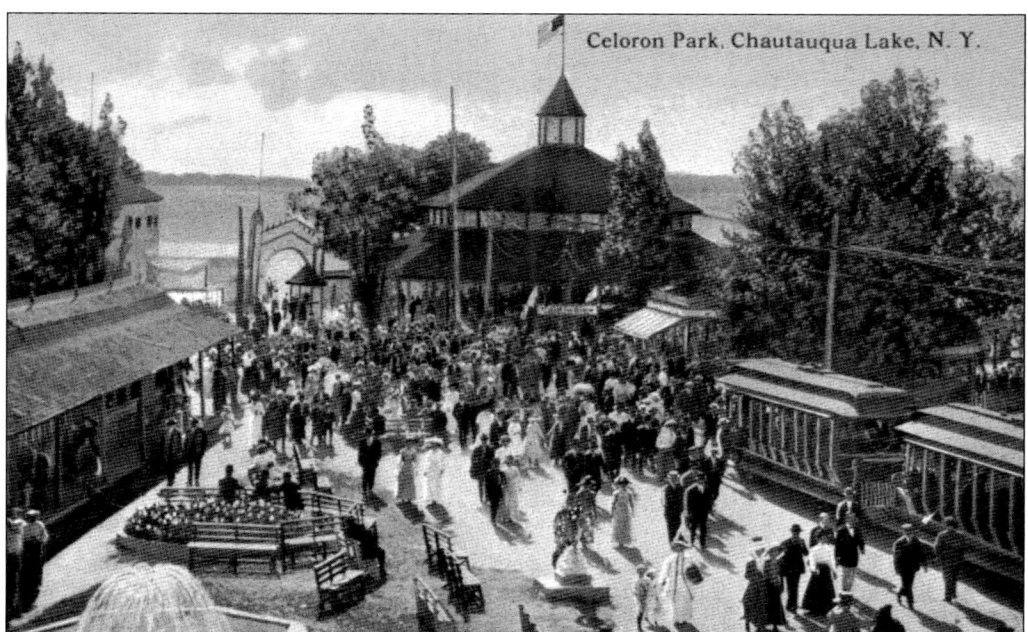

Two of the open summer trolley cars are seen here in the park. Moved from the other end of the park, the merry-go-round is in the circular building. The end of the long building of refreshment stands and concessions is at left. This view is looking west and could have been taken from the bandstand on the second level of the pavilion.

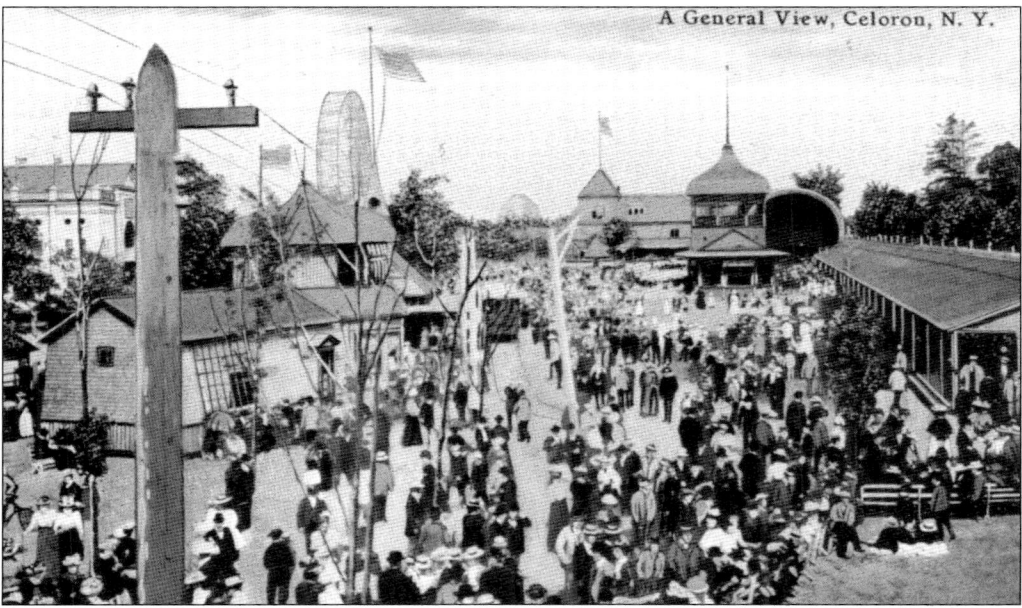

Looking east, this view could have been taken from the merry-go-round building. The trolley track is the cleared area in the center, and a trolley is approaching. The Hotel de Celoron in the center background still has a pointed roof, which means this image was taken before August 1902. Celoron Park's photographer's stand is the pointed roof on the left in front of the Phoenix Wheel.

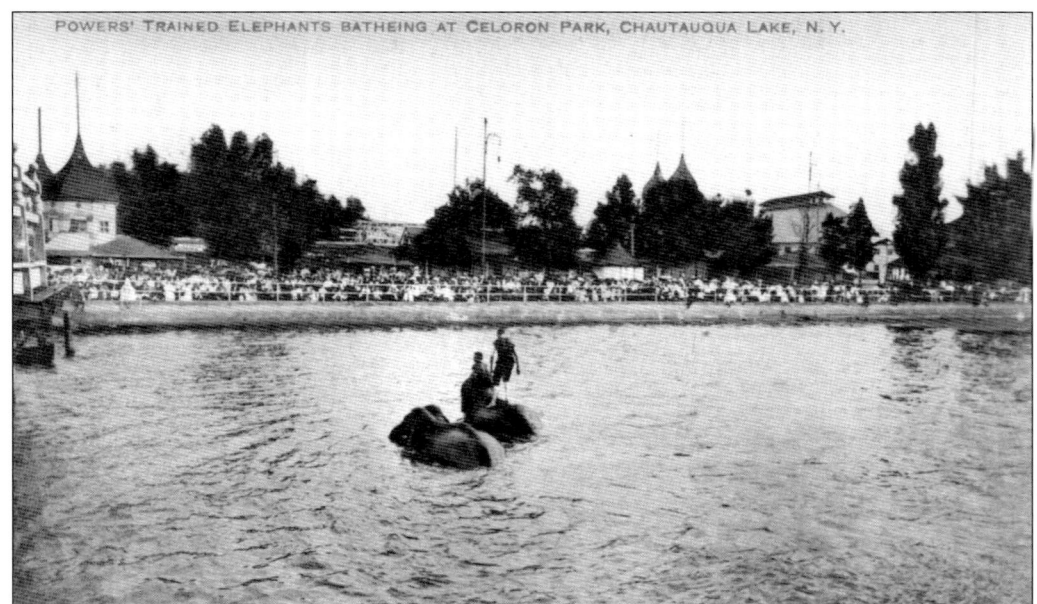

July 1910 found Powers's Trained Elephants at Celoron Park. The act had played the Hippodrome in New York City for more than 1,000 performances. For one week every day at 4:30 p.m. and 8:00 p.m., the elephants did trick work and swam in the lake. As can be seen in the postcard, crowds gathered along the seawall to watch. This was a free attraction that brought families to Celoron Park. (Courtesy of FHC.)

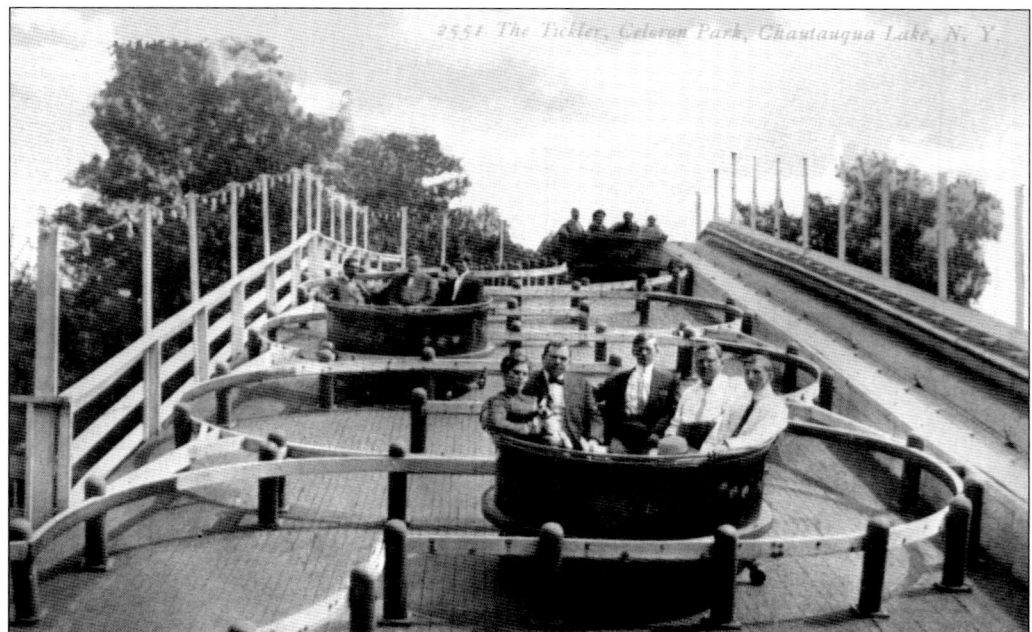

The Coney Island Tickler was brought to Celoron Park in 1908 and remained for seven seasons, leaving in May 1915. It cost about $8,000 and was billed as "the best amusement attraction ever brought to Celoron." Up to 10 people could ride in a round padded car as it careened down an incline on caster-type wheels, bumping guide rails and spinning on the way to the bottom.

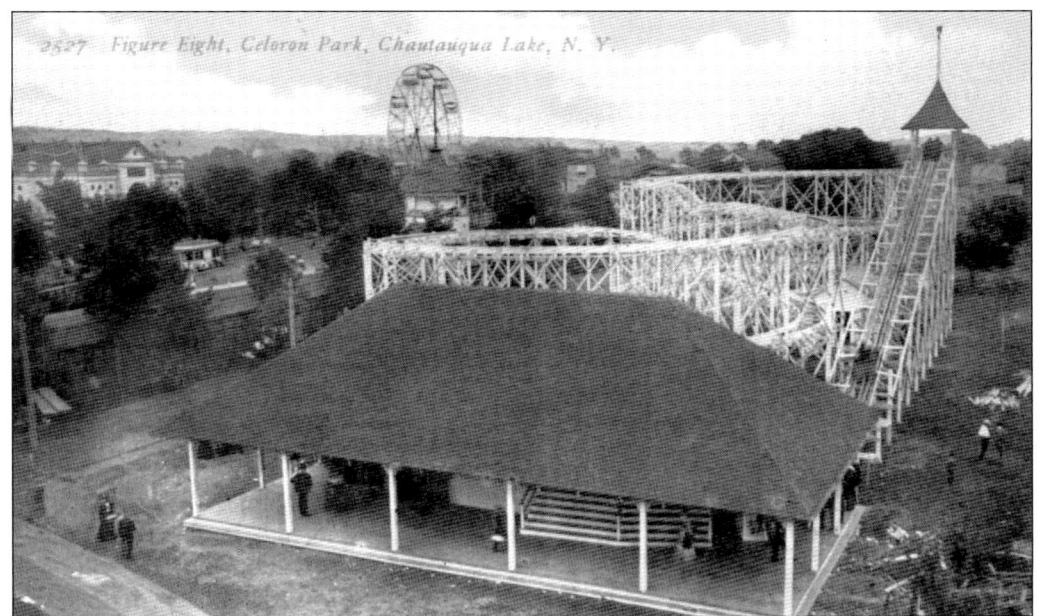

The Figure Eight was the second of the five roller coasters in Celoron Park's history. It came to the park in 1903 and gave thrills to summer visitors through the 1932 season. It was located behind the long building of refreshment and concession stands. The Gravity Railway, the first roller coaster, was destroyed by fire in 1900.

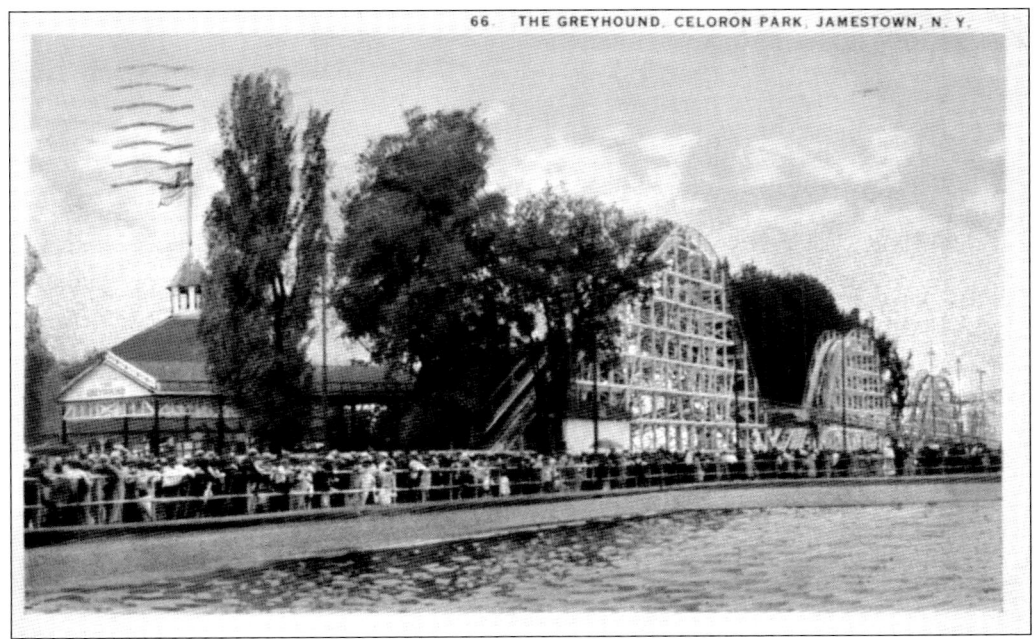

The ill-fated Loop-the-Loop of 1904 and the Scenic Railroad for the next three years were the third and fourth coasters. The Greyhound was the last coaster in the park. The Greyhound paralleled the lake past the bathhouse and the merry-go-round. The Greyhound was built in 1924 and was destroyed by a tornado in 1959. It was not rebuilt.

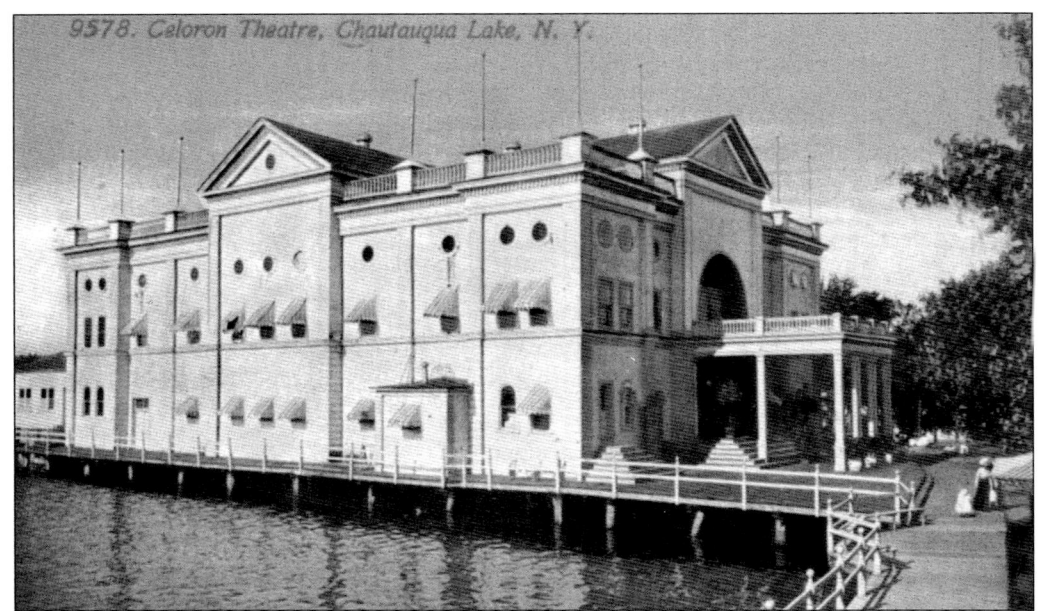

Additions to the park in 1897 included an indoor theater with the capacity to seat 2,000 people. Built on piles driven into the lake, it was located where the dome-shaped outdoor theater had been. The floor of the auditorium sloped from the entrance toward the stage. The theater was booked the first month with first-class vaudeville attractions and continued excellent entertainment for years.

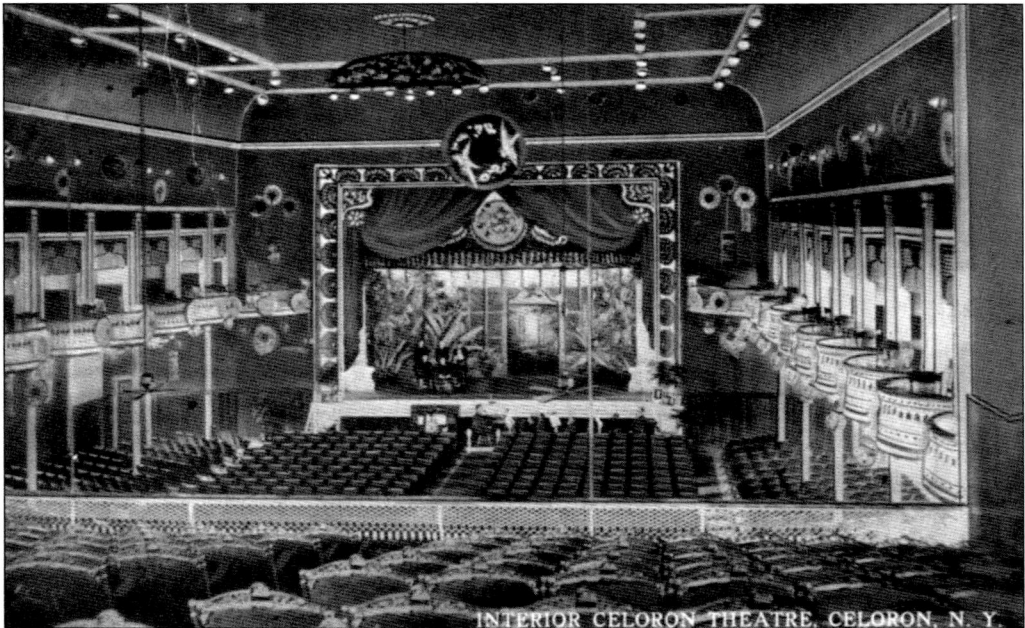

The interior of the theater had rich and artistic ornamental work. Opposite the stage was a large gallery with 18 boxes along the sides. Prices were 10¢ a seat or a box for four for $1. The stage opening was 24-by-34 feet, and the stage was 32-by-50 feet. Twelve dressing rooms were ready for the performers.

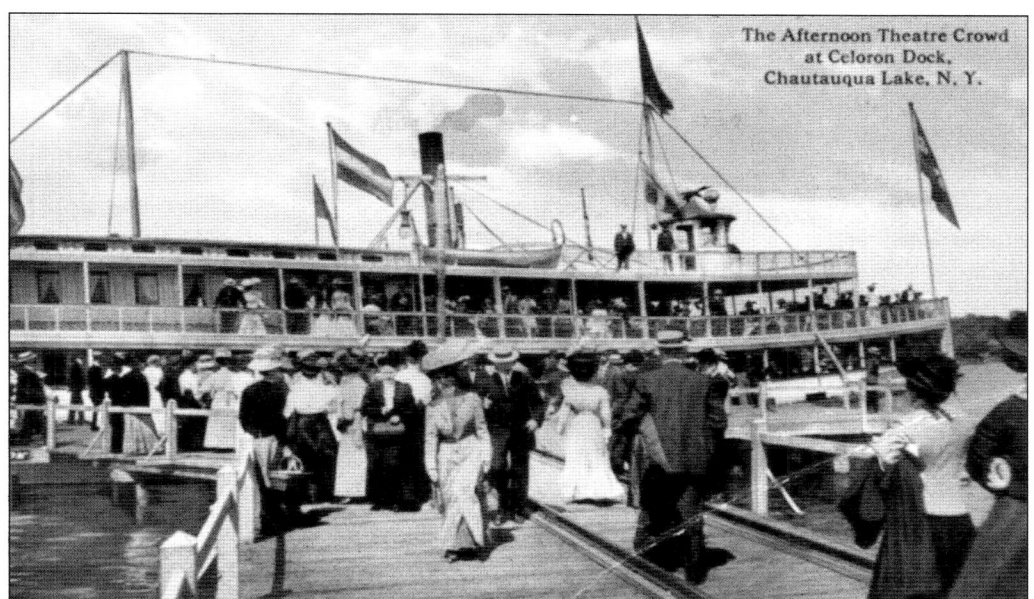

Steamboats stopped at Celoron Park with large crowds of passengers eager to enjoy the variety of entertainments and amusements offered at the park. Passengers can be seen getting on and off the boat. Headed down the lake, a few of the passengers may be getting off to catch the trolley, which can get them to Jamestown in 10 minutes instead of the half-hour the steamboat would take.

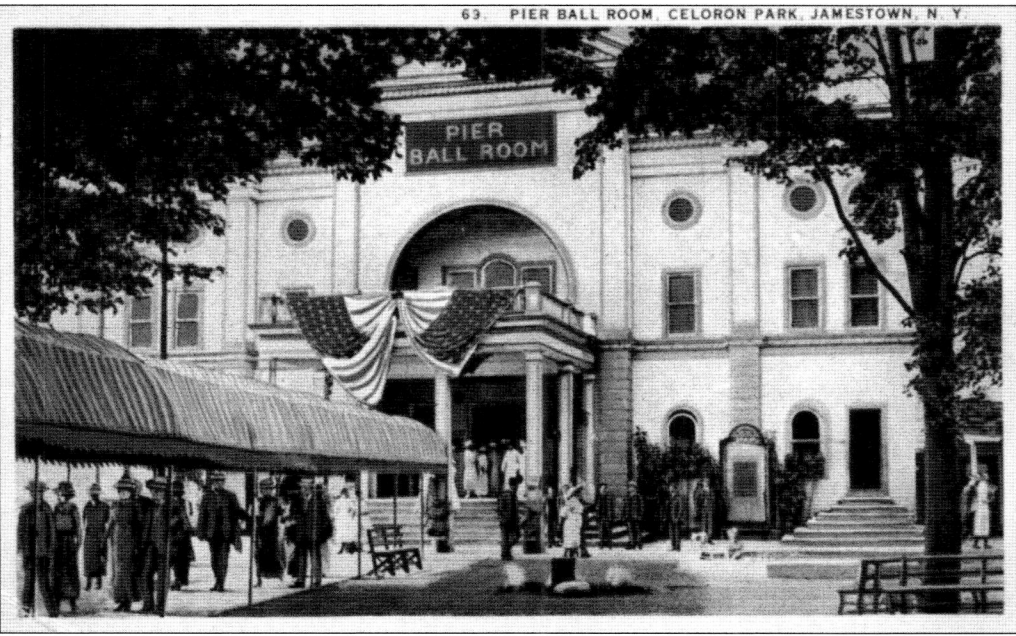

The Celoron Theater became the Pier Ball Room in 1924. The floor was raised, leveled, and covered with hardwood to make a large dance floor. Many big bands of the time played here for the dancing and listening enjoyment of the many summer visitors and local residents. The Pier Ball Room was destroyed by fire in 1930, along with some concessions stands on the east side.

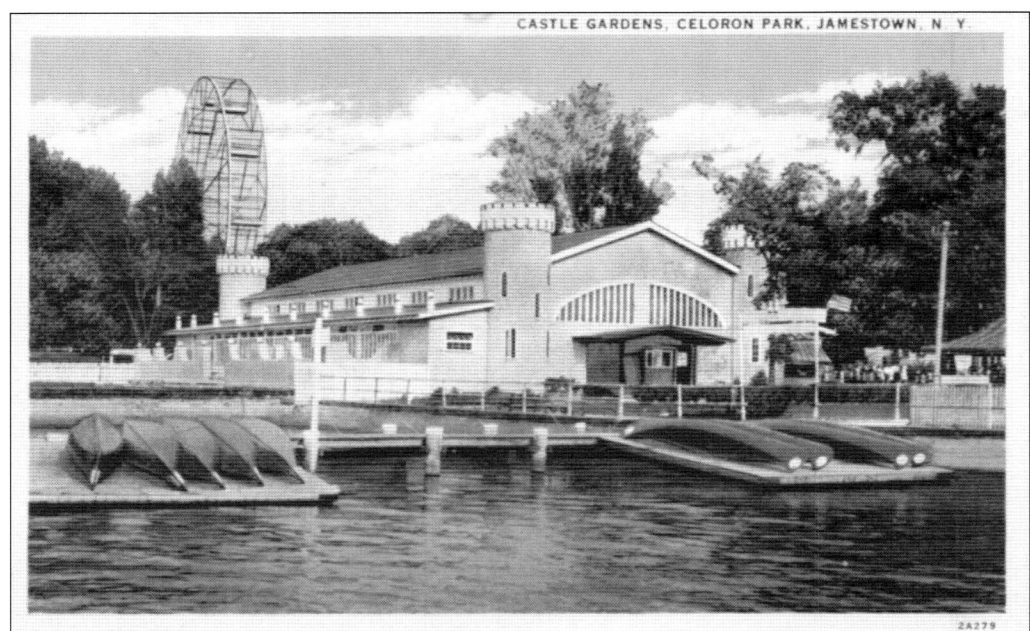

To continue the dancing at Celoron Park, this dance hall was built in three weeks and opened on July 24, 1930, six weeks after the Pier Ball Room burned down. It was located just inland from the old Pier Ball Room site. Called Castle Gardens in the beginning, the public continued to call it the Pier Ball Room. This new Pier Ball Room burned on June 1, 1962. (Courtesy of MC.)

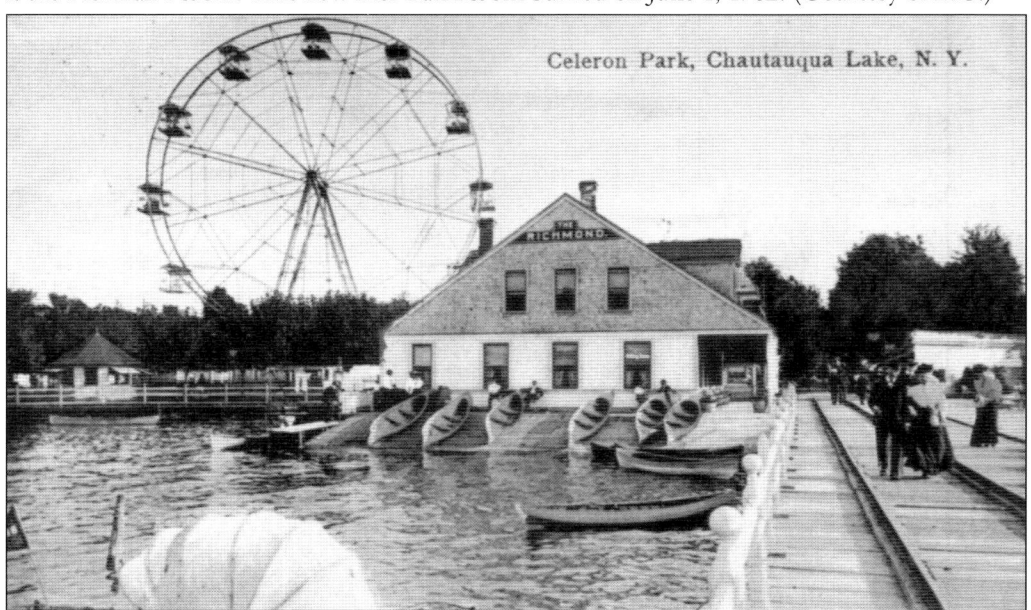

The Phoenix Wheel was dismantled in 1952 and shipped to California. The last steamboat dock washed away in 1945. The Richmond Hotel, which sat close to the water, was flooded during high water, damaged by fire, and torn down in 1960. This image shows how wide the dock was with the trolley tracks on it. Small boats could be rented here and at many other places on the lake. (Courtesy of MC.)

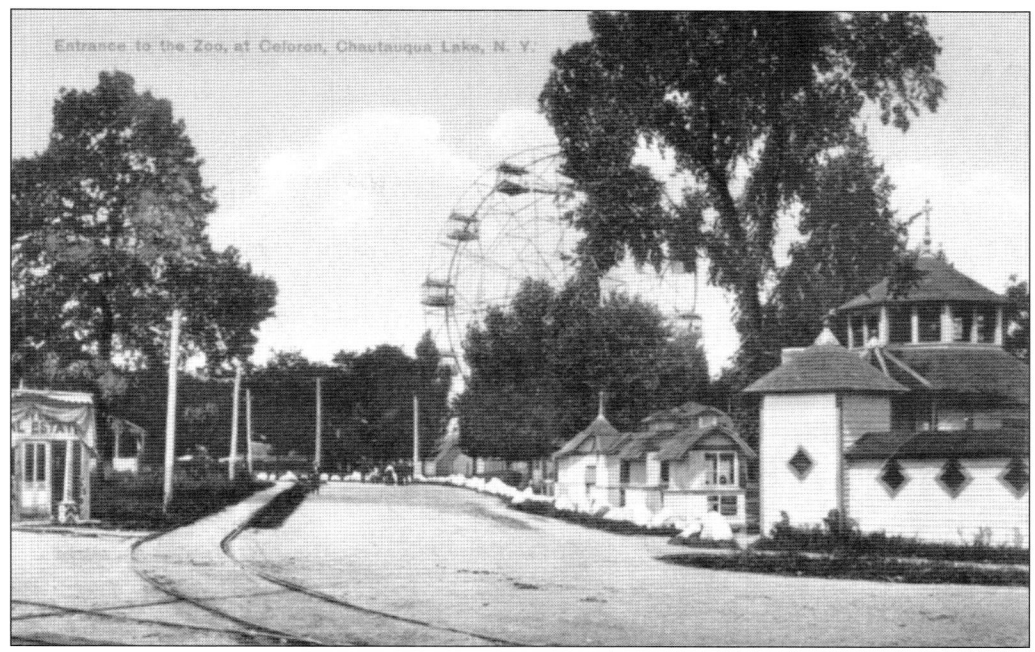

The zoo, or the menagerie, was at the east end of the park. Beginning in May 1895, it had a variety of animals throughout the summer. In May 1912, Tom, the big bear, who had made his home at the zoo and had sometimes lived at the streetcar barn during the winters, left for a new home in Pennsylvania. The rest of the animals left soon after Tom.

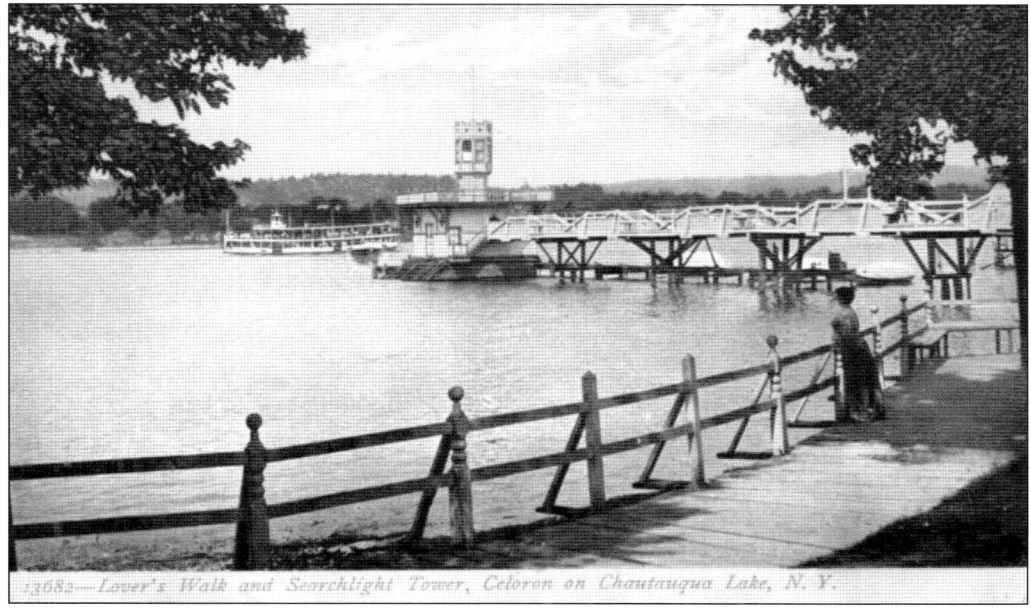

Lovers Walk was the bridge that connected the searchlight tower with the shore. The bridge, built in 1894, was 280 feet long and had a handsome entrance and seats all along it at intervals. It went to the old waterworks crib on which was then built a boathouse. On the roof was a tower for the searchlight.

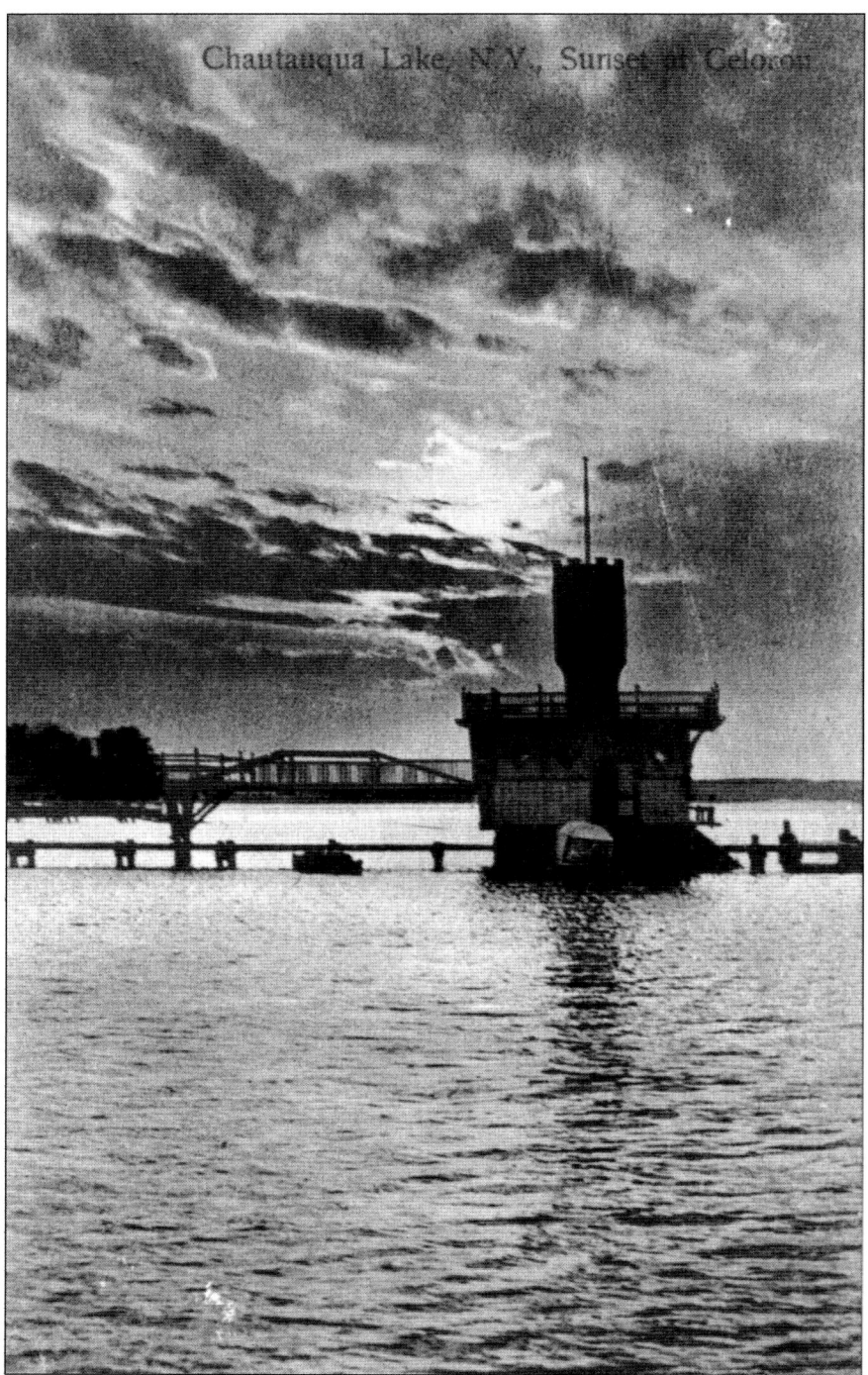

This structure was built on the old wooden crib of the unsuccessful waterworks company. This was the headquarters of the Launch Owners Association. The tower on the roof held the powerful searchlight that was brought to the park in 1894. This searchlight's beam was thrown over the park, the lake, and along the far shores.

Two

Town of Busti

The town of Busti, stretching from the New York–Pennsylvania border to the shore of Chautauqua Lake, was formed in 1823 and was named for the general agent of the Holland Land Company, which sold land to individuals in western New York. The village of Lakewood, first known as Lakeview, developed along the lakeshore and was incorporated in 1893.

John Cowing, one of the individuals who purchased lakeshore land, built a lakeside hotel in 1870, which became known as the Lakeview House. The Packard brothers built summer homes and rental cottages near the hotel. A second hotel, the Kent House, was built in 1875 and burned in 1887. The new Kent House was built in 1888. The old Lakeview, after several fires, was rebuilt as the Sterlingworth Hotel in 1889. Lakewood's permanent residents numbered 600 in 1893, and the summer population was two to three times that number.

Lakewood became a summer stop on the Erie Railroad. The summer visitors could stay in the lakeside hotels, cottages, and smaller hotels or boardinghouses, or continue along the lake by steamboat to reach their final destination. By the early 1900s, they could transfer to the trolleys to continue their trip.

Lakewood developed as a summer place for wealthy industrialists from the larger cities. The hotel business declined in the early 1900s, leaving the Sterlingworth, renamed the Waldmere, as an annex to the Kent House if needed for extra rooms. It burned in 1902. The Kent House was permanently closed in 1909. Many summer visitors chose to build cottages along the lakeshore to the east and west of the hotel area. A country club built a clubhouse on the Sterlingworth property, which eventually became the present lakefront park.

Many of the summer cottages in the village of Lakewood and the town of Busti have become year-round homes, while some remain as summer cottages for distant owners. Lake privileges remain with many of the homes and cottages in the early developments.

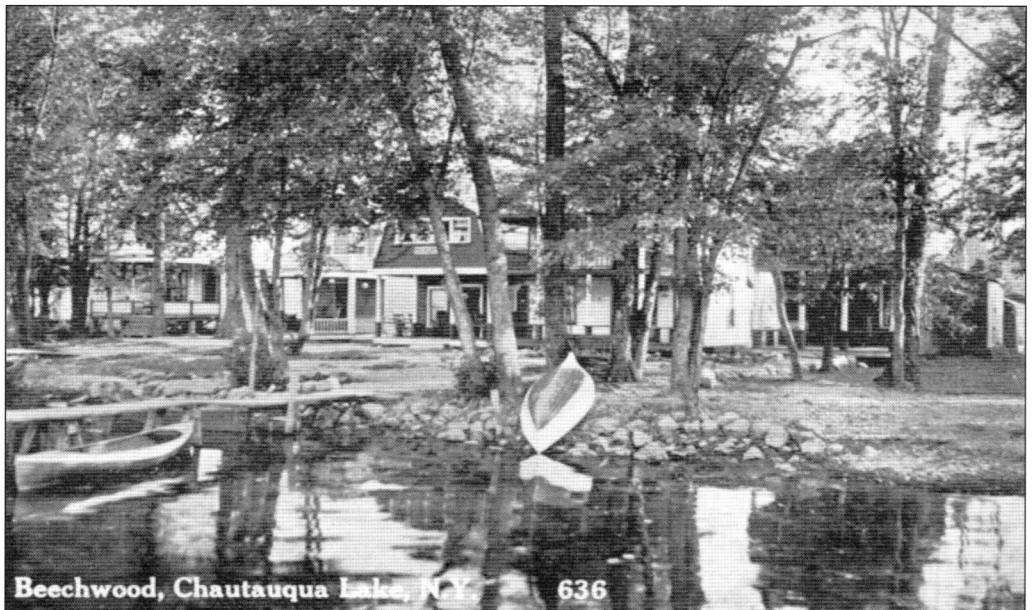

Beechwood, one of the developments built by Ziba Squier, between Lakewood and Celoron, provided cottages close to the city of Jamestown and near Chautauqua Lake. Conveniently located near a trolley stop, commuting to the city was an easy trip for anyone working through the summer. Cottages were perched on narrow lots that afforded a lakefront for many.

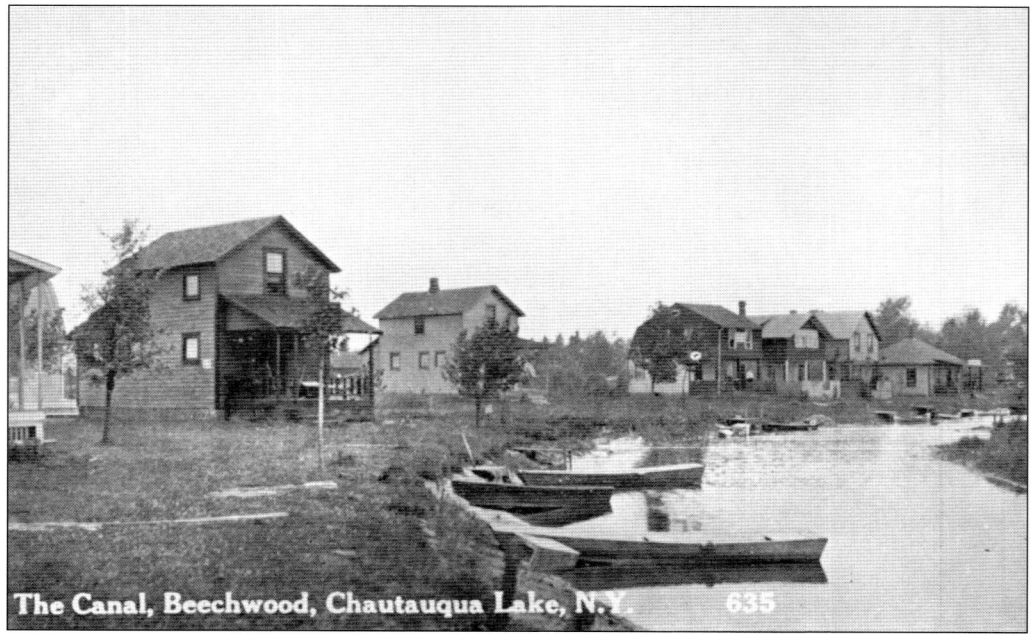

Some of the cottages were waterfront only because Squier dug a canal connected to the lake. This gave cottagers the chance to have a boat at their front door with access to the lake. Eventually the canal was filled in, and the cottages had only a field in front of them. The area still has many of these cottages, some of which have been winterized to be used as year-round homes.

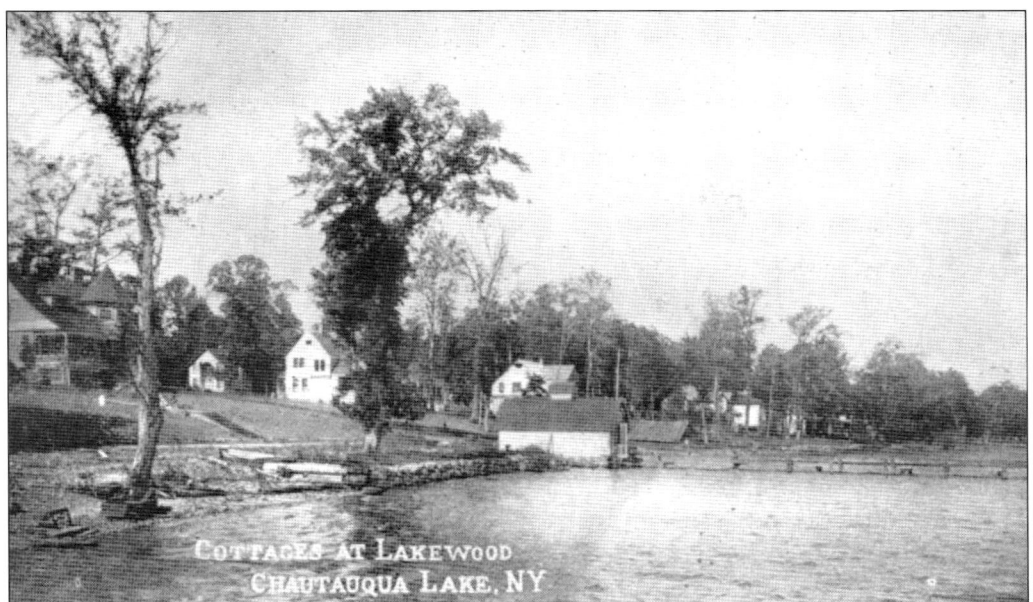

Which cottages these are has not been determined. The Packard brothers built cottages close to their summer homes near the two hotels, and the Kent House had cottages they rented. Other developments were Clement Park and Shadyside to the east and Howard Park and Waldmere Park to the west. Many businessmen from Jamestown built cottages here, along with families from Pittsburgh and other large cities.

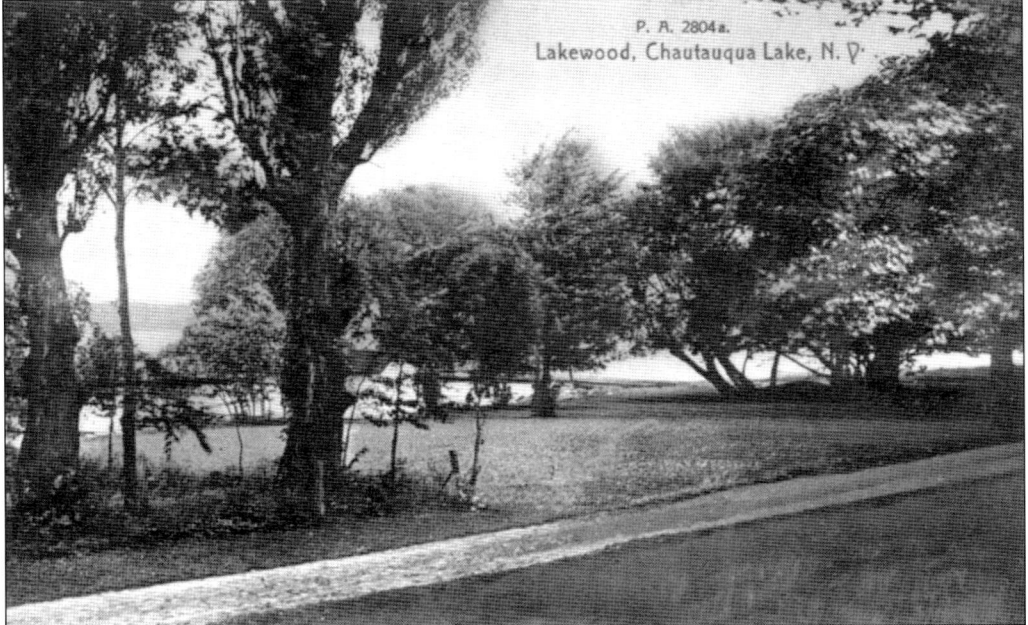

Lakewood's waterfront stretched for a few miles. Pictured here is a pleasant open area with some shade trees, a dock (maybe used for small boats and not the scheduled steamboats), and a road that runs near the lake, giving access to many. The scene was similar in many places along the lake that had not yet been developed around the beginning of the 19th century.

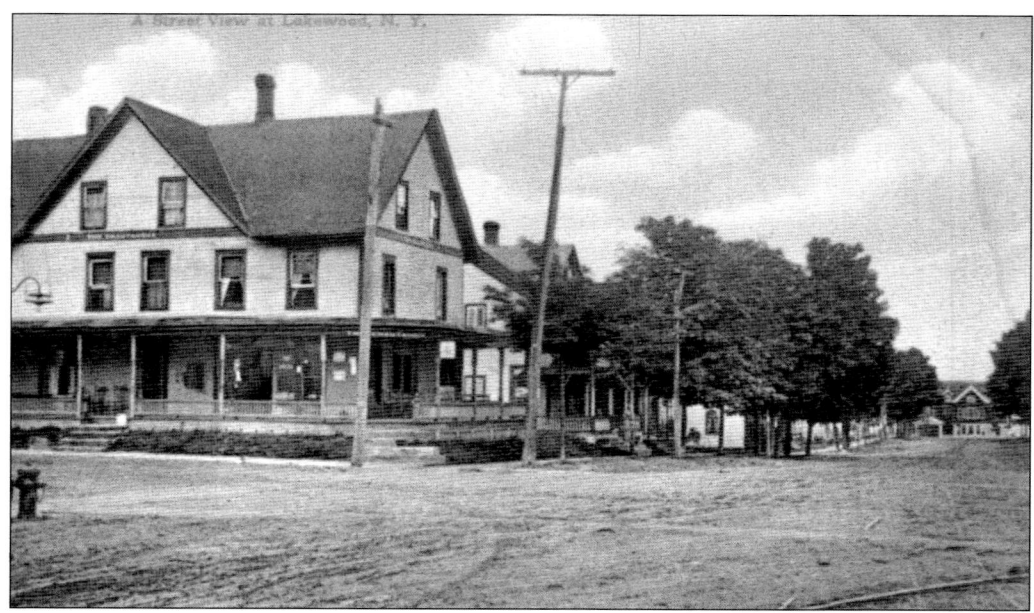

The Chautauqua House was the small hotel on the northwest corner of Chautauqua and Summit Avenues in Lakewood. This hotel catered to summer visitors who did not patronize the large lakefront hotels. Chautauqua Avenue runs north toward the lake. This photograph was taken after 1906, when the country club was built and blocked the view of the lake at the end of Chautauqua Avenue.

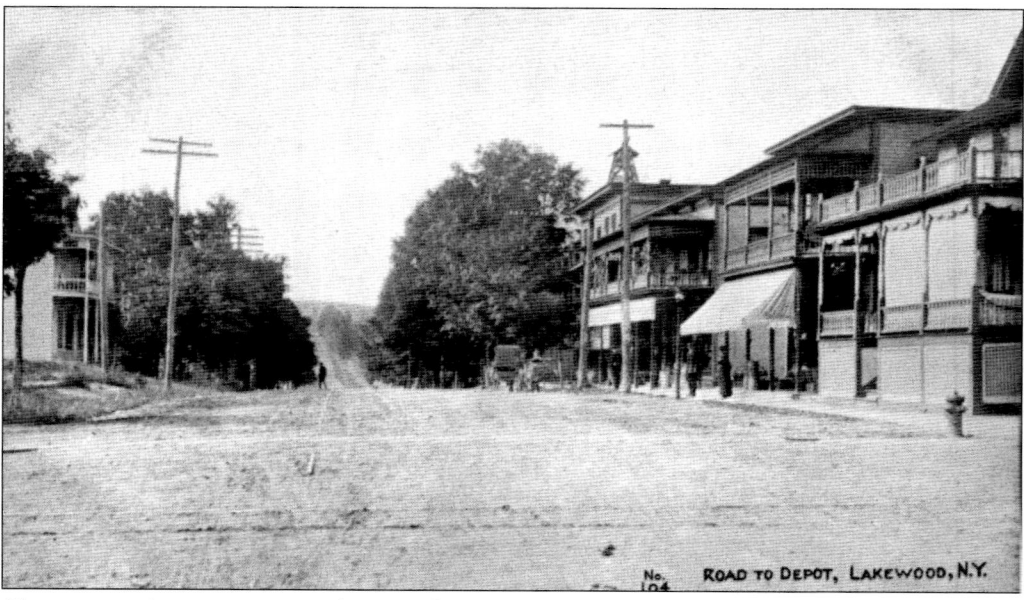

Chautauqua Avenue runs south toward Fairmount Avenue. The Erie Railroad tracks cross Chautauqua Avenue about where the trees are in this picture. In the summer, Lakewood became a stop on the Erie, and many visitors transferred from train to trolleys or steamboats to reach destinations along the lake or stayed in Lakewood. Baggage carts of trunks could be seen traveling this avenue whenever a train had arrived or was due.

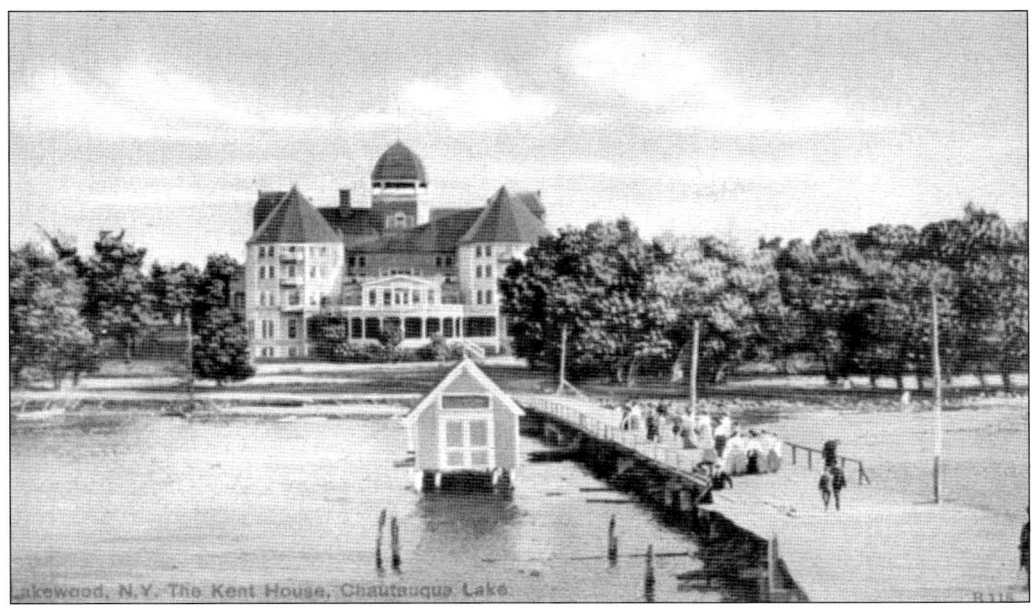

Alba Kent of Jamestown built the first Kent House in Lakewood in 1875 and enlarged it the next year. It could accommodate up to 500 guests. Guests could arrive by steamboat or train and later by trolley. A popular lakeside hotel, it was consumed by fire in 1887. The Kent House (pictured above) replaced the first one in 1888 and for a few years used the adjacent Waldmere Hotel as an annex.

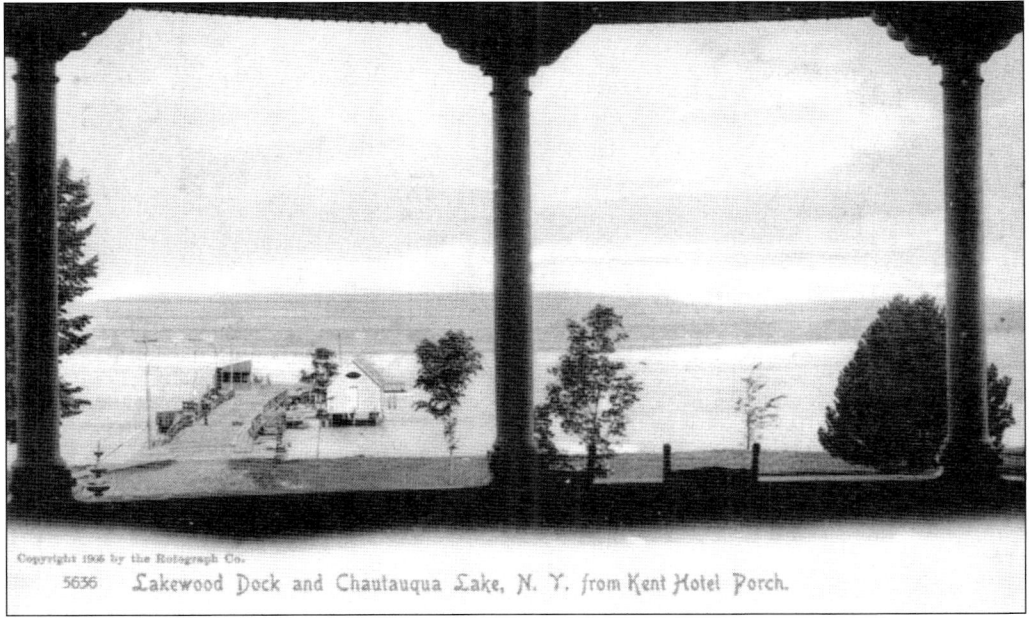

The verandas of the Kent House overlooked the long lawn extending to the lake and the Kent House dock. The neighboring hotel burned in 1902. The Kent House struggled to survive but ceased operations in 1909, and the contents were sold at auction. It is said that when it was dismantled in 1915, much of the lumber went into building many of the homes in the area.

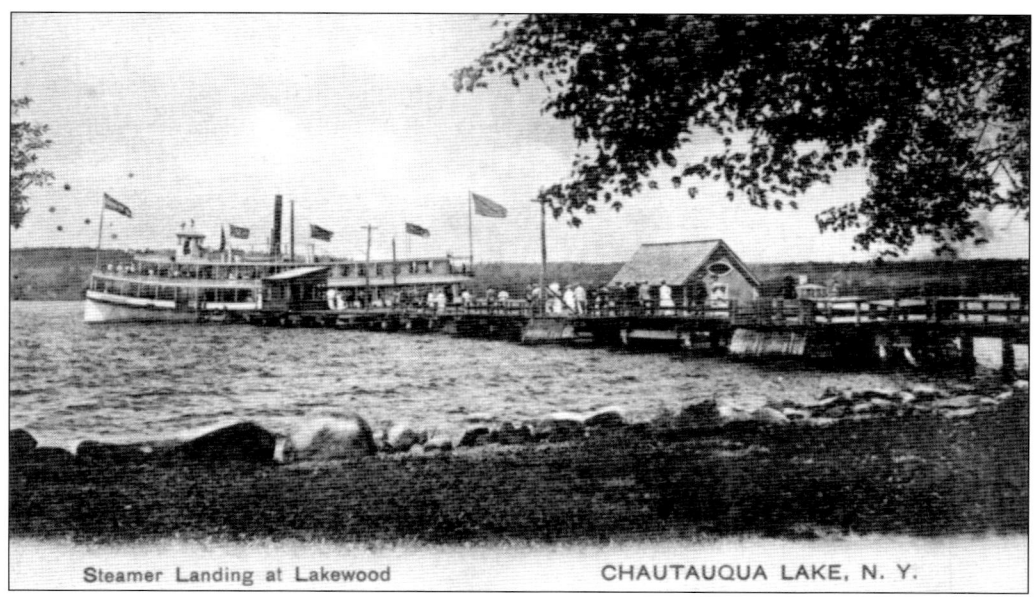

This is the Kent House dock. At one time, the two hotels—the Kent House and the Sterlingworth/Waldmere—had separate docks where the steamboats stopped. The schedule showed a 10-minute interval between the dockings. The Kent House had fine dining rooms and dancing, which brought visitors from other resorts along the lake.

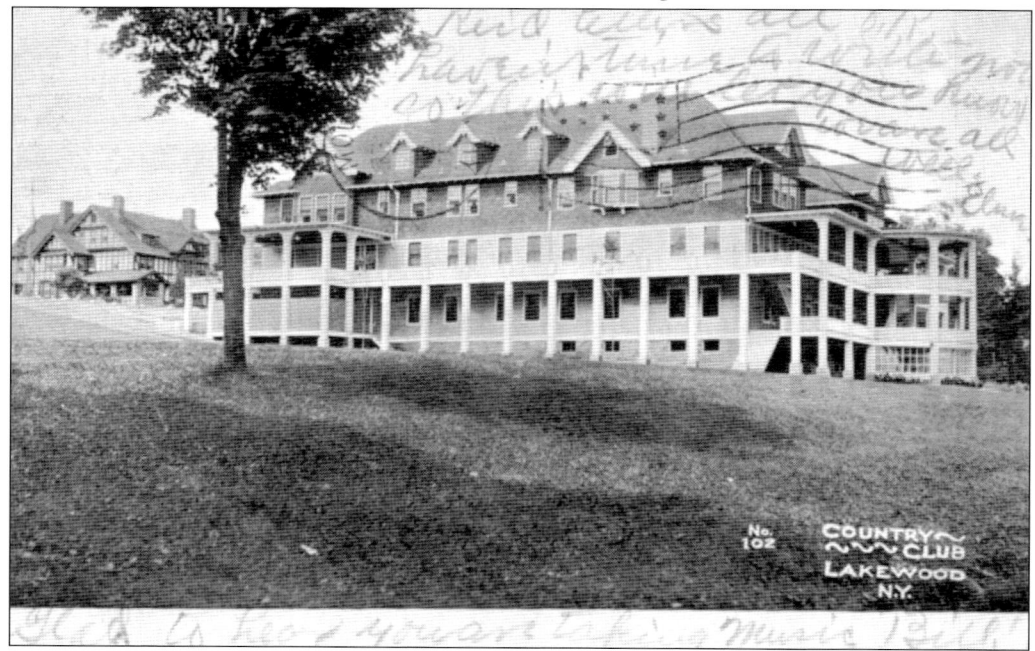

The Lakewood Country Club, formed at the beginning of the 20th century by wealthy residents of New York, Pittsburgh, Cleveland, Cincinnati, and others around the lake, erected this clubhouse in 1905–1906. Built on the site of the former Sterlingworth/Waldmere Hotel, the clubhouse opened in July 1906. It became a restaurant in 1919. In 1933, with the building gone, the property was purchased by the Village of Lakewood for a public park.

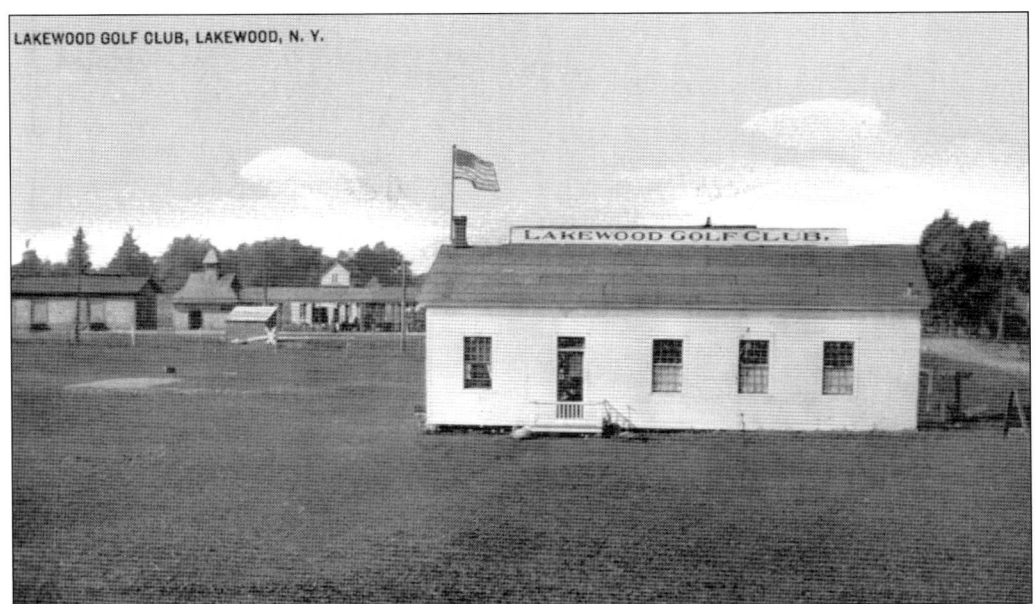

The members of the Lakewood Country Club created a golf course located to the south beyond the Erie Railroad tracks. At an earlier time, it was announced that the Lakewood hotels would develop a golf course west of Waldmere Park on their grounds. One of the managers was an avid golfer. The one pictured here, though, is probably the later golf club developed by the country club.

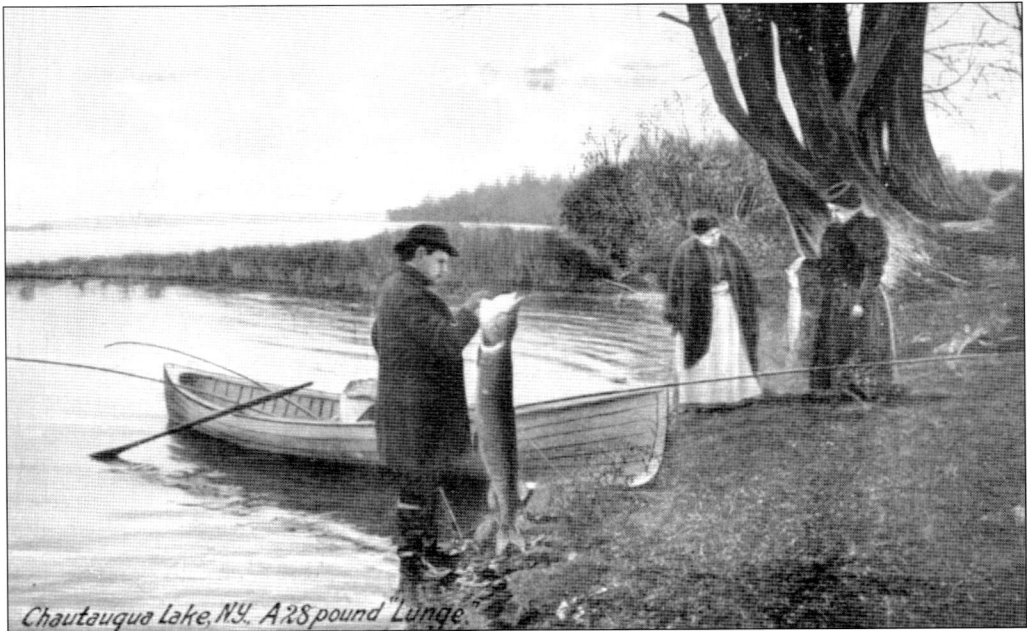

Fishing in Chautauqua Lake provided hours of pleasure for visitors. Locals supplemented their income by providing fish to the numerous hotel dining rooms along the lake. Rowboats could be rented at boat liveries, and most came equipped with fishing gear. The man has a 28-pound muskellunge, the lake's famous game fish. Note that the woman is also holding a fish.

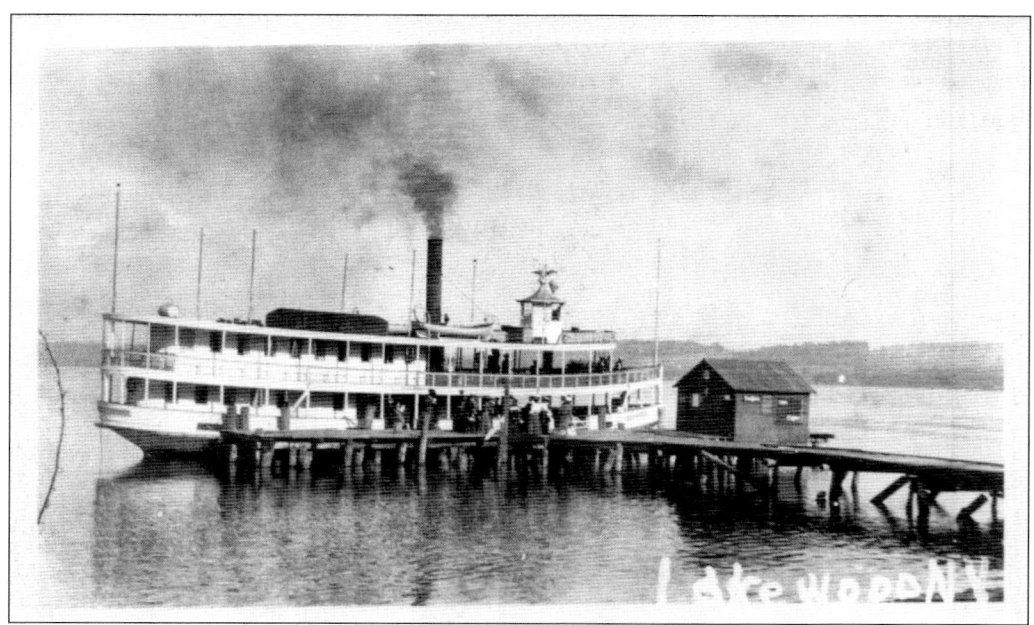

This image is labeled "Lakewood, NY." In 1912, the only Lakewood dock was carried away by ice. In 1913, it was rebuilt, and steamboats began stopping again. This photograph may have been taken with a Kodak Autographic camera, which allowed the photographer to write on the film while it was still in the camera. These cameras began appearing in 1916.

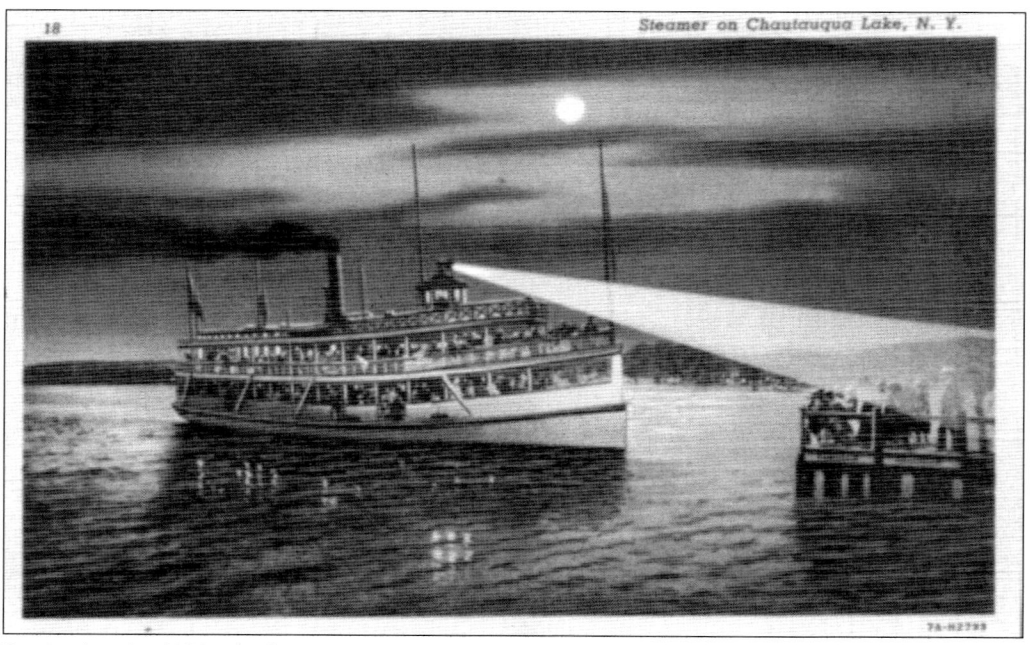

Beginning in 1890, the large steamers were being equipped with electric light plants. Night runs and evening excursion cruises became a bit safer when searchlights were added, beginning in 1901. The *City of Buffalo* was the first steamer with an electric light plant and was used for night trips from Lakewood to Chautauqua and back.

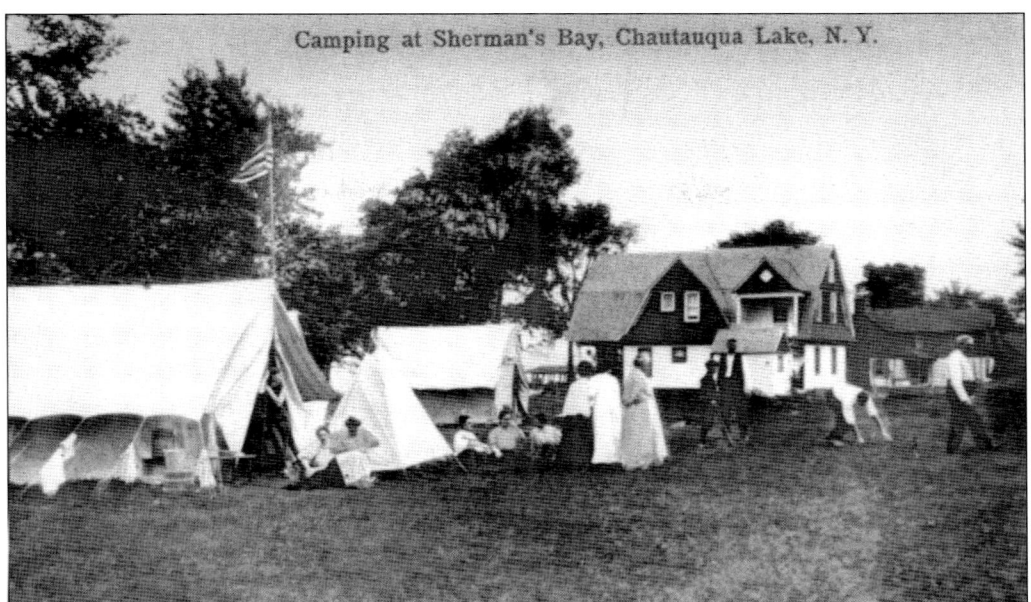

Sherman's Bay is up the lake from Lakewood. Like other shoreline areas, there were summer homes and, as this picture shows, places for tents. Camping was a favored activity by many from the local areas. They could transport all the paraphernalia needed and enjoy a few days or weeks by the lake. On one day in February 1899, there were 105 ice-fishing huts counted on Sherman's Bay. (Courtesy of MC.)

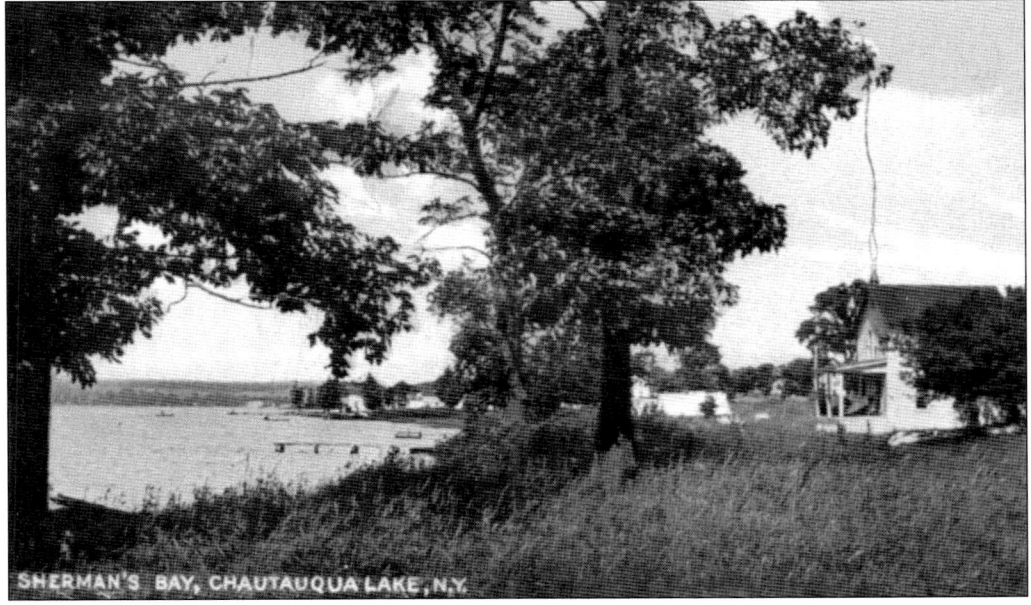

Sherman's Bay, served by the Chautauqua Traction trolley line as it stayed close to the lakeshore, is just west of the development of Waldmere Park. On Sherman's Bay's west side, an area named Vukote was developed with summer homes on canals. Dug in the wetlands, the canals helped to drain the land and provided boat moorings and lake access. These canals continue today, while the Beechwood canal does not.

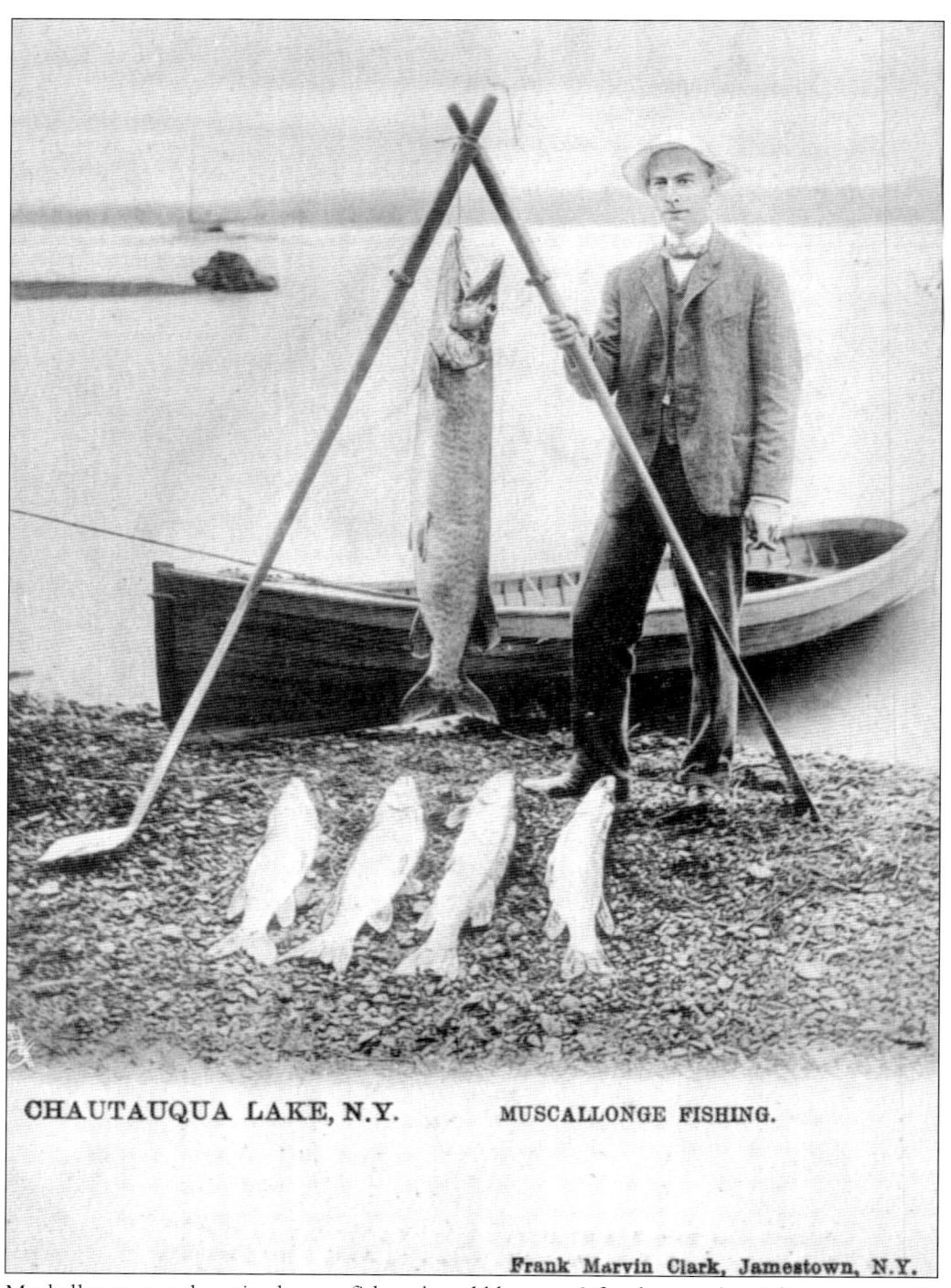

Muskellunge was the prized game fish and could be over 3 feet long and weigh many pounds. This fine catch of Chautauqua Lake muskellunge is a good day's work. Any fisherman would happily pose with these fish. Daily limits were not set as low as they are today. Today the season is limited, as is the total number of fish that can be taken by one person. (Courtesy of FHC.)

Three

TOWN OF NORTH HARMONY

North Harmony did not become a town until 1919. Before that, it was a part of the town of Harmony, which included territory between the New York-Pennsylvania border and Chautauqua Lake. The distances residents had to travel for town business was an influence in the decision to split Harmony into two separate towns. Early settlers located homes on the lakeshore in what was then the town of Chautauqua and later became the town of Harmony in 1816.

Thomas Bemus was the earliest settler on land his father, William, had articled in January 1806. William settled across the lake at what became Bemus Point, so there will be more about him when the book reaches the section on the town of Ellery. Jonathan Cheney had land on the east side of the lake but chose to settle on the west side. The Bemuses and the Cheneys, along with the Prendergasts, came from Pittstown, Rensellaer County, New York. Thomas Bemus and William Bemus, on opposite sides of the lake, were at the narrowest part of Chautauqua Lake, referred to as "the Narrows." The lake there is about 1,000 feet wide. Other parts of the lake are up to 2 miles wide.

Development along the lakeshore in this town did not include large hotels similar to the ones in Lakewood. Smaller hotels and boardinghouses with individual cottages were the rule along this part of the lakeshore. Victoria, with a hotel, is up the lake from the Narrows. Clusters of cottages lined the shore at intervals below the Narrows. These developments remain today, with many of the cottages remodeled into year-round homes. Signposts along the road retain the names of Neit's Crest, Connelly Park, or Quigley Park and remind motorists that these clusters of cottages are still here.

At the Narrows, where Thomas Bemus established his ferry, the settlement of Lakeland grew. The name was later changed to Stow. Today the Chautauqua County Veterans' Memorial Bridge spans the Narrows, carrying Interstate 86; however, the ferry continues to be used each summer.

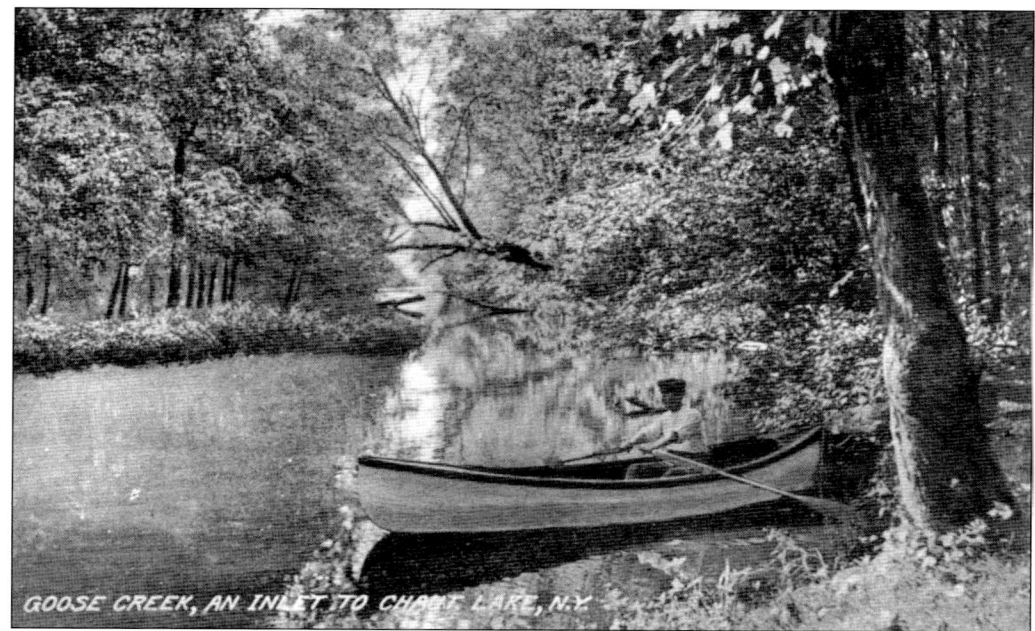

Goose Creek, considered today a great trout stream, is one of the larger tributaries flowing into Chautauqua Lake. It meanders through the towns of Busti and North Harmony, emptying into the lake between Loomis Bay and Ashville Bay. Like other streams entering the lake, it provided a quiet place for boaters to rest and even picnic.

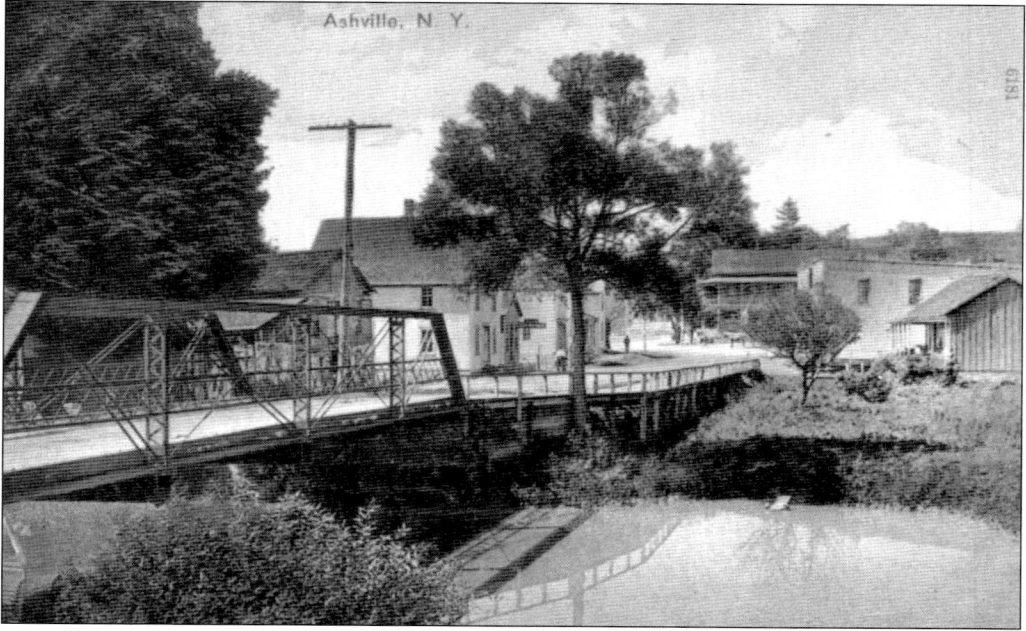

The trolley line kept close to the lakeshore until it reached Sherman's Bay. Here it began to swing inland, crossed the highway, and headed toward Ashville, a hamlet located on Goose Creek. The building with verandas near the center is the hotel, only a short walk from the trolley station that is off to the left end of the bridge. (Courtesy of FHC.)

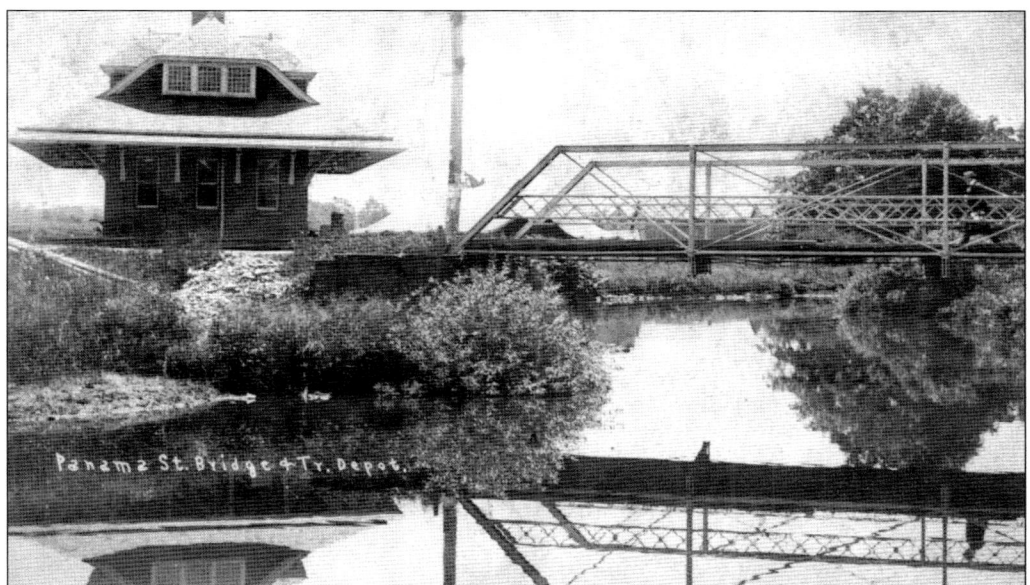

This is the Ashville trolley station. The bridge takes the Panama Road toward the hamlet of Ashville and on to the village of Panama. This bridge crosses Goose Creek, which then curves away from the station heading for Chautauqua Lake. A short walk takes the passenger to the center crossroads of the hamlet of Ashville.

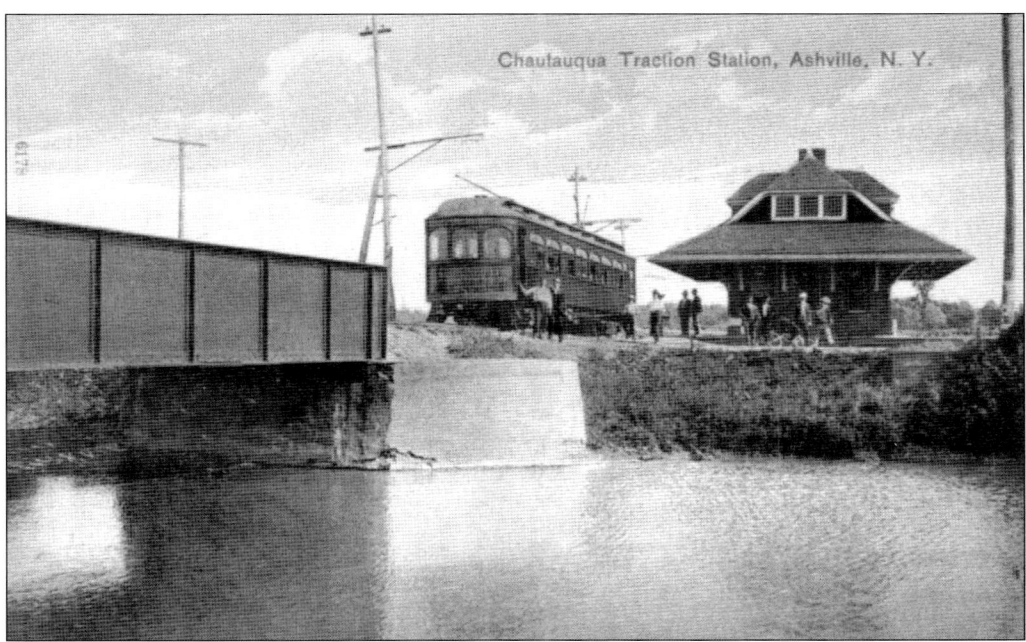

Another view of the trolley station in Ashville is seen here, but this time it is showing the trolley car alongside the station. It is ready to cross the bridge over Goose Creek and head back toward the lakeshore. The bridge shown in the postcard above is just off to the right in this view. The Ashville station was similar to the station built at Cheney's Point.

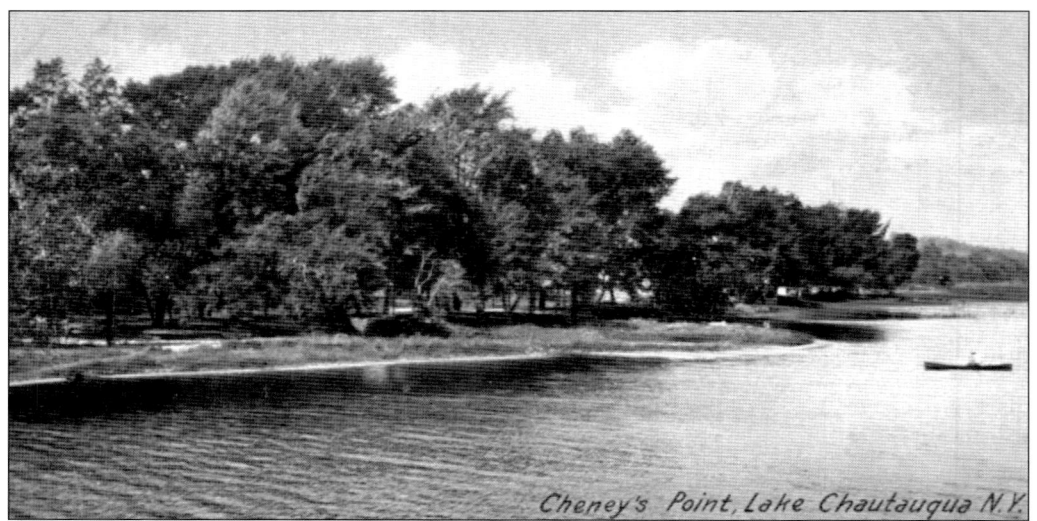

The YMCA established a summer camp here for a number of years, where boys from age 12 to 17 ate, slept, swam, and participated in planned activities. The undeveloped west side of the lake began to change when the Chautauqua Traction Company's trolley line reached Mayville in 1904. Cheney's Point gained a trolley station but lost the camp, which moved to a new site near Dewittville. (Courtesy of FHC.)

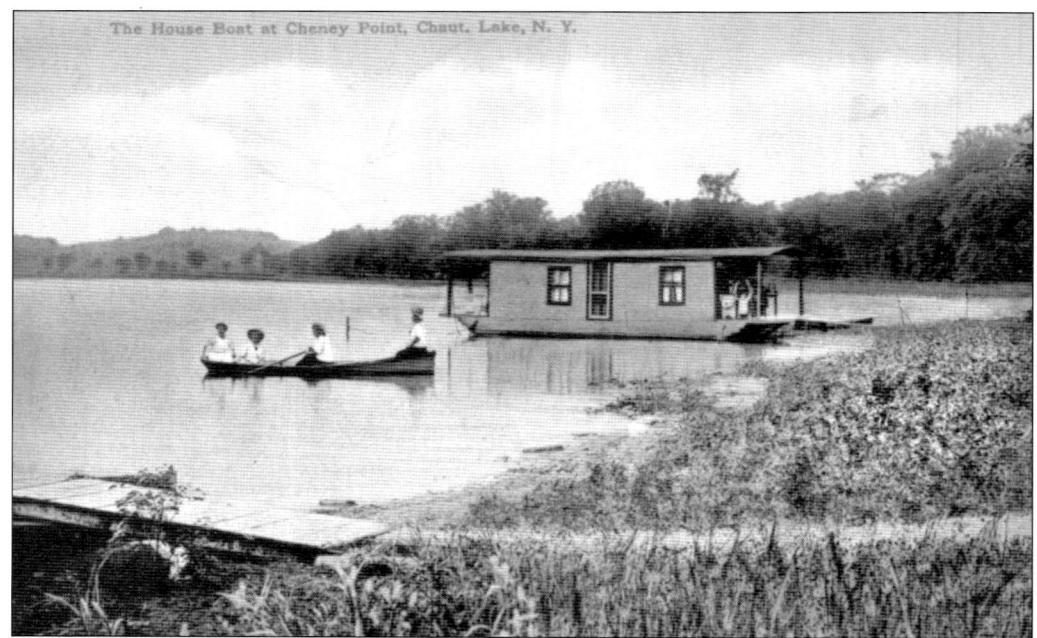

Fred H. Wilson and family passed the summer on a houseboat opposite Celoron in 1894. Whether this is the same houseboat is unknown. In the report about Wilson, it was commented that it was surprising that more people did not use a houseboat on Chautauqua Lake, as was done on eastern lakes. Eventually cottages were scattered along the west side of the lake. (Courtesy of MC.)

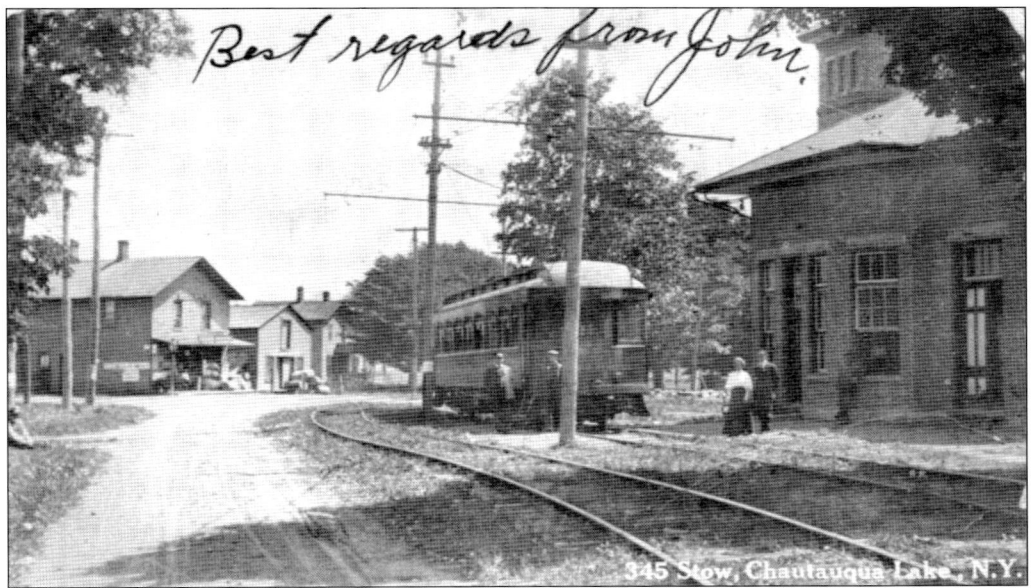

Stow, at the Narrows, is the location of this powerhouse and station for the trolley line. This was necessary to produce additional power for cars on a long line. Built before the trolley line reached Stow, the bricks had to be brought up the rail line on the east side of the lake and transferred over by ferry to avoid the bad springtime roads.

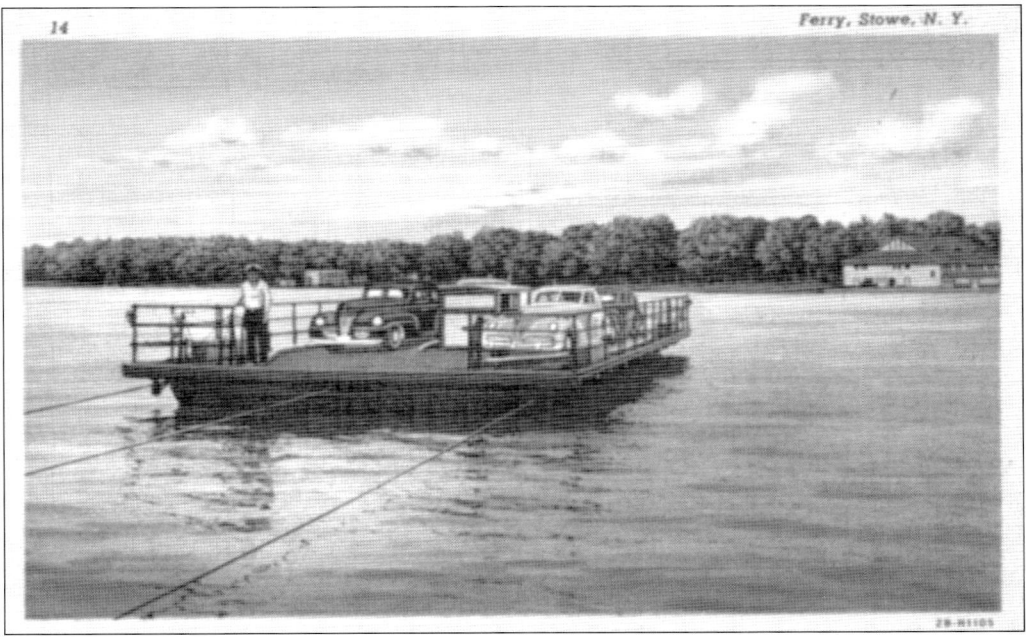

The ferry crossed the Narrows between Stow and Bemus Point. Beginning with a log raft, Thomas Bemus received a license to operate a ferry here in 1811. This postcard is from a later time period but is labeled Stow, whereas most ferry postcards are from Bemus Point. The Casino at Bemus Point is on the far shore. The ferry saved a 20-mile trip around the end of the lake.

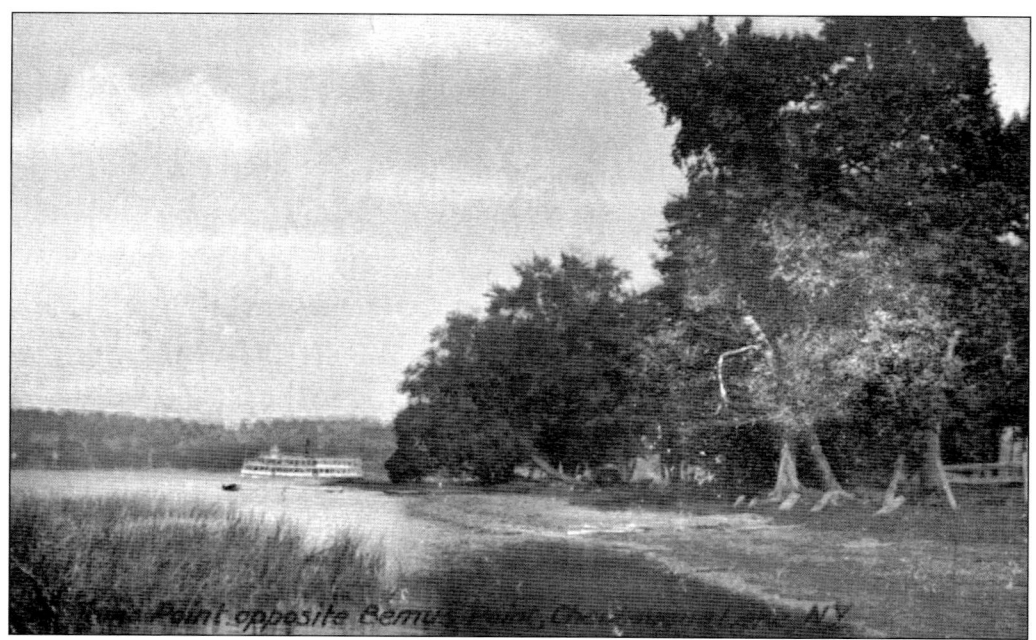

Tom's Point, located up the lake from Stow, was named for the early settler, Thomas Bemus. Steamboats, after passing through the Narrows on the way up the lake, would pass Tom's Point and turn left to approach the Long Point Dock or pass Long Point on the east side of the lake. Tom's Point was a popular place for picnics into the mid-20th century. (Courtesy of FHC.)

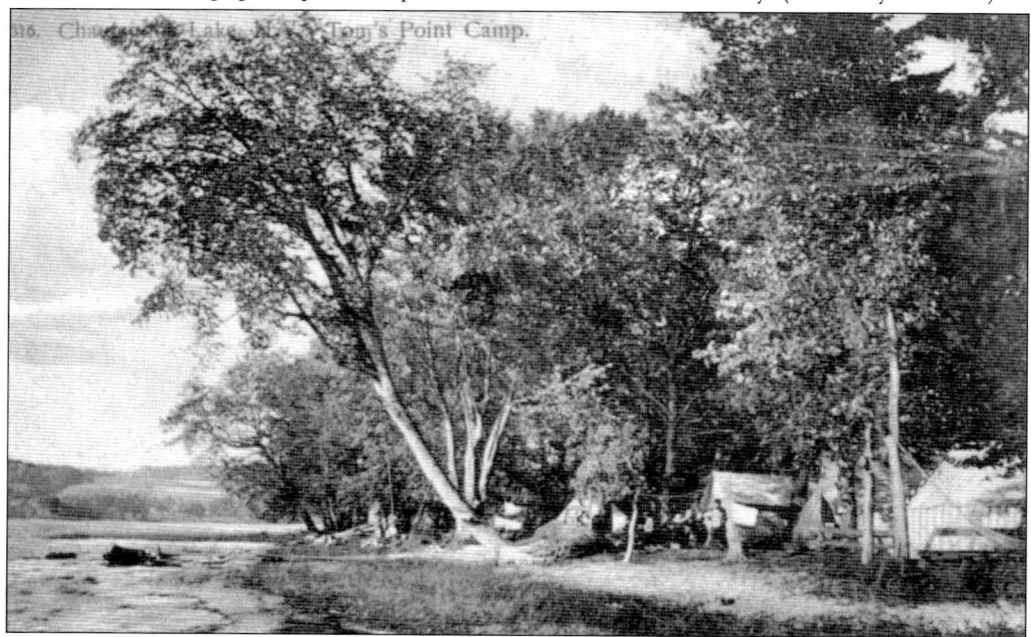

Tom's Point was never developed with cottages and amusements like many lakeshore areas. The White family's dairy farm provided camping areas on Tom's Point for the numerous families or groups of friends that wanted a spot to relax and enjoy the cooler lake breezes. It is now a Wildlife Management Area overseen by New York Department of Environmental Conservation.

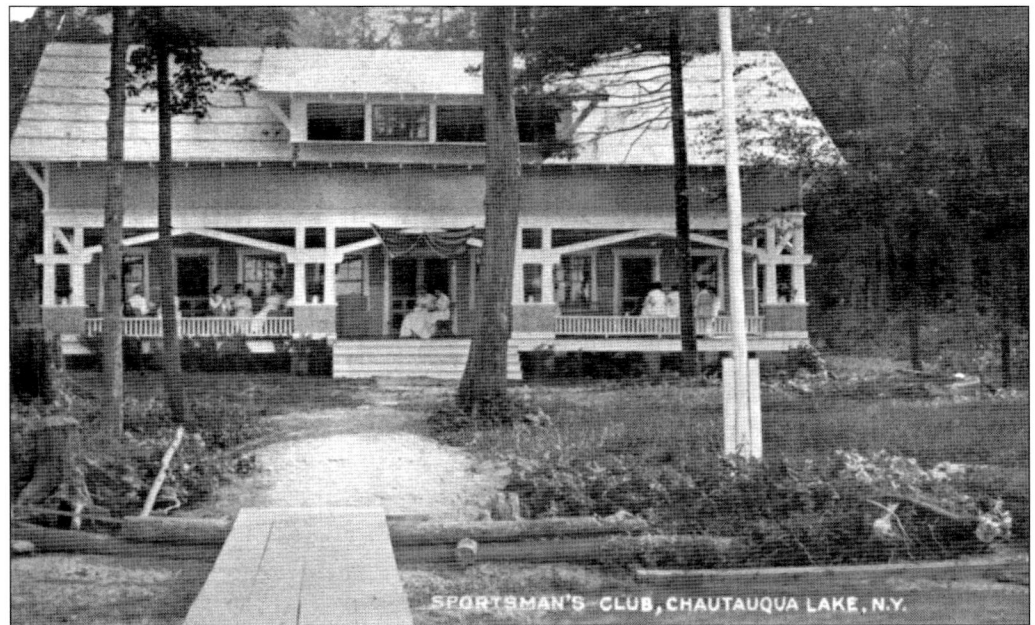

Twelve charter members founded the Sportsmen's Club of Lake Chautauqua for hunting and fishing in 1907. This clubhouse, built in 1910 on 10 acres just northwest of Tom's Point, burned in 1939. The second story was a dormitory used during hunting and fishing seasons. A new clubhouse was erected and still serves the club, now in its second century.

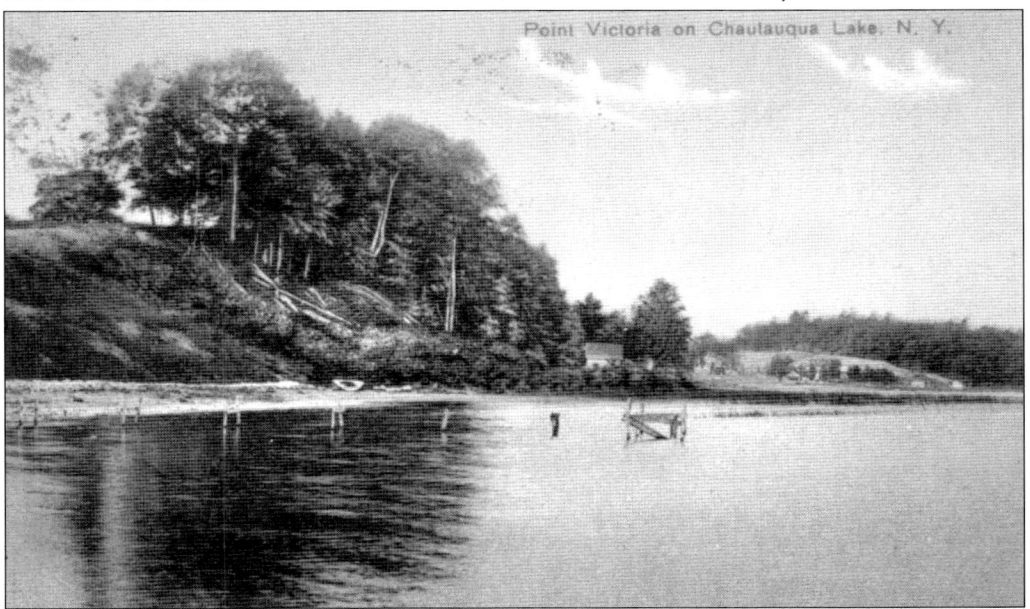

Willard Marcy began the development of Point Victoria in 1890. Named for his wife, the area soon boasted a small hotel and cottages. Farms benefitted from the arrival of the trolley line, as did the resort business. In April 1904, Loudy Green, a farmer near Point Victoria, had the distinction of being the first to ship dressed hogs to market on the trolley, thus avoiding the muddy wagon road.

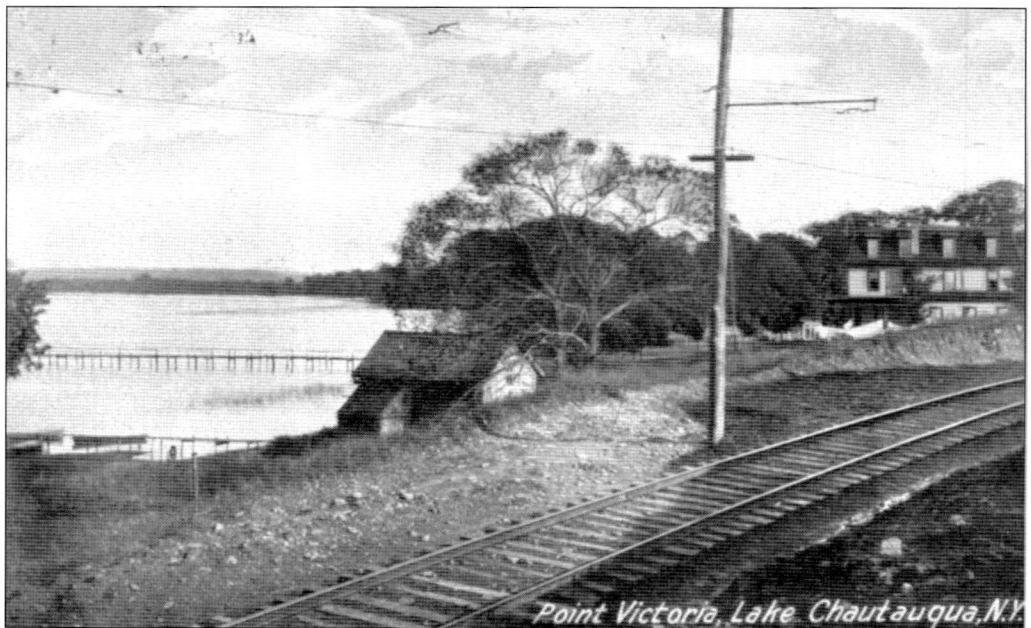

Point Victoria was a flag stop for steamboats. A second dock for pleasure boats can be seen in this view. A hotel is on the higher hill, offering a lake view. The steamboats or the wagon road were used to access this resort area until the trolley arrived in 1904. The trolley line served Point Victoria from 1904 to the end of trolley service in March 1926.

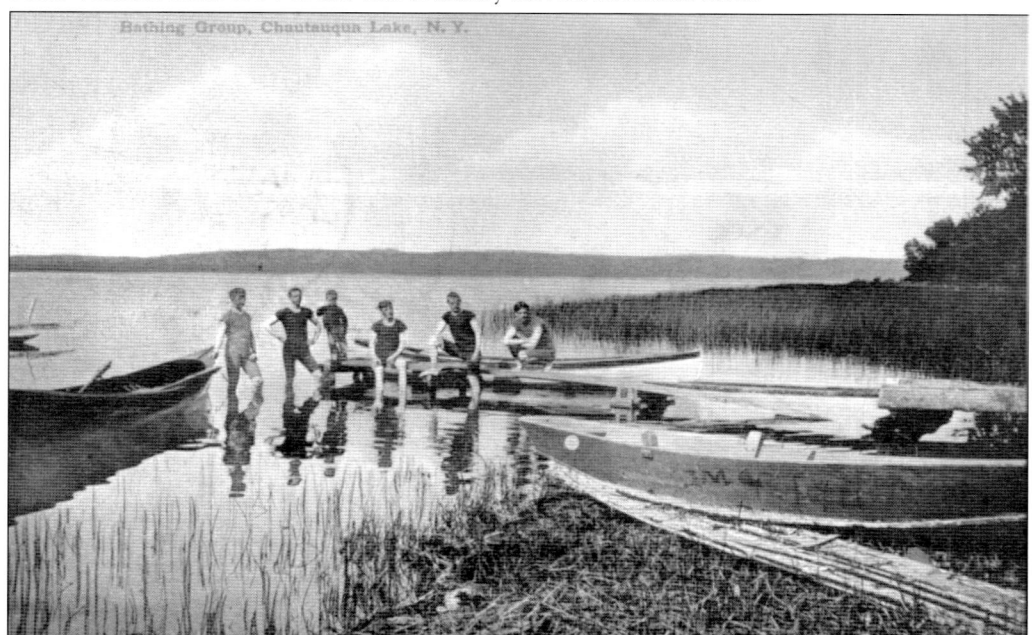

This bathing group could be at any shoreline shallows along the lake. With rowboats, these men could leave their respective cottages or hotels and meet for an afternoon of bathing and social time or even a picnic. They seem to be on a small dock that someone constructed for tying up a boat and getting to shore, rather than getting wet while pulling the boat up onshore.

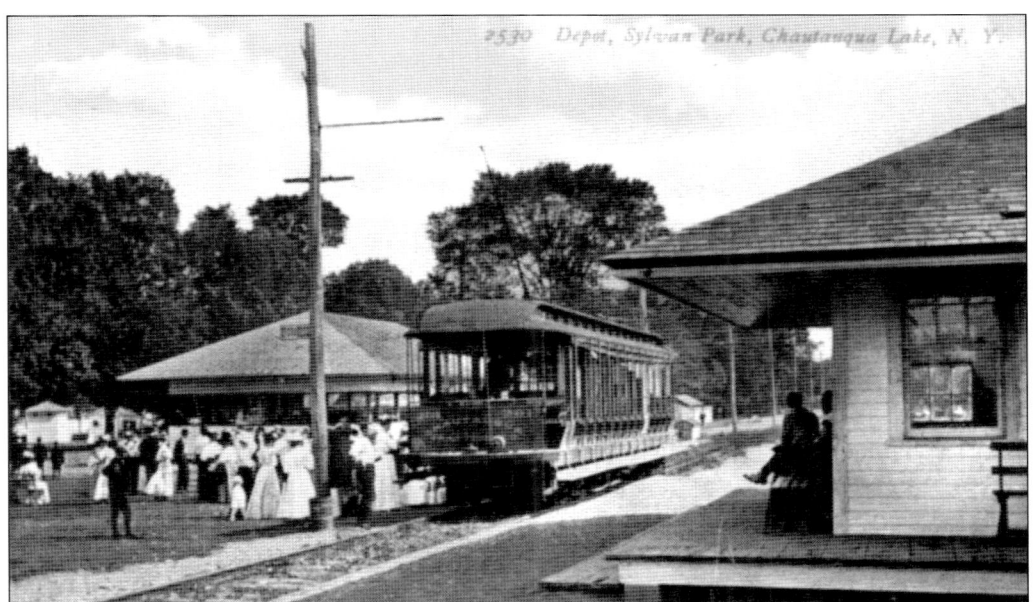

Shortly after the Chautauqua Traction Company expanded its trolley line along the west side of the lake, the company needed a picnic area on that side, too. The Hewes and Morris tract, up the lake from Point Victoria, was leased, and a picnic park was established. This became known as Sylvan Park. There was a small trolley station where people could wait for the trolley out of the weather.

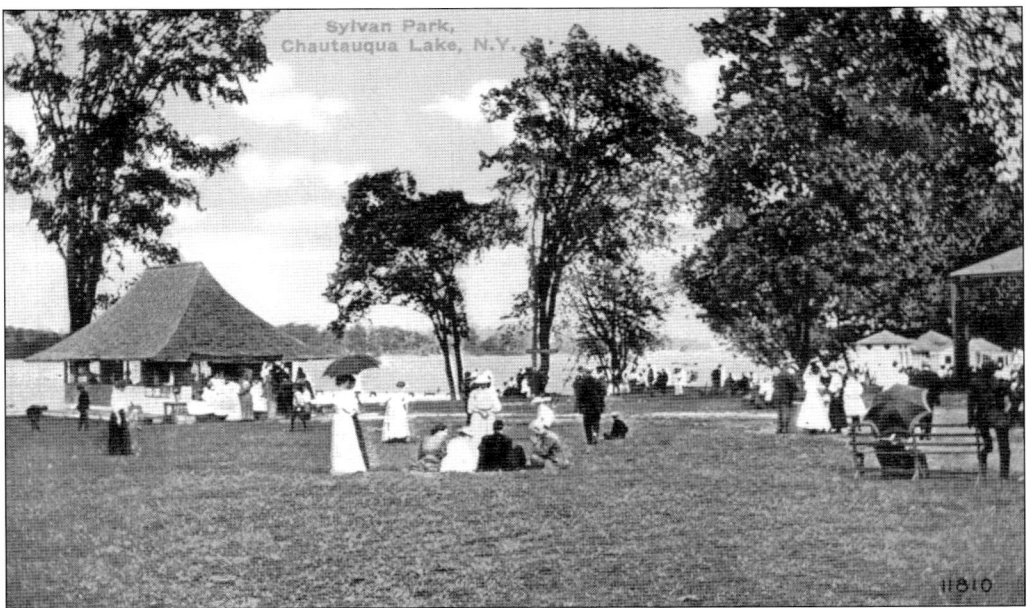

These are the grounds of Sylvan Park on Chautauqua Lake. The bathhouses with the pointed roofs are in the far right background. Sylvan Park provided the lake's west side with a simpler picnic area than Celoron Park. The level lakeshore provided playgrounds and ball fields for athletic contests. A picnic pavilion offered an area for large groups to enjoy picnics, and drinking water was piped to Sylvan Park.

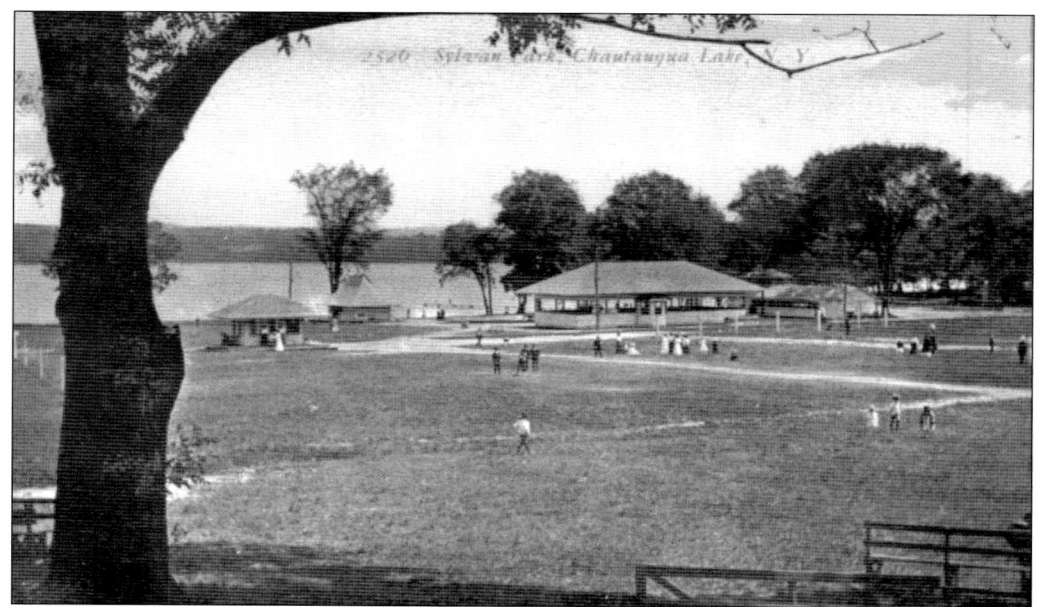

Sylvan Park was the site of many company and Sunday school picnics. The large picnic pavilion sheltered the groups from sun or rain. The small stands gave the participants places to sell refreshments to those who did not pack a picnic basket. At one time, there was a dance hall. The lakeshore provided a beach, considered one of the finest along the lake. (Courtesy of FHC.)

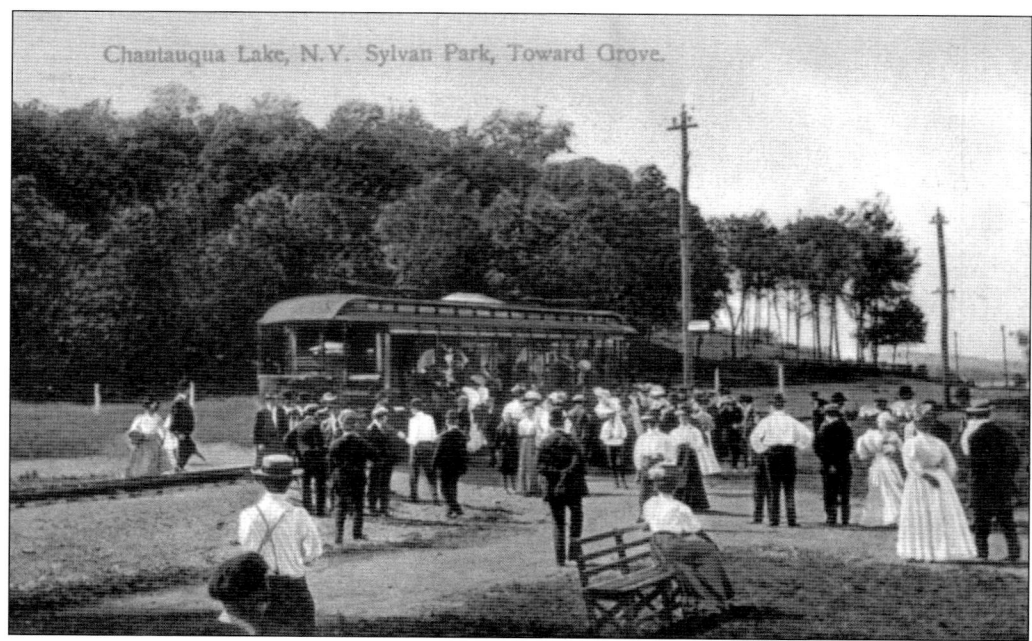

The grove of large trees that gave the park its name was cleaned up and provided a cool place to stroll, sit, or picnic on the higher hill away from the lakeshore. When trolley service ended in 1926, Sylvan Park became Camp Twa-ne-ko-tah, a girl's camp, until the early 1960s. It is now Camp Chautauqua, considered one of the best RV parks in the country.

Four

Town of Chautauqua

The Prendergast family purchased a large number of acres located in the present town of Chautauqua from the Holland Land Company. The extended family founded the city of Jamestown, opened stores in Mayville and Jamestown, farmed many acres, acted as county judges and town supervisors, and contributed to the town and county in other ways. More settlers arrived, and settlements expanded.

As the county seat, people from throughout the county came to Mayville. The county poor farm was established in Dewittville, east of Mayville. As time went on, Chautauqua became home to Chautauqua Institution, which has now celebrated 135 years. Across the lake, Point Chautauqua, planned by landscape architect Frederick Law Olmsted, still adheres to his plan. Hotels and cottages came and went. Wealthy industrialists found the lake for their summers out of the large cities, and the "wealth" of Chautauqua, town and county, became known beyond its borders. Families escaping the cities found the simple pleasures of the lake, and generations later continue to return to the area. The ice industry was a winter activity, and huge wooden buildings occupied lakeshore lots, holding the ice until it was shipped via rail to large city markets. These have gone.

Walking, horseback, stagecoaches, and boats were the early modes of transportation for these people. In 1828, the first steamboat was built in Mayville, providing a quicker way to get between Mayville and Jamestown and points along the lake. Mayville's dock continued to have steamboats stay overnight so an early-morning run could begin after the morning train arrived, dispensing passengers ready to continue to the resort of their choice along the lake. Rail lines came to Mayville from different directions and helped move visitors from place to place. Eventually the automobile began to replace the older modes of transportation. Between the larger resort areas, small cottages or camping spots hosted short-term vacationers.

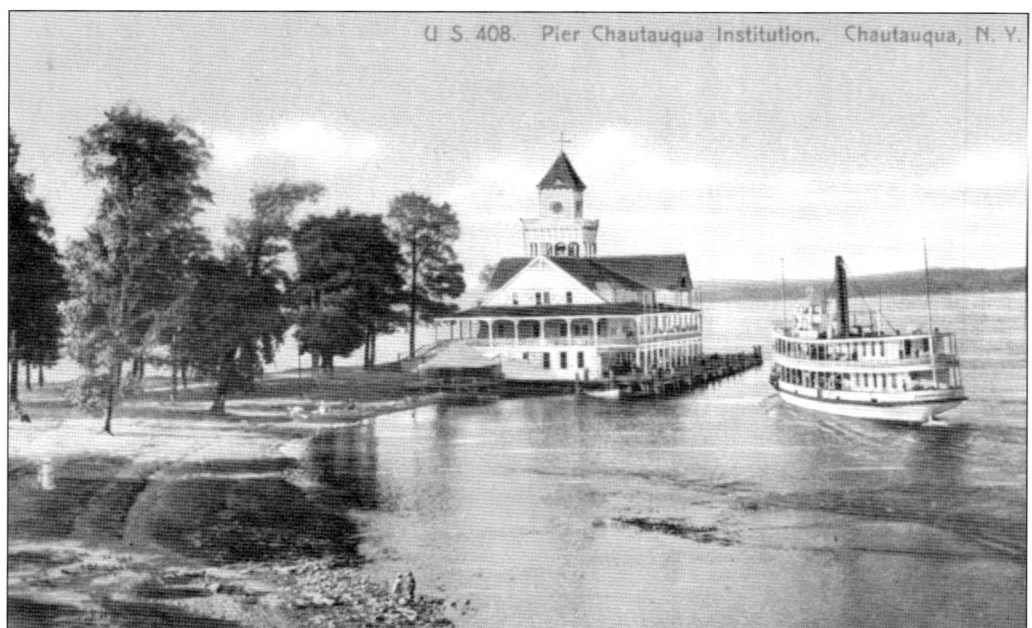

In 1886, a new dock and dock house was built at Chautauqua. The dock level had a ticket office and baggage and waiting rooms, with shops on the next floor and dormitory space and classrooms on the top level. The tower was 100 feet high and contained a large $900 clock and a fine set of chimes that called Chautauquans to lectures and other activities.

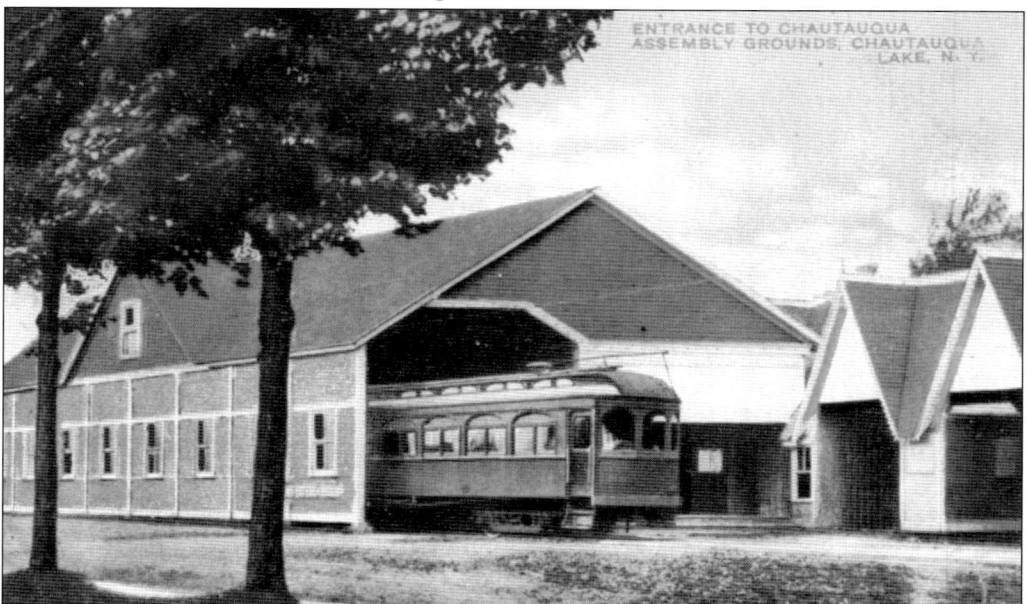

By 1904, Chautauqua Traction Company's trolley line arrived at Chautauqua and completed the rail system that connected all points on both sides along Chautauqua Lake. Before the trolley reached Chautauqua, most visitors arrived by steamer, making the steamboat dock the main entrance. This is the trolley station with the main gate for horse and buggies. It was replaced in 1916–1917 with the building that still stands.

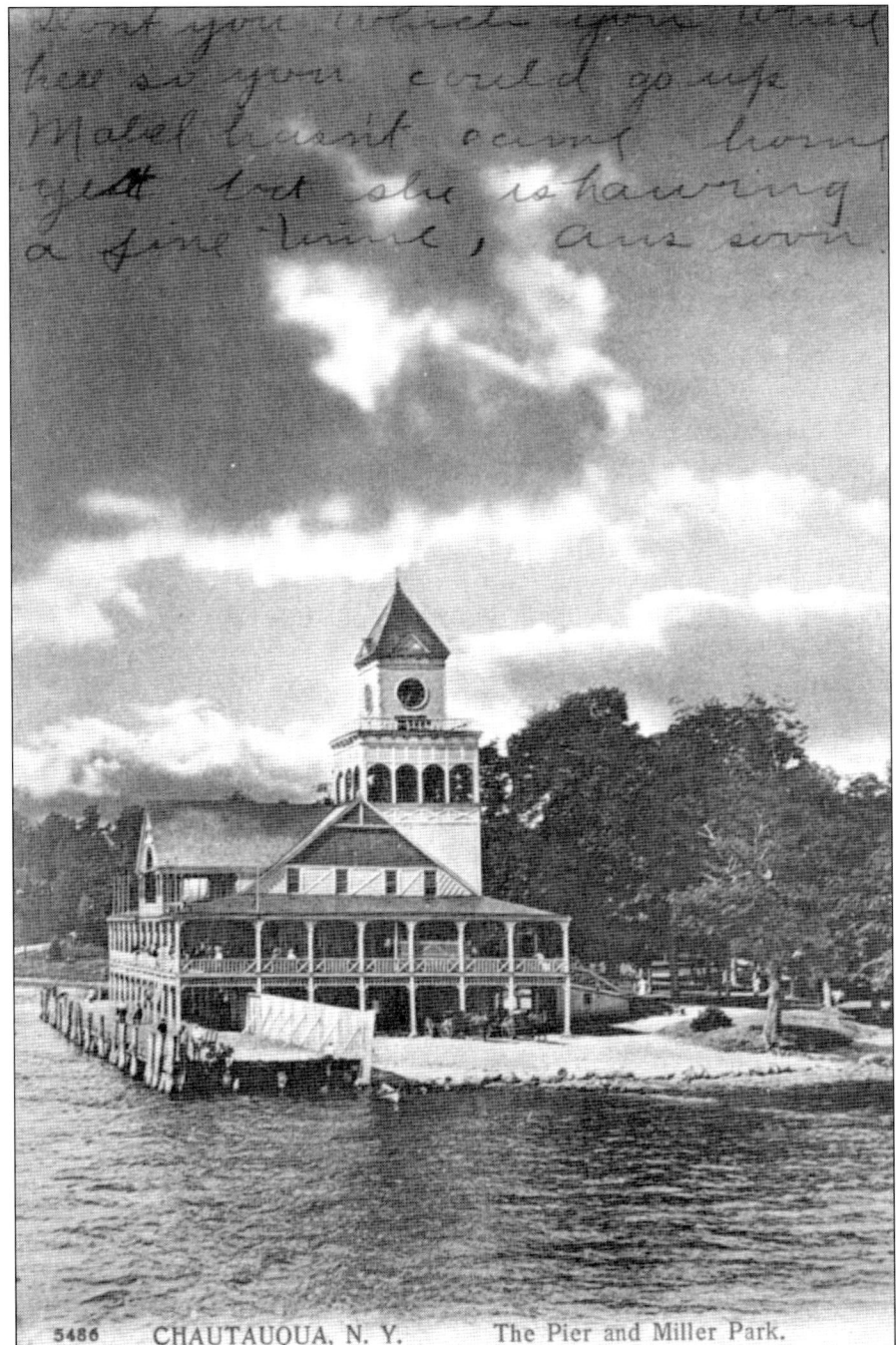

The 1886 Pier Building stood at the point near where the original outdoor auditorium of the Chautauqua Assembly was located. Behind the auditorium, Lewis Miller, cofounder of the Chautauqua Assembly, built his cottage. The auditorium was abandoned at that site before the Pier Building was constructed, and the resulting open area has remained a park, named for the cofounder. Miller Cottage still overlooks the park today.

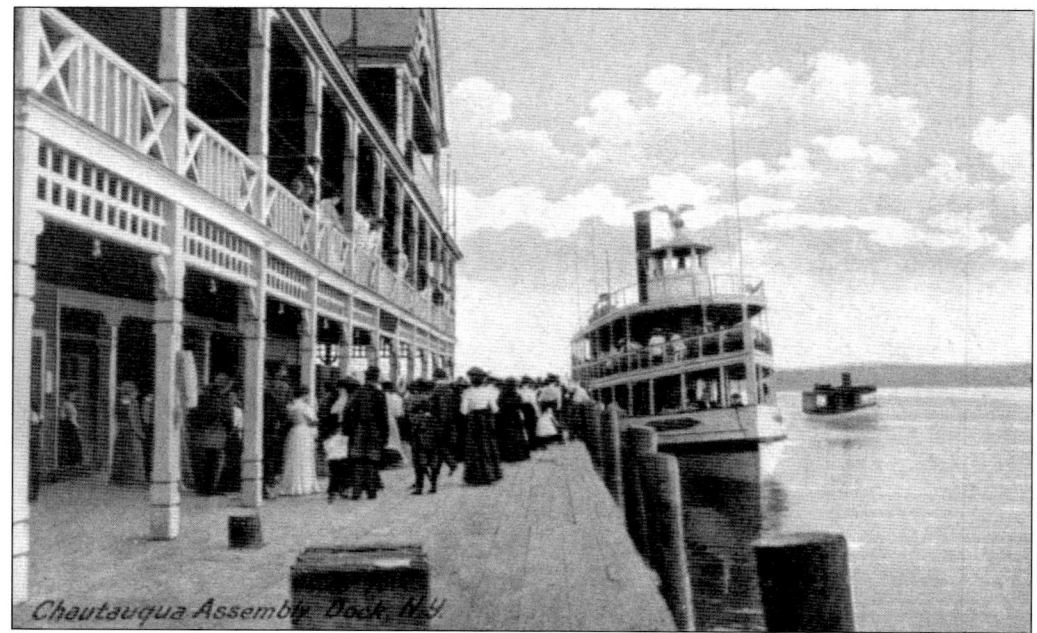

A close-up view shows the steamer dock and veranda of the dock building. It was quite a busy place, as hundreds of summer visitors could arrive by steamer at once. Many arrived with trunks and baggage for the season, creating a crowded dock. Stores and concessions were available on the second story.

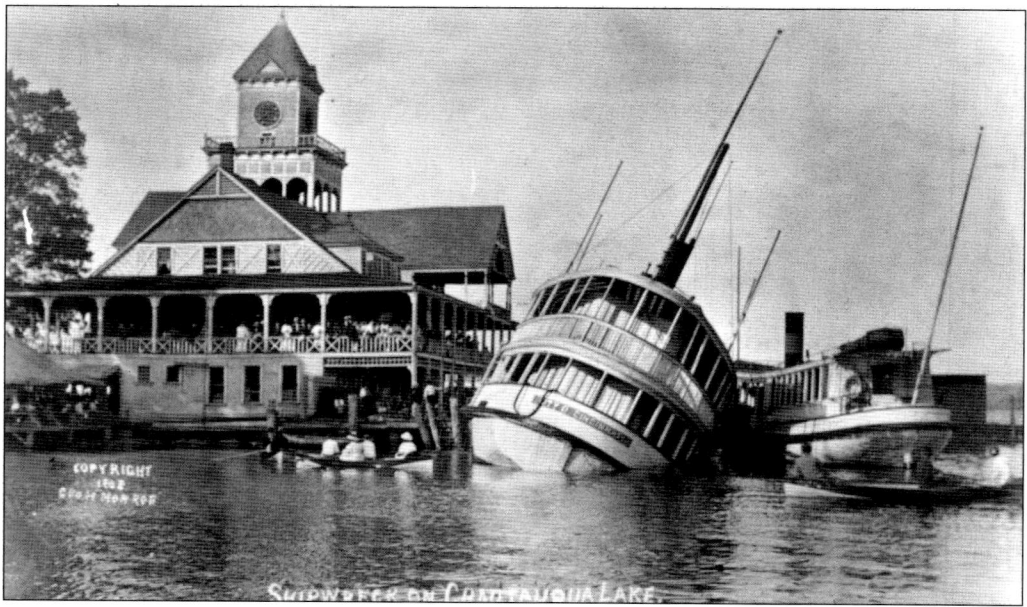

On August 8, 1908, the *City of Cincinnati* struck a submerged pile at the dock at Chautauqua. The hull was pierced, and water rushed in, causing the steamer to list away from the dock. It happened within a few feet of the dock, so the passengers were able to disembark over a gangplank from the bow. The *City of Cincinnati* was soon pumped out, repaired, and back in service.

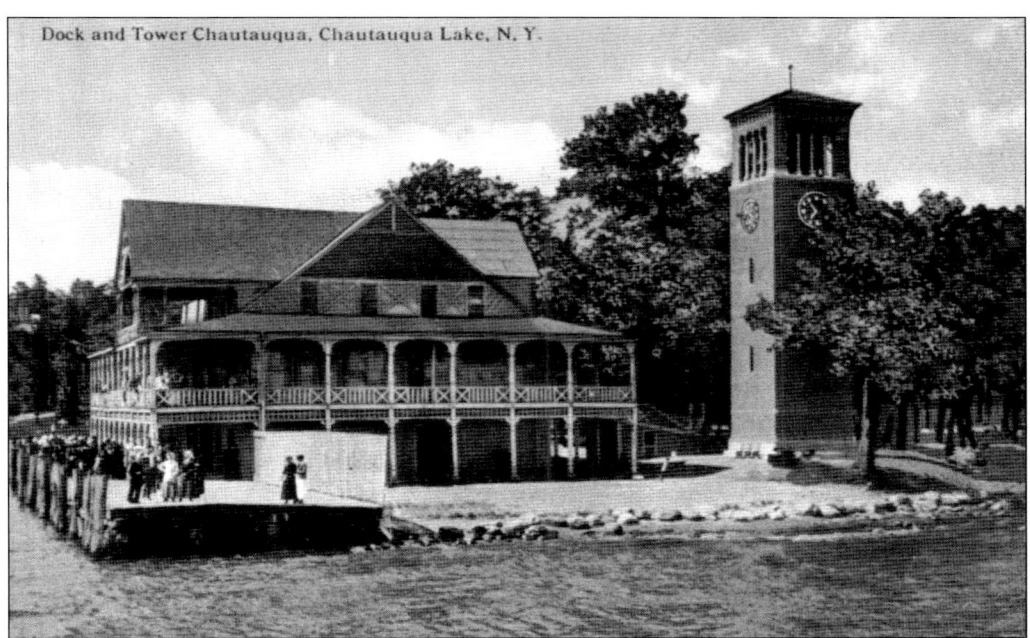

The more than 5 tons of bells became too much for the wooden tower after a number of years. A new 69-foot-high, 16-foot-square, brick bell tower was constructed next to the Pier Building to hold the bells. On August 1, 1911, it was dedicated and named the Miller Bell Tower. The Miller Bell Tower has become the recognizable symbol of Chautauqua Institution.

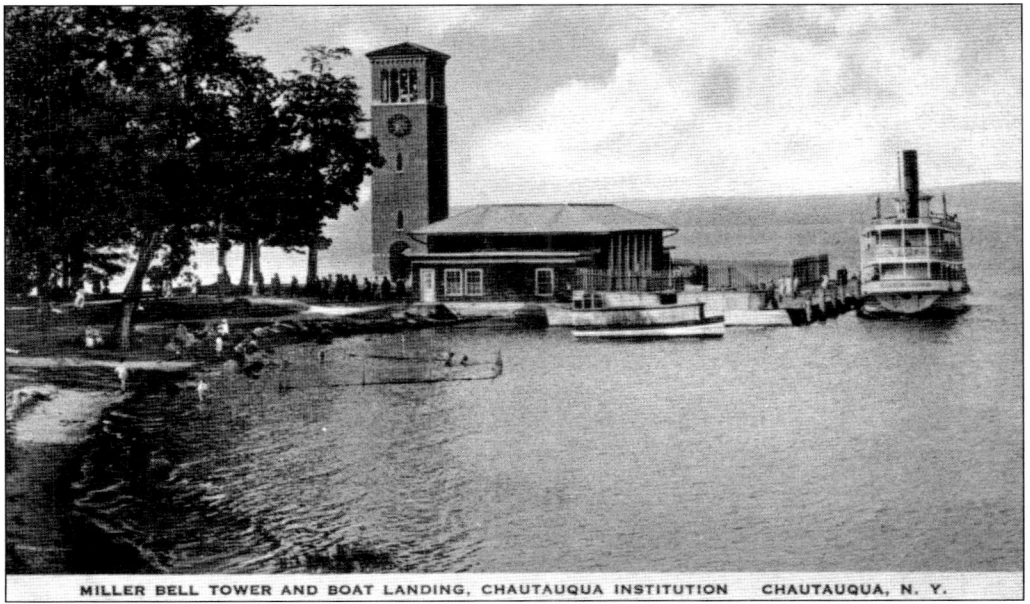

The old Pier Building was replaced with a smaller structure in 1916 since fewer people were arriving at Chautauqua by boat. The steamboat dock remained for a number of years until the steamboats were gone from the lake. At the end of the steamboat era, the building became the College Club, where college-age Chautauquans could meet for activities. It has since become a multiuse building.

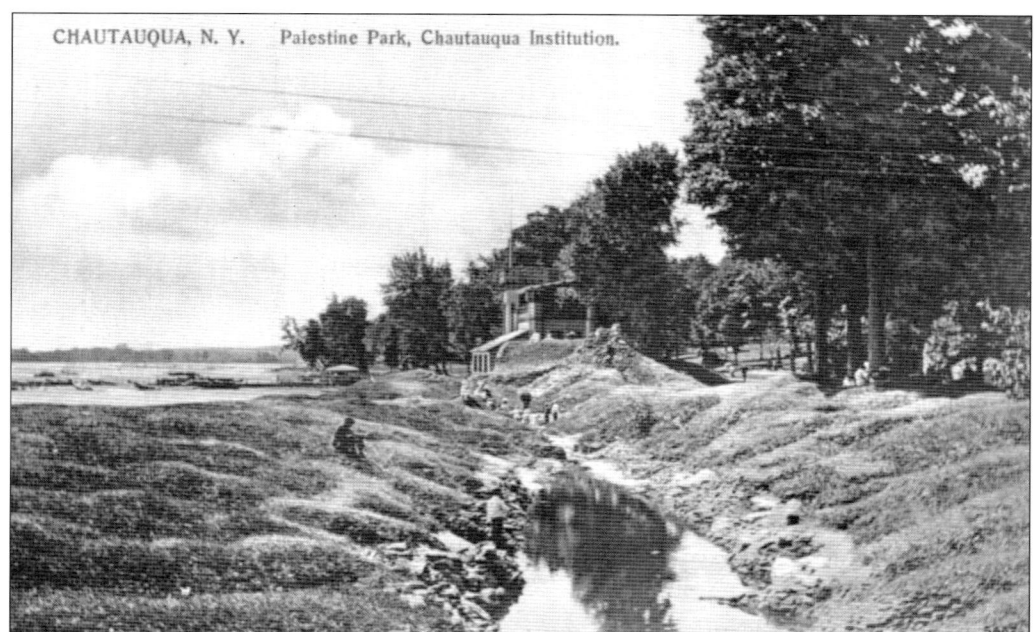

Palestine Park was created to teach the geography of the Holy Land. After all, Chautauqua began as a training assembly for Sunday school teachers. Model cities were placed in the correct areas of mountains, hills, and rivers, with Chautauqua Lake as the Mediterranean Sea. Palestine Park is located south of Miller Park and is still a good geography lesson for young and old.

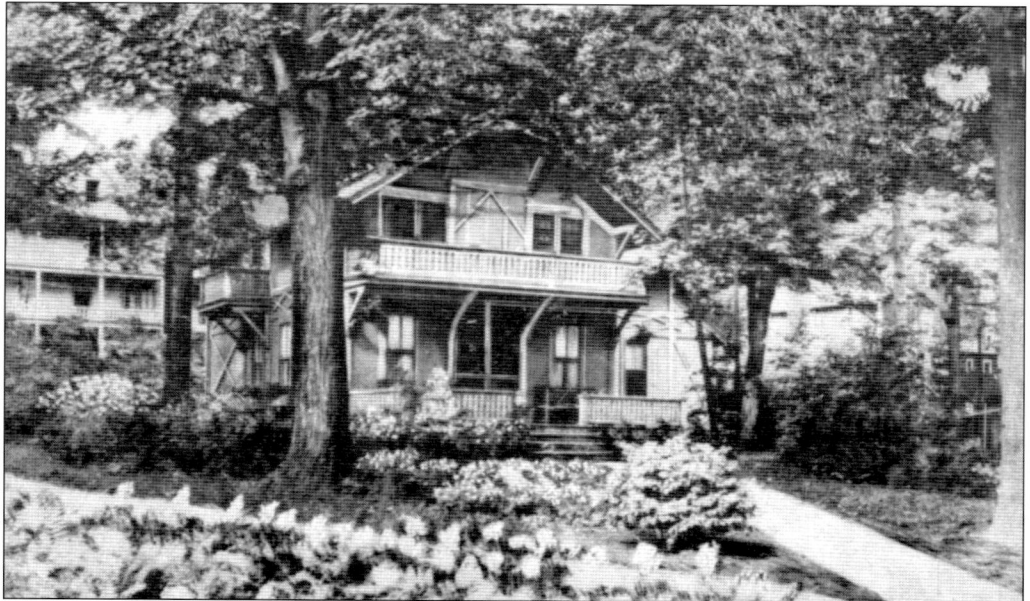

This is a mid-20th-century picture of the Miller Cottage, which overlooks Miller Park today. Lewis Miller built it in 1875, the second year of the assembly. Because some of the lumber was precut in Akron and brought to Chautauqua, it is the first prefab house on the grounds. Some call it the Edison Cottage since Thomas Edison resided there with his wife, Mina, who was Lewis Miller's daughter.

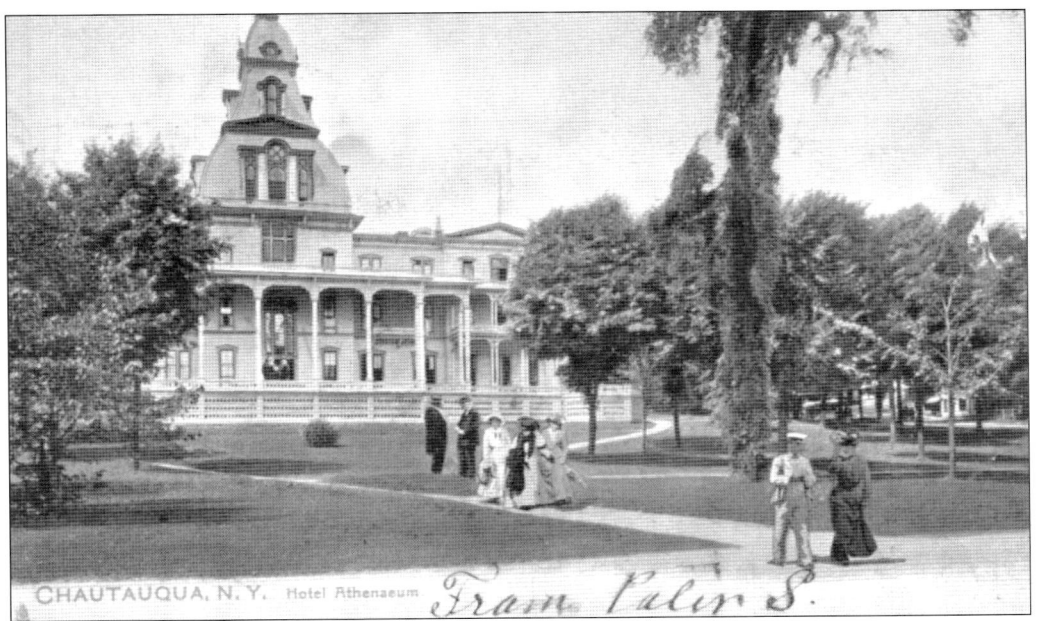

Built in 1881 to accommodate the many visitors arriving at Chautauqua, the Hotel Athenaeum is one of the two remaining hotels along the lake from this era. It has had visitors from around the world through the years. Today, with the Victorian-styled parlor, complete with wicker furnishings, or the comfortable rocking chairs on the wide verandas, one can relax and almost see the steamboats of yesterday on the lake.

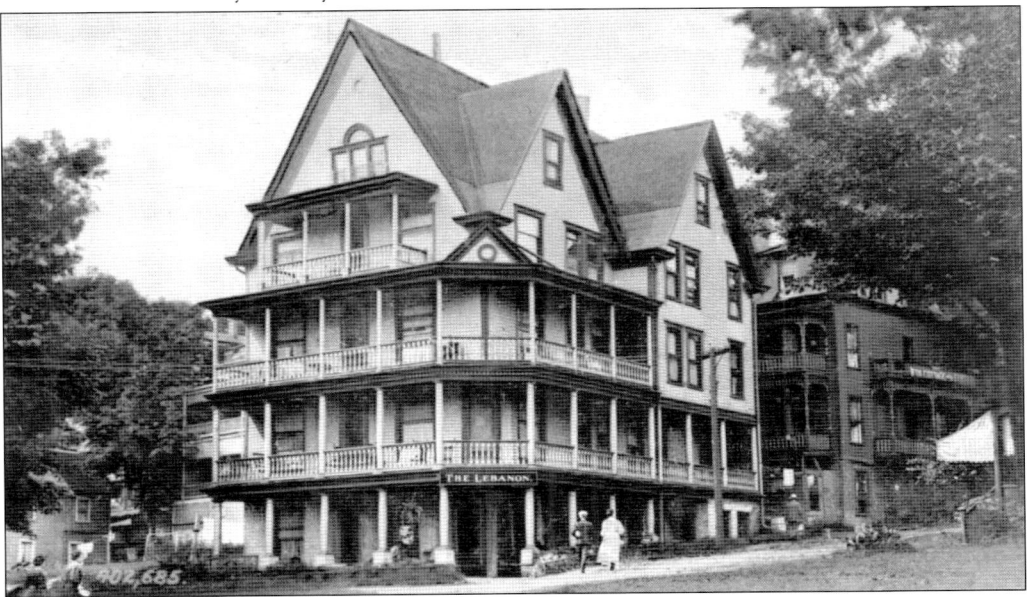

Smaller hotels and boardinghouses catered to visitors throughout the season at Chautauqua. The Lebanon Hotel, on the corner of what is now Miller and Simpson Avenues, and was one of three hotels in a row along the lakeshore. The Windsor and the Belvedere were the other two, and all three hotels overlooked the lake near Palestine Park. The Lebanon later became the Hotel William Baker.

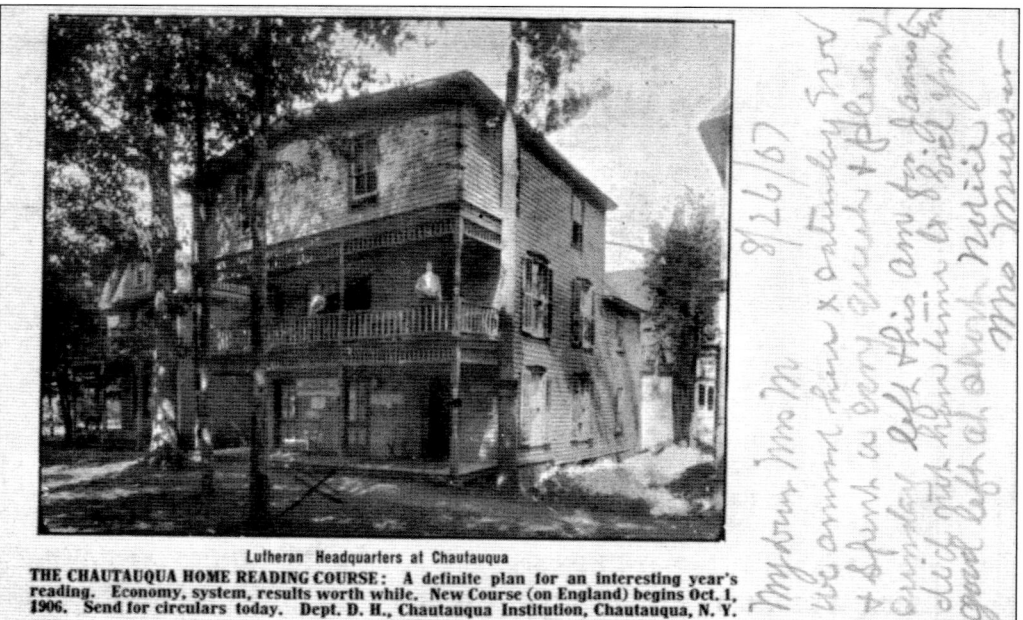

Chautauqua Institution began as a Methodist campground, but soon other denominations established a presence on the grounds. Pictured is the Lutheran headquarters, but the postcard carries a message about the Chautauqua Literary and Scientific Circle (CLSC), now the oldest book club in America. It was an integral part of the Chautauqua movement, enabling people to further their education through a home-study course of recommended reading.

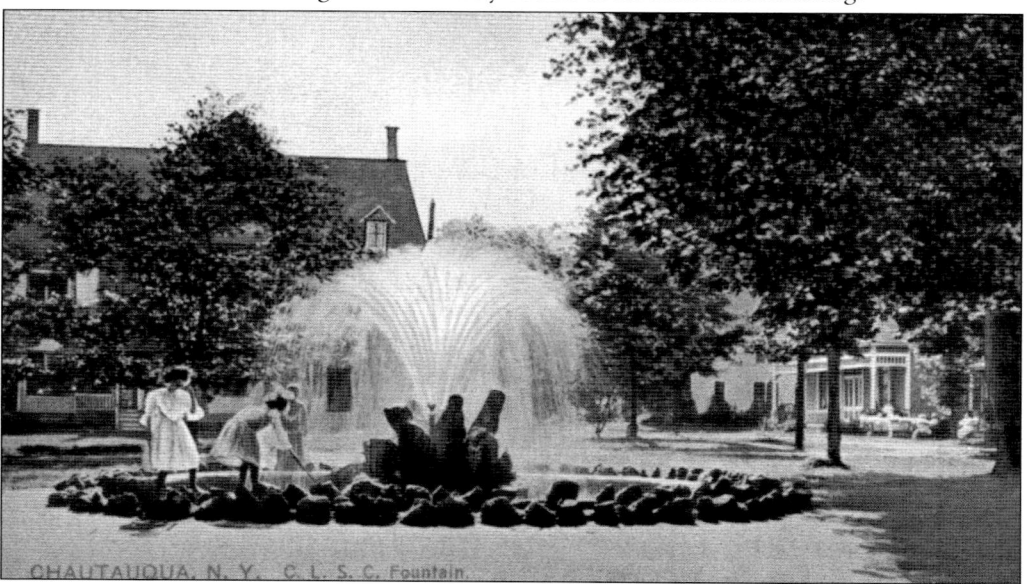

The first CLSC class to graduate from the four-year-long reading course called themselves the Pioneer Class. On their 10th anniversary in 1892, they built this fountain near their class building, Pioneer Hall. The porches of Pioneer Hall can be seen on the right through the trees. Fountains were a popular landscape element at that time. Subsequent CLSC classes often gave a gift to Chautauqua on their 10th anniversary.

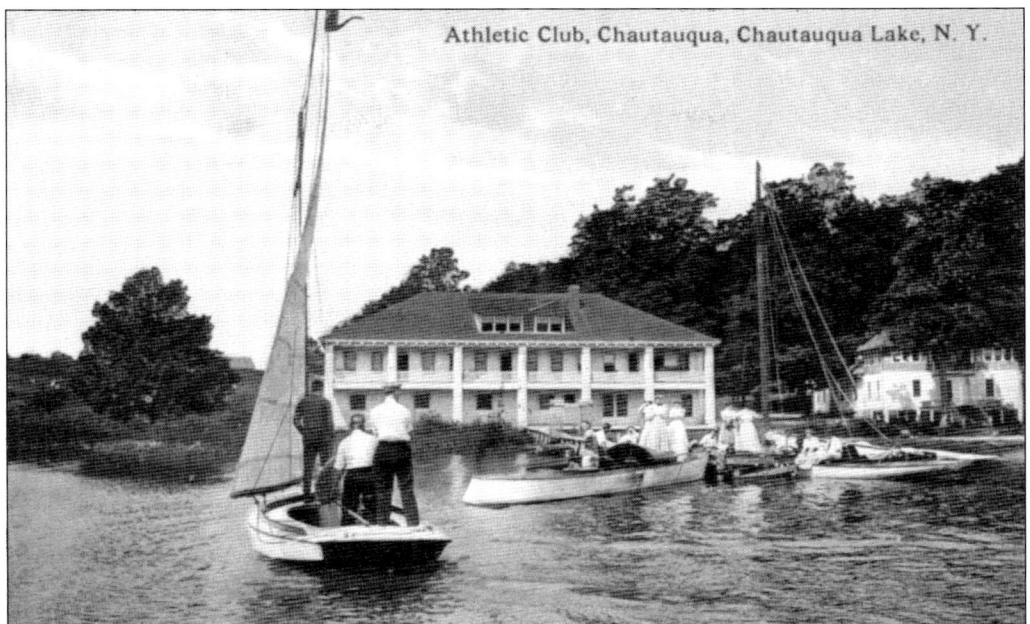

The Athletic Club, located on the lakeshore to the south of the Athenaeum, provided sailing, rowing, and other athletic pursuits for visitors and season residents of Chautauqua Institution. Tennis courts were located behind the building, and the Boys Club and Girls Club were nearby. The athletic field was behind this building and up the hill. It was torn down and replaced by the Beeson Youth Club building in 1968.

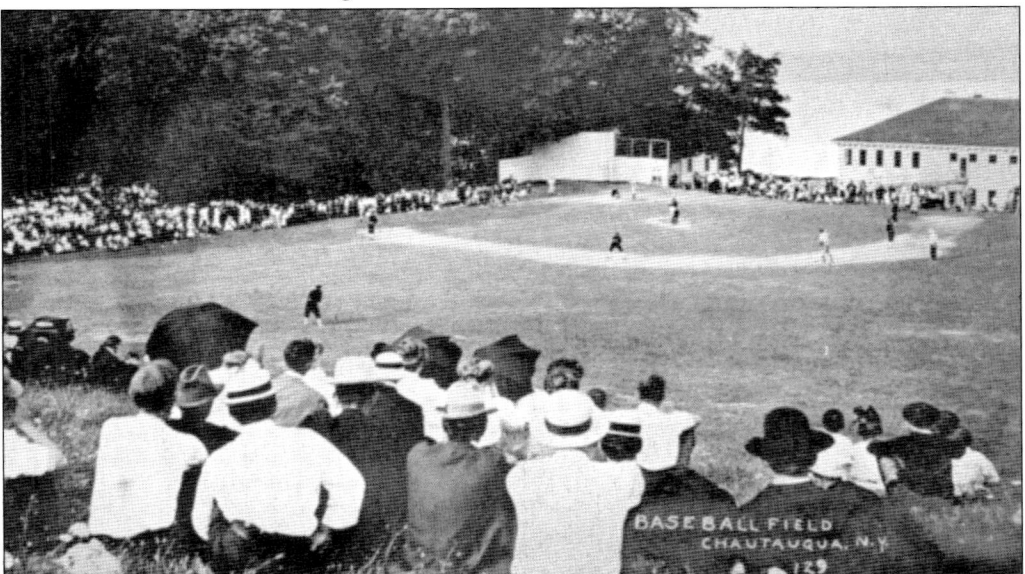

Chautauqua's athletic field was the site for many baseball games between teams of all ages. Chautauqua had at least one team that played other community teams from around the area. This view was taken in 1906 or before and does not show the covered bleacher seats, which were built later. Look closely to see the bridge that connected the Athletic Club's upper floor to the top of the field. (Courtesy of FHC.)

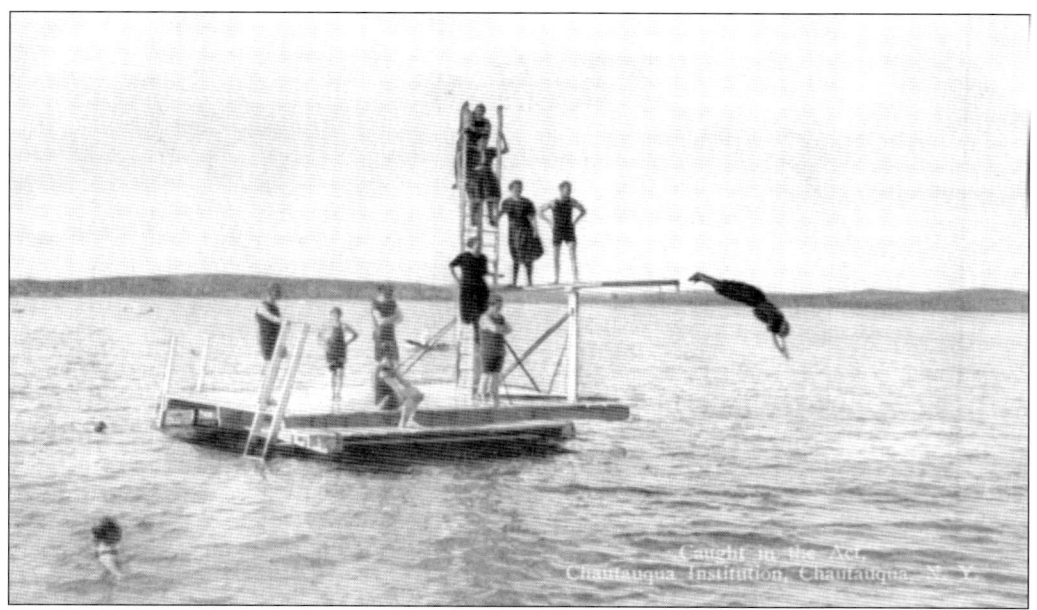

Chautauqua had an early School of Physical Education, so it is not surprising to see swimming and diving taking place on the waterfront. Note that both men and women participated in athletic pursuits at Chautauqua. Other sports also took place here. The Boys Club and Girls Club both had many athletic games and field days. Tennis, quoits, and golf all had a place at Chautauqua.

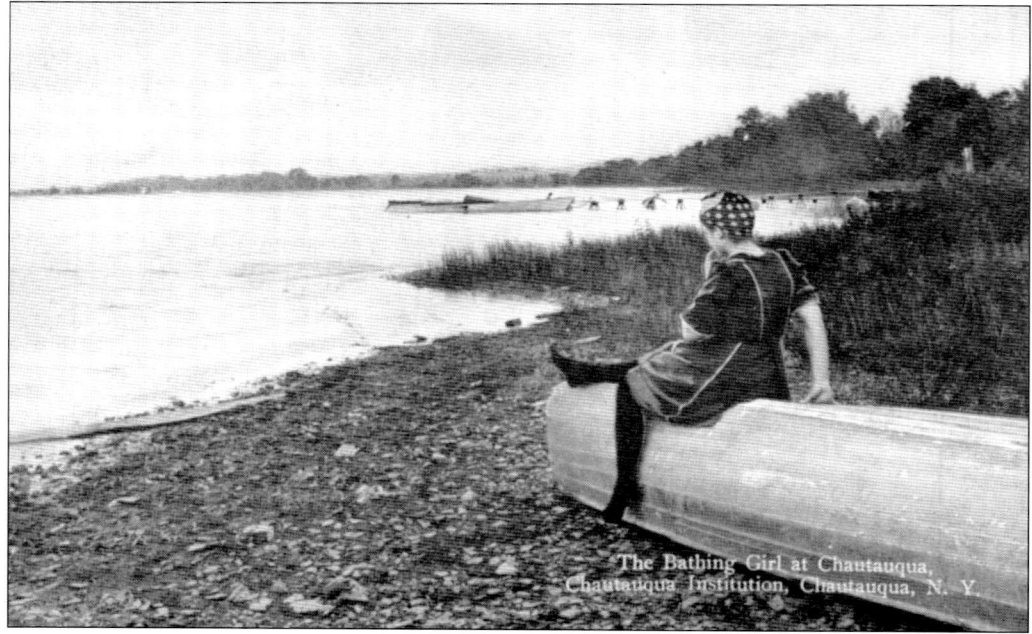

This bathing girl sure is well covered! She won't get a suntan, and that heavy costume is not made for much swimming. Is she posing for the photographer or wishing she could be out in the water to swim and dive as the people in the above postcard? Or is she just resting and relaxing in a quiet place along the shore?

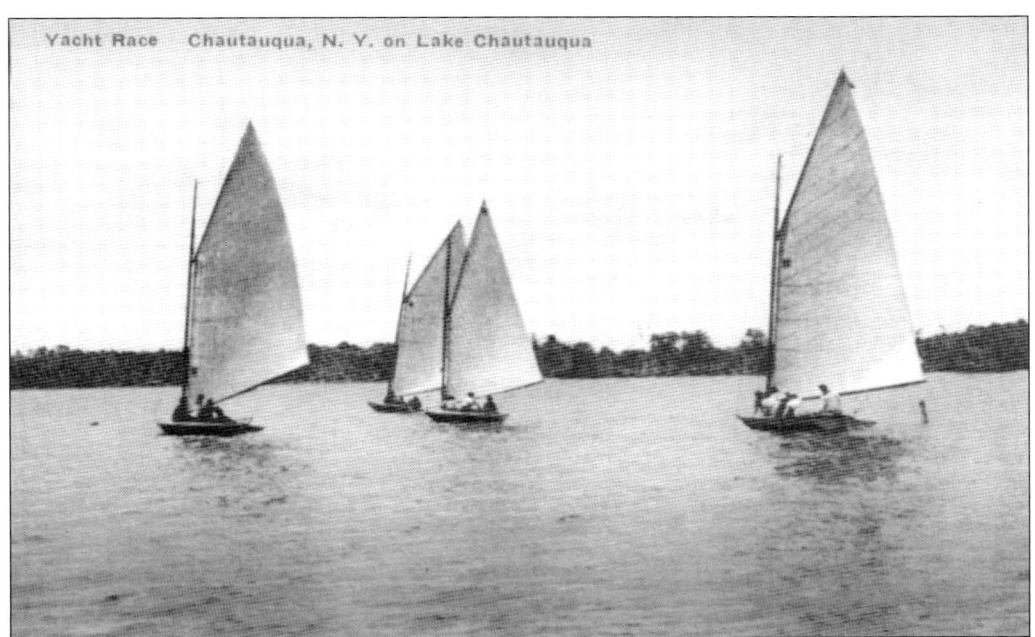

Chautauqua Institution's Athletic Club had sailboats, rowboats, and canoes for their members, and some members had their own boats. Sailing races were a weekly event during some years. The Chadakoin Boat Club, located in Greenhurst (and later in Lakewood), gave Chautauqua's club competition in the races. (Courtesy of FHC.)

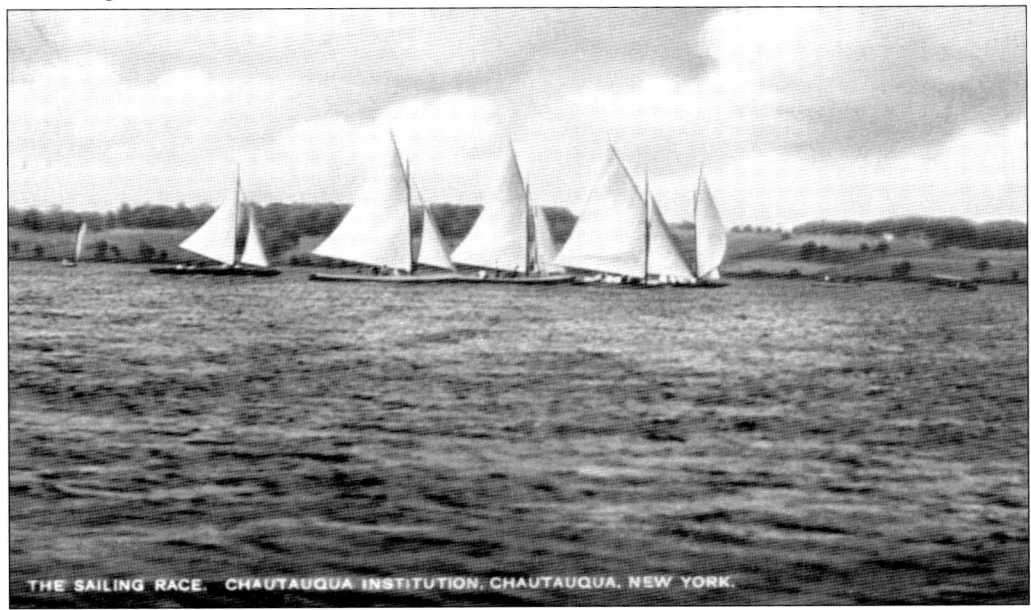

Chautauqua Lake is considered a very good place for sailing because of the orientation of the lake to the prevailing northwesterly winds. Many different kinds of sailboats can be seen on the lake, and today's sailboats differ from the earlier ones. But the sailors are still the same, enjoying their boats, the races, or just a nice day relaxing with only the sound of the wind in the sails. (Courtesy of FHC.)

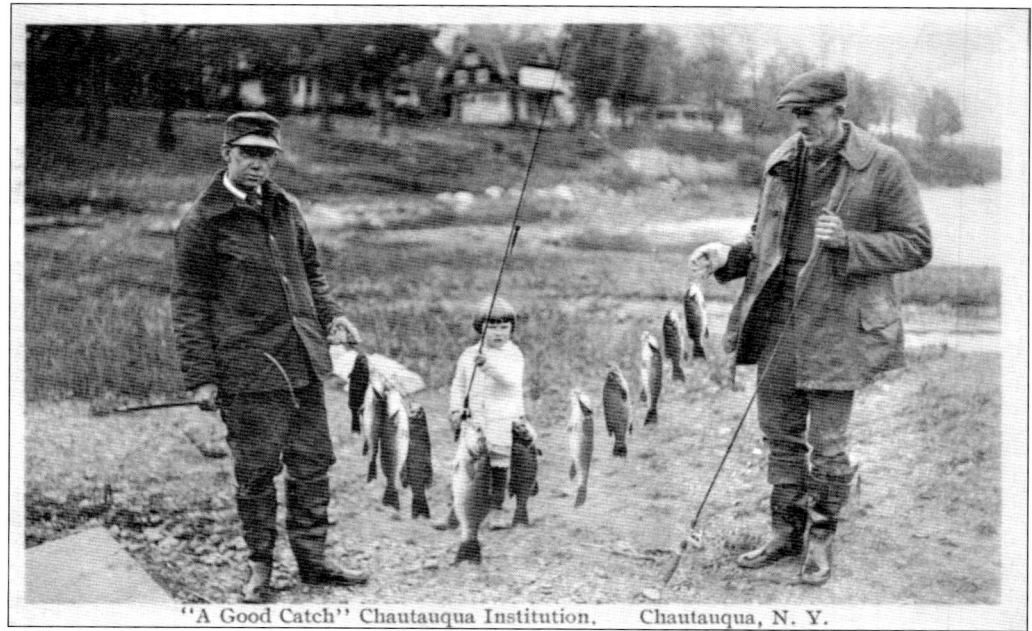

"A Good Catch" Chautauqua Institution, Chautauqua, N. Y.

Fishing has always been an activity enjoyed by visitors of all ages. Chautauqua Lake offers a variety of fish, from the large game fish, the muskellunge, to the smallest sunfish. Fish was on the menu in many homes and in the dining rooms of the lakeside hotels. The start of fishing season in the late 1800s and early 1900s helped fill the hotels with people before the summer visitors came for the season.

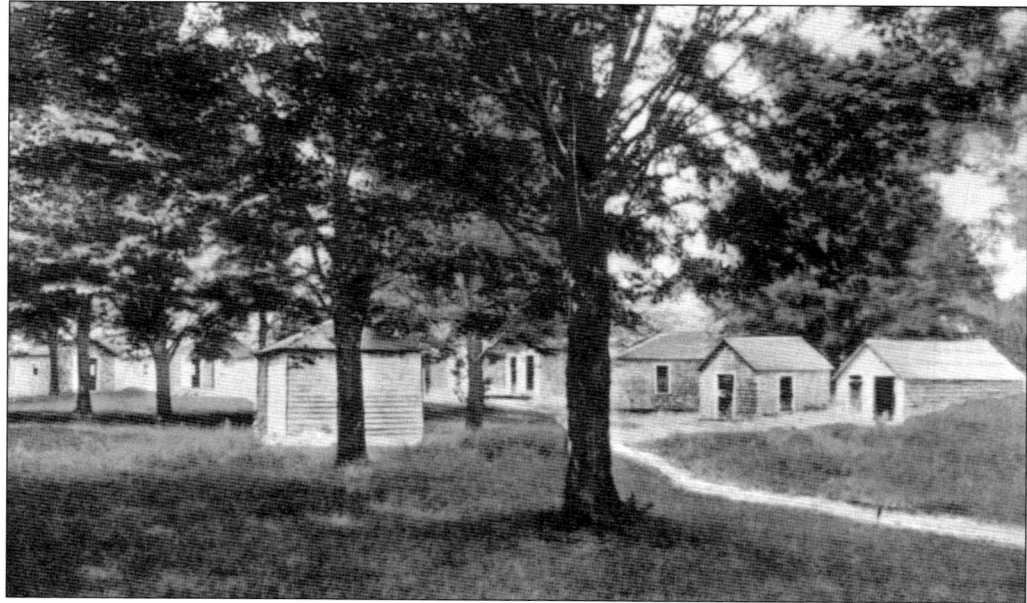

These small cabins are the practice shacks used by music students and other musicians. Located near the road and away from the lectures and the quiet pursuits of the institution, the number of shacks grew over the years from the original nine sponsored by piano manufacturers to as many as 40 for use by all musicians.

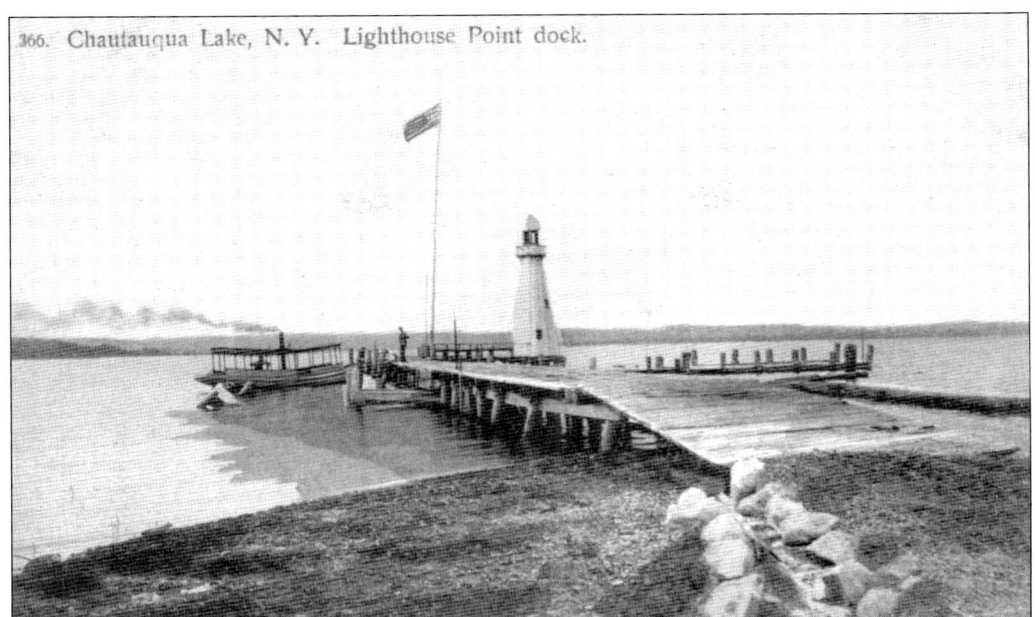

Lighthouse Point did have a lighthouse. It was located at the end of the dock and was lit by an acetylene gas plant. Seen up and down the lake, it served as a navigation aid. The trolley line along this side of the lake reached Lighthouse Point by 1904. The trolley station established there is today an active, small grocery that serves area residents and summer visitors.

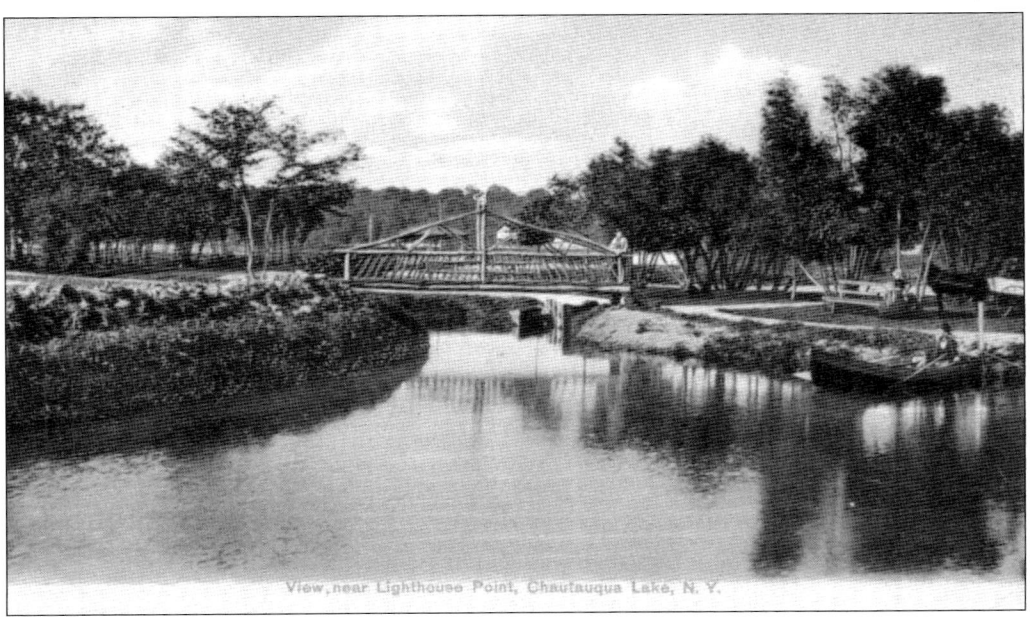

In 1898, the report of the development of three new summer resorts between Chautauqua and Mayville appeared in the newspaper—Duquesne Heights, Wahmeda, and Lighthouse Point. Pictured is part of the grounds of Lighthouse Point. Wahmeda and Lighthouse Point remain in today's vocabulary, while Duquesne Heights has disappeared. An 1895 announcement mentioned only Duquesne Lawn to be developed by Pittsburgh investors.

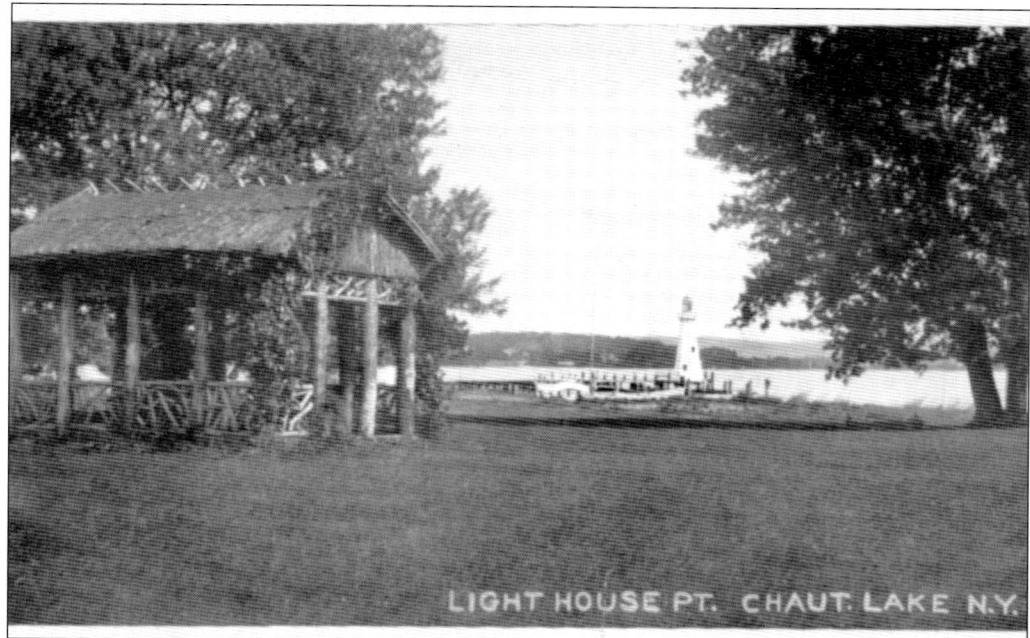

A pavilion was built at Lighthouse Point and could be used for picnics or just a pleasant place to sit and enjoy the view. The lighthouse on the dock can be seen. A launch named the *Lighthouse Tender* was provided for the resort visitors, with its headquarters at the resort's dock.

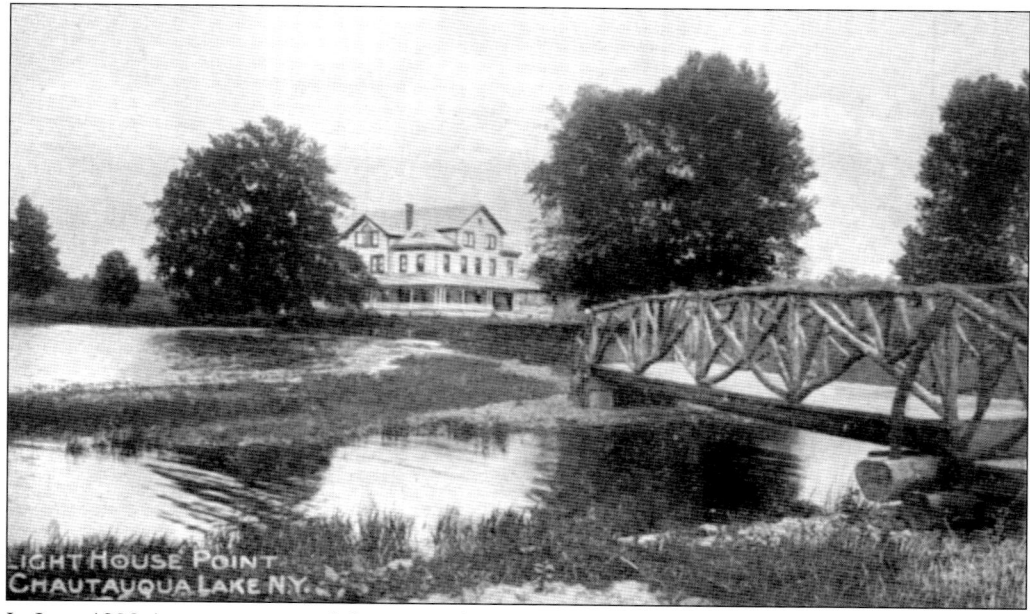

In June 1899, it was announced that a new hotel at Lighthouse Point was complete and would be open to the public about July 1. It was to have a water system as well as the acetylene gas-plant lighting. Wahmeda and Duquesne Lawn also had small hotels. Close to Chautauqua Institution, the hotels offered bars and dancing not available at the institution. All were gone by 1904.

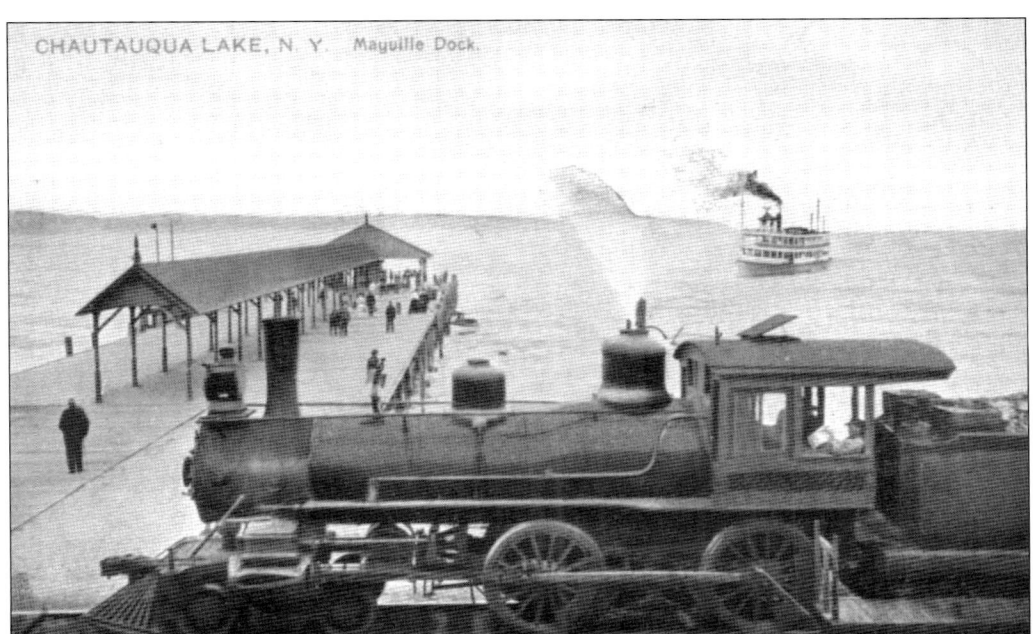

Mayville was the connect point for the Pennsylvania Railroad, which came from Pittsburgh, and the local transportation system along Chautauqua Lake. The steamboats delivered visitors to points along the lake, as did the rail service on the east side of the lake. Trolley service on the west side began in 1904. The steamboat dock was across the street from the railroad station.

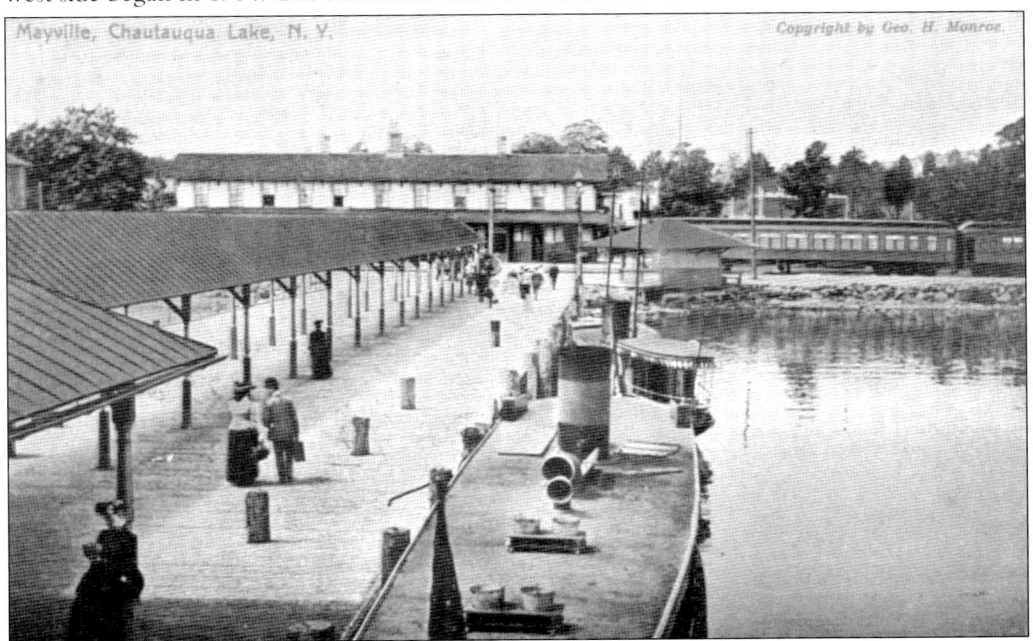

The 1883 dock, built at Mayville, was to be 350 feet long and 50 feet wide. A promenade floor with a roof was to be erected on it. This is one of few, if not the only, dock that had a roofed area for the passengers' comfort. This was a busy dock when trains discharged passengers with baggage, who then hurried to steamers to arrive at destinations along the lake.

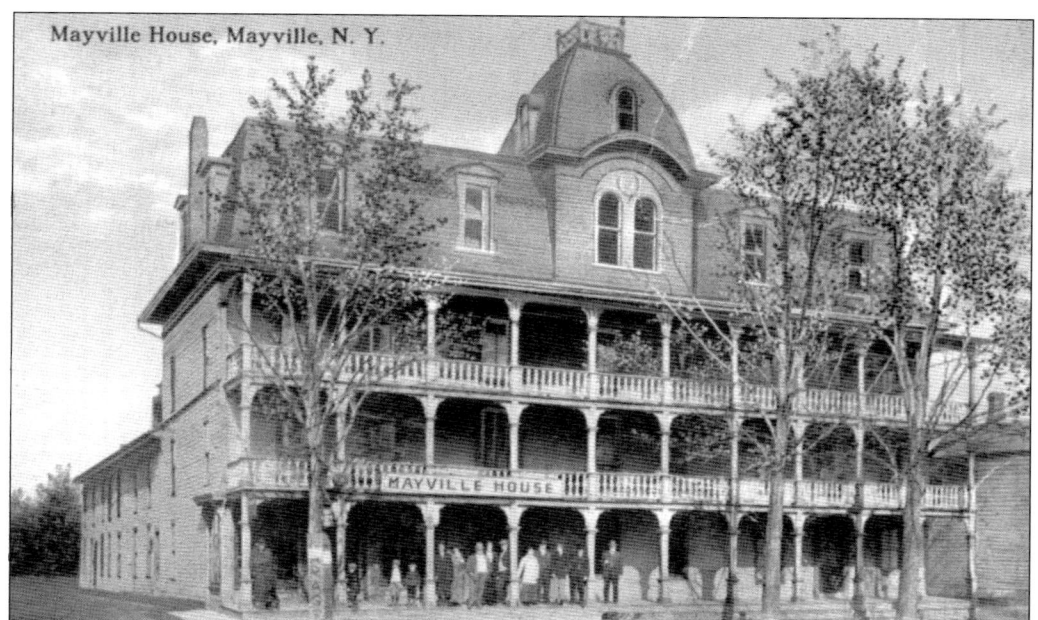

The Mayville House played host to many visitors to the county seat, Mayville, New York. Judges, attorneys, jurors, and court officers were among the hotel's guests. Built in 1850 with a different name, it was in the business district near the county courthouse. With a tower on the fifth level, the view of the lake was one of the best, until fire consumed the hotel in 1914.

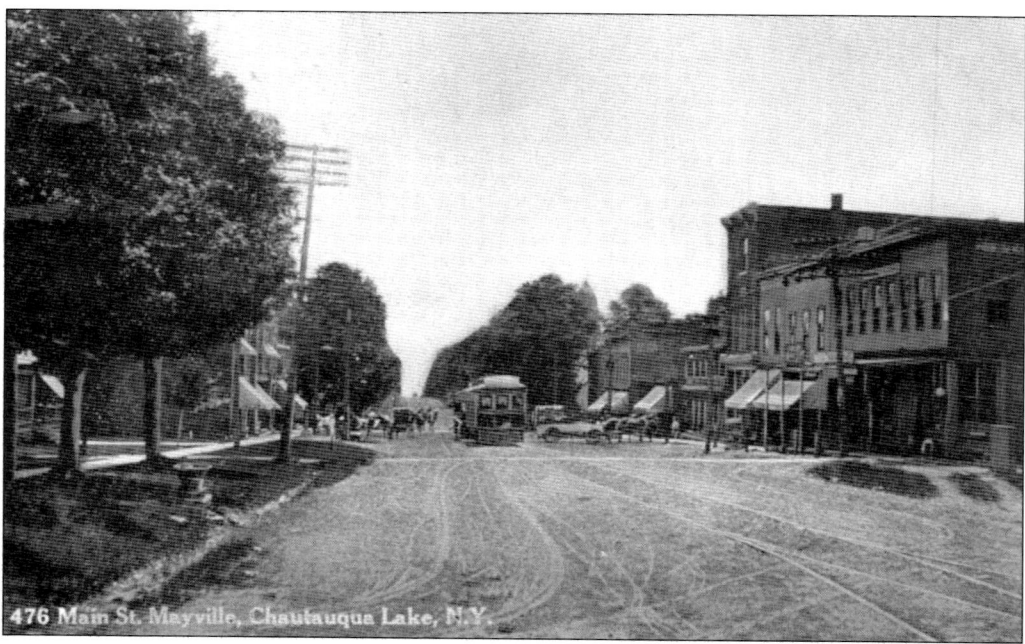

The trolley has moved to the center of the street as it comes through the upper business district. The courthouse is the next stop before it continues over the hill to Westfield to make connections with the New York Central Railroad system. The west-side structures were rebuilt after the 1901 fire. In 1913, some of these building would have a third story added to them.

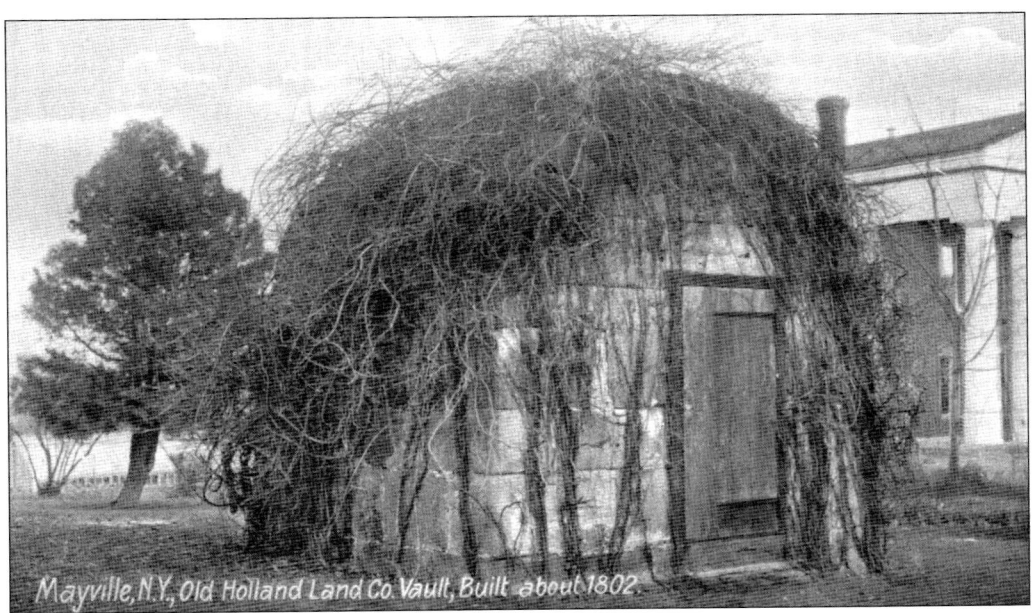

Mayville, N.Y., Old Holland Land Co. Vault, Built about 1802.

William Peacock, a surveyor, laid out the county seat of Mayville and marked the boundaries of most of the towns in the county. In 1810, he was sent to Mayville as the subagent for the Holland Land Company. He established a home and an office, and constructed this vault for keeping company papers. The vault is still located by the present courthouse. Note the 1835 courthouse in the background.

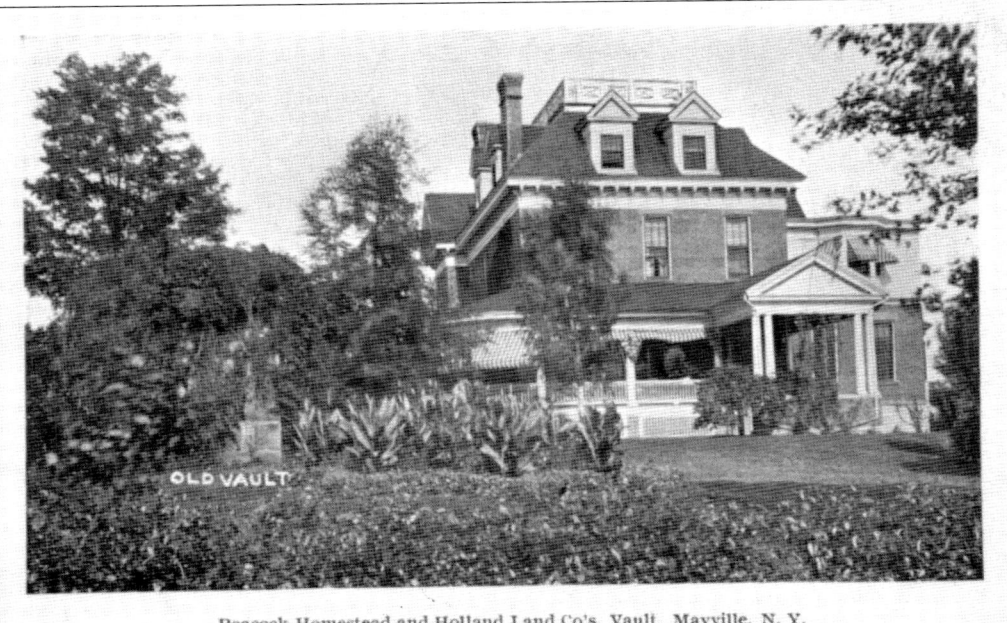

Peacock Homestead and Holland Land Co's. Vault, Mayville, N. Y.

Peacock's home was this large mansion next to the county courthouse. Peacock retired from the Holland Land Company in 1836 and died in 1877. He donated some of his large land holdings to Mayville for a cemetery, the academy, and schools. His mansion became a restaurant but was torn down in 1971 to make way for new county office buildings and parking lots.

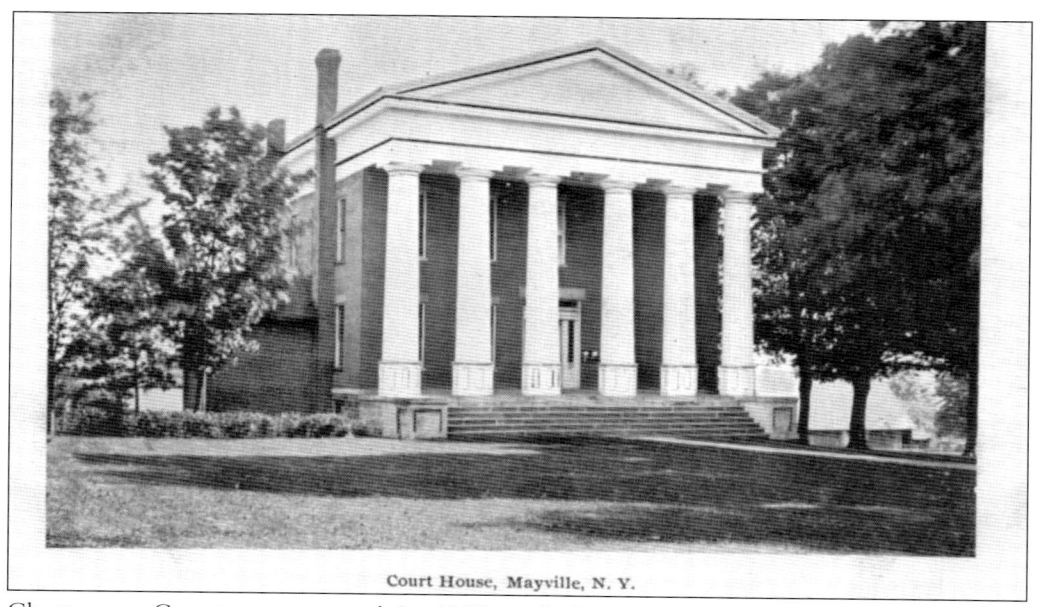

Court House, Mayville, N. Y.

Chautauqua County was created in 1808, and the government was organized in 1811. Chautauqua County erected a small wooden courthouse in Mayville. By 1832, citizens felt a new courthouse was needed. Money was raised, and the building was constructed, but all the funds had been spent, with nothing left to finish the inside. With more funds raised, it was finally finished in 1835.

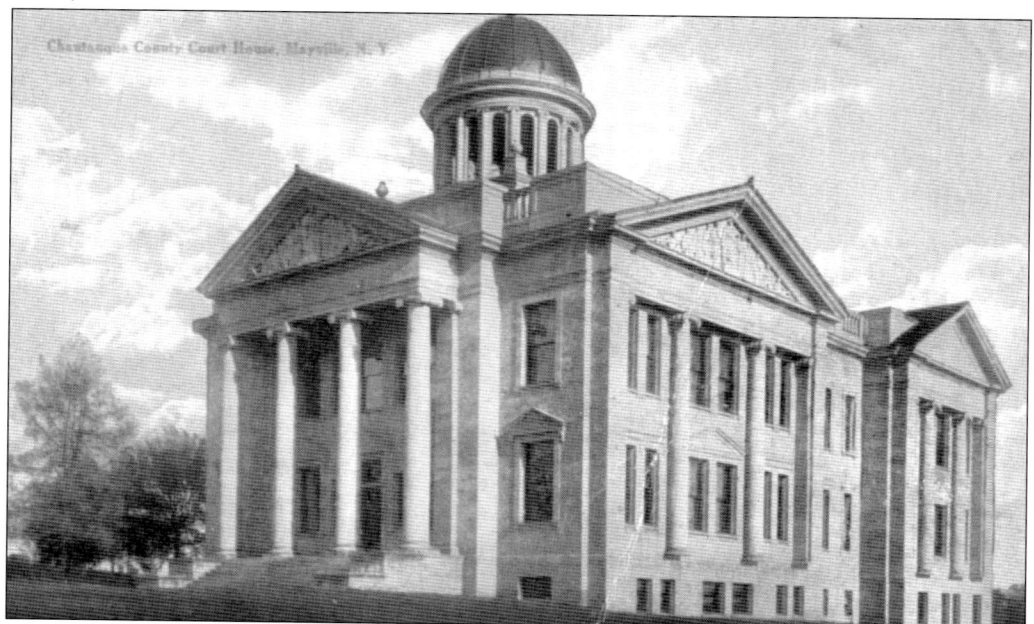

The third and present courthouse was built in 1907 and has just been renovated. Additional county office buildings have been constructed adjacent to the courthouse. Like the earlier courthouses, it occupies the northeast corner at the top of the hill north of the business district. Originally the county clerk and county treasurer had separate offices across the street, but today they are within the county buildings.

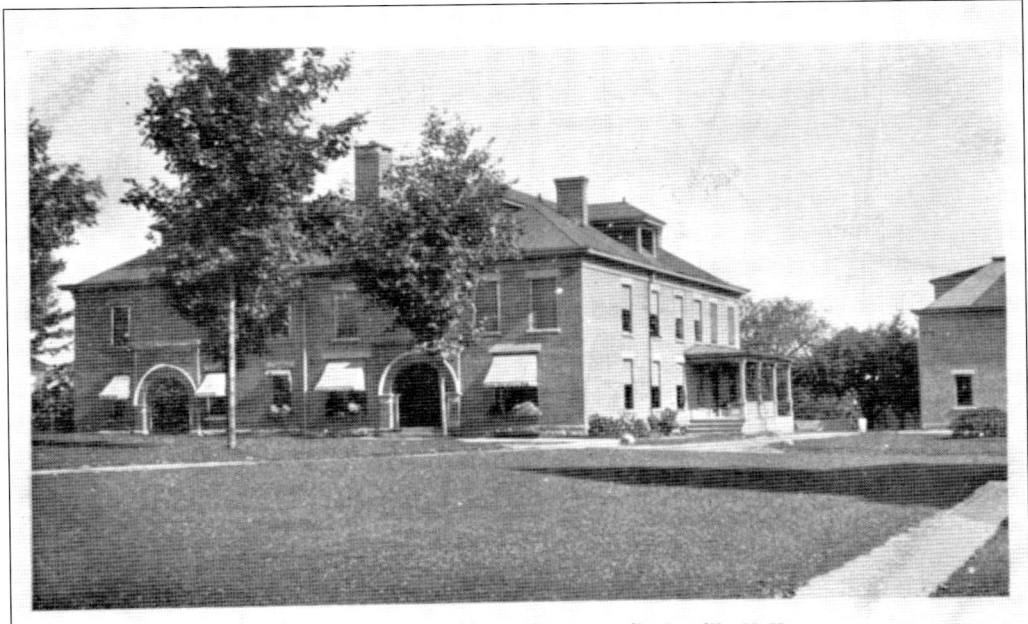

Located across the street from the county courthouse, the jail and sheriff's residence overlooked the park above the business district in Mayville, New York. With his residence close by, in the late 1920s, Sheriff Axel Levin was able to go home for lunch and leave his best guard, Judy, on duty. Prisoners soon learned that Judy, the police dog, was indeed the best guard.

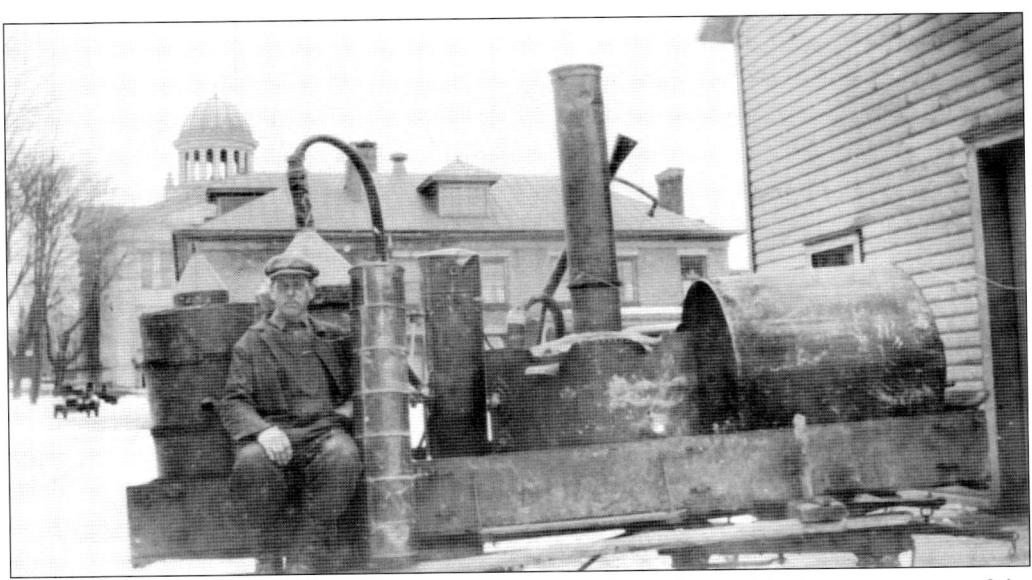

Sheriff Axel Levin (Granddad Levin to the authors) is shown here with the components of the largest still confiscated in Chautauqua County while he was in office during Prohibition. The county courthouse can be seen in the background. This real-photo postcard may have had a limited circulation, but the Woman's Christian Temperance Union (WCTU), started just up the road in Fredonia, could have used it in its campaign.

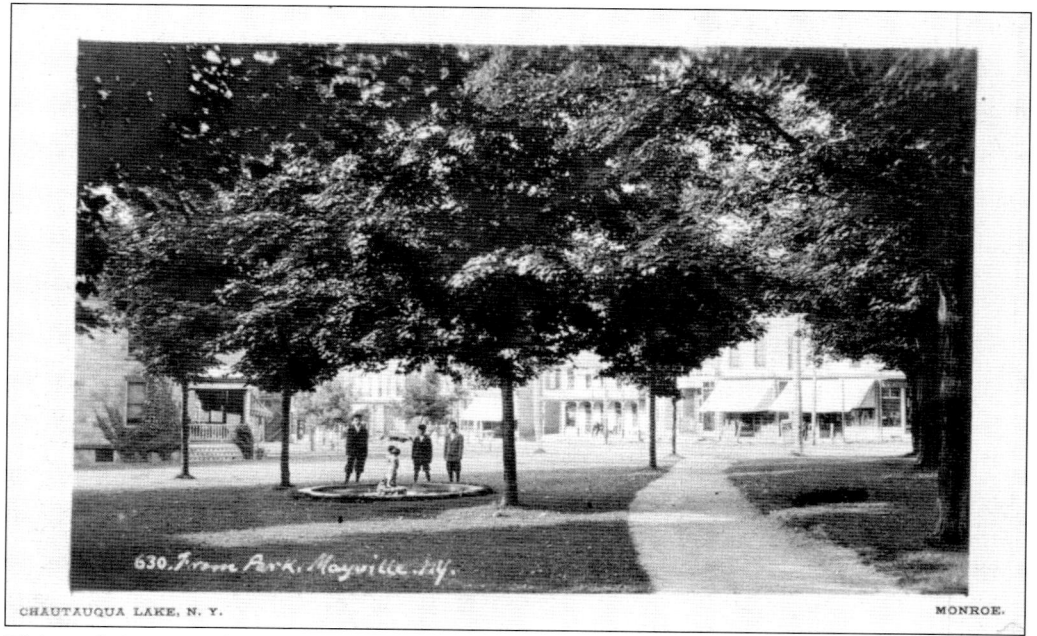

This park in Mayville continues to occupy the corner by the jail. It still has the fountain in which Judy, the police dog, was given permission to get in and cool off on hot days. The statue in the fountain has been a favorite with residents for years. Despite occasional vandalism and repairs, the statue is one of the few remaining originals that were popular during the late Victorian period.

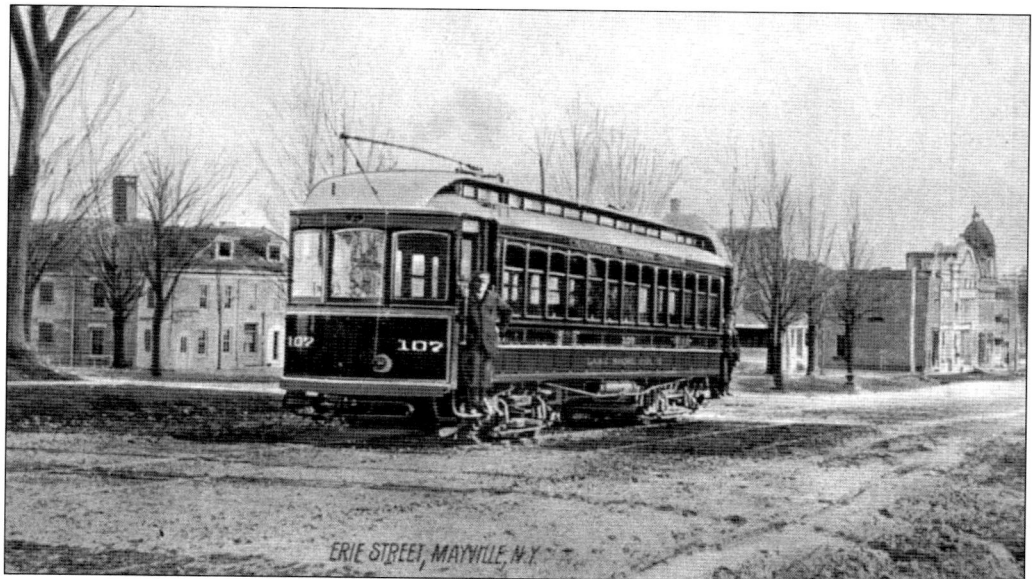

This trolley is on Erie Street, which runs from the lake toward Westfield. Seen in the background is the jail and some of the business district, including the Mayville House at far right. Although it says Lake Shore Route on the side, this car fits the description of Chautauqua Traction's Car No. 107. One other Chautauqua Traction car had Lake Shore Route on it when it arrived. (Courtesy of MC.)

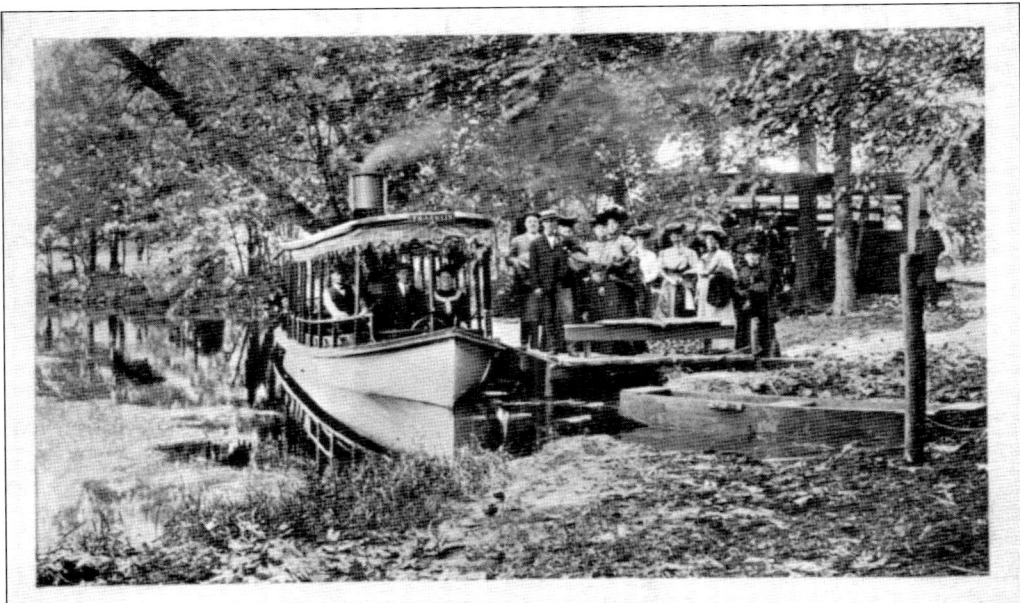

Designated as an inlet of Chautauqua Lake, this is probably Big Inlet (pictured above). This stream enters near the head of the lake to the east of Mayville and would have been large enough for the small steamer. Other streams that enter the lake have created points that extend into the water by depositing sediments at the entry point. These inlets provided a destination for boaters, and some were favored by fishermen.

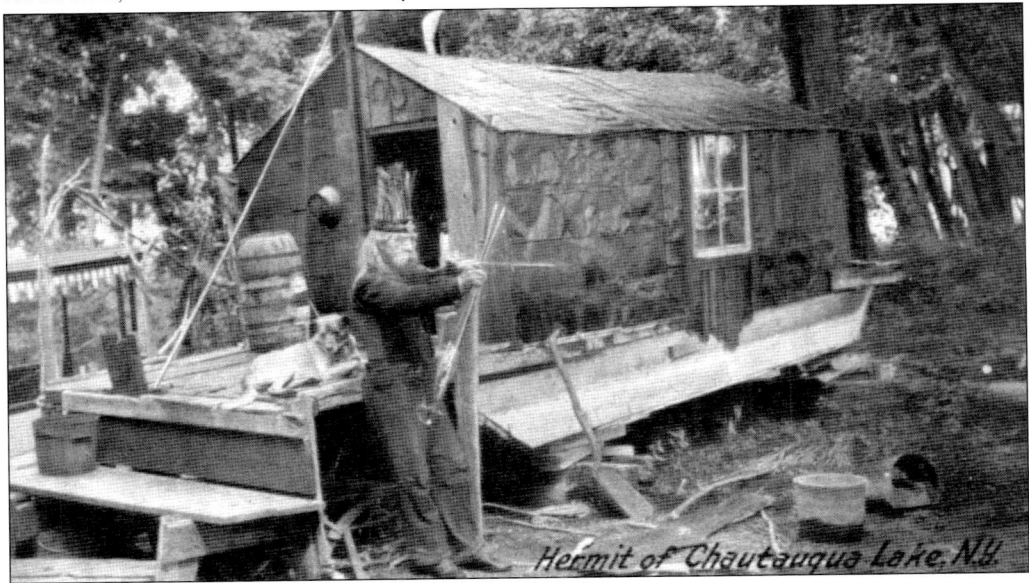

"Left-handed Charlie" Cowden, a well-known hermit of Chautauqua Lake, often had his portable abode at the Big Inlet near Hartfield. He entertained people in 1891 by giving concerts on his over 100-year-old violin and on his specialty, the "bones." He said that he planned to fish and whittle out curious things with his jack knife. He was an old soldier and had been a cowboy for 19 years. (Courtesy of MC.)

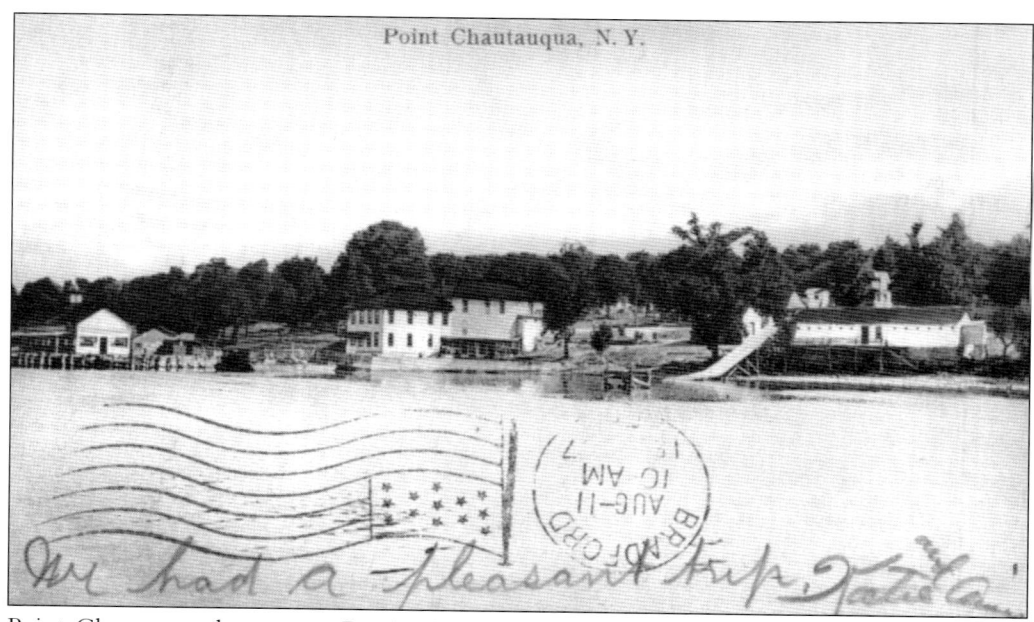

Point Chautauqua began as a Baptist Association property. Fredrick Law Olmsted executed the original plan for the property in 1875. The lakefront includes the dock at the far left. The middle building was the Breeze Hotel at one time. To the far right is the 1899 boathouse and toboggan slide. The association declared bankruptcy and sold off its properties. In the late 1880s, Point Chautauqua reemerged as a resort area.

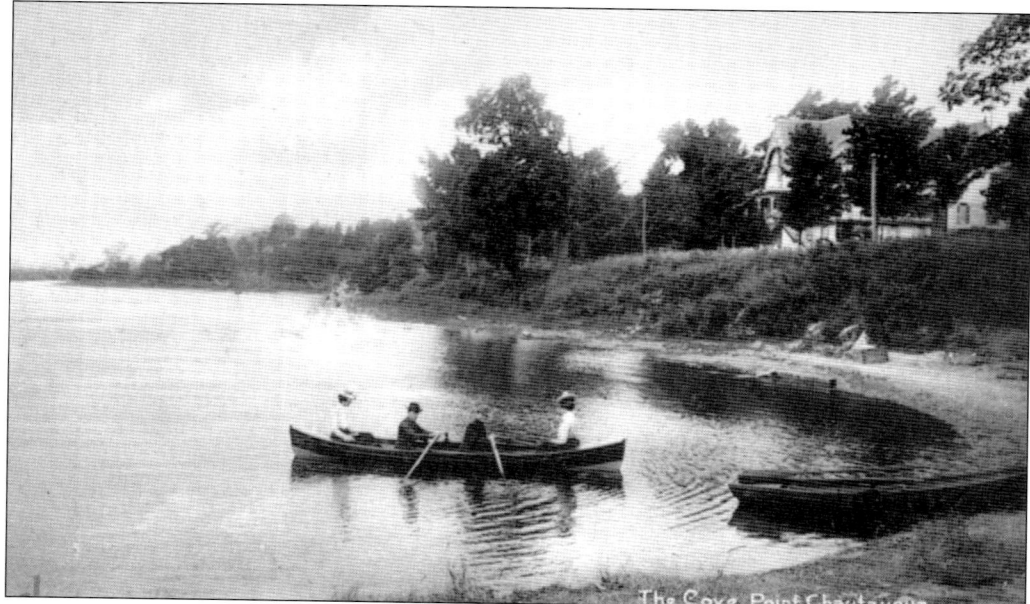

This is a typical shoreline along much of Chautauqua Lake, which has a narrow beach with a few cottages overlooking the lake. This view seems to be south of the steamboat dock access point to Point Chautauqua since the top of the Grand Hotel or the Hartson Tabernacle building can be seen over the treetops on the far left. From looking at the map, this is probably Dewittville Bay.

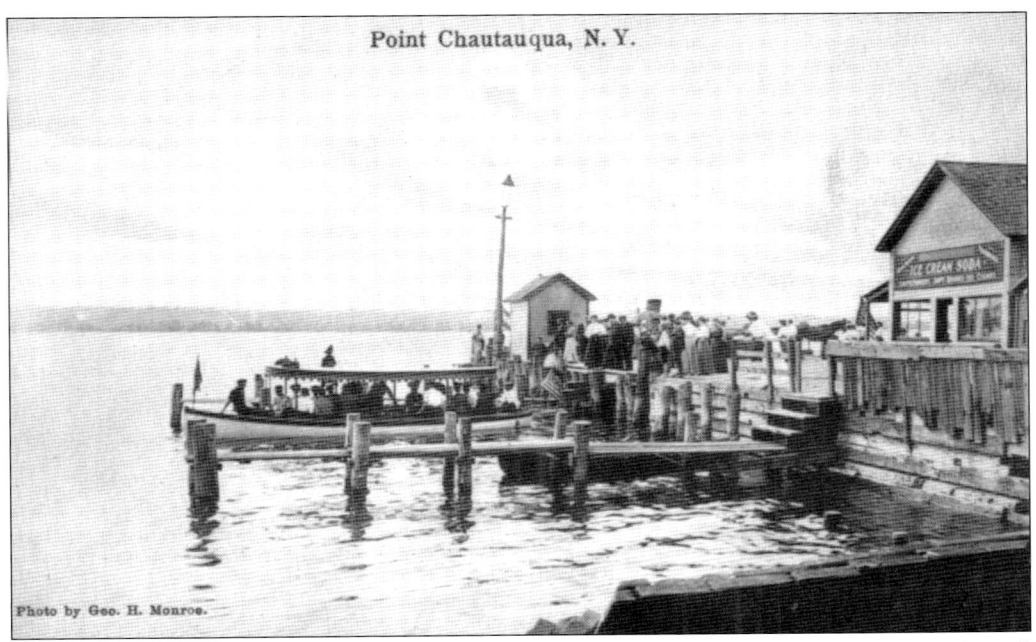

The steamboat dock was an important waterfront site for Point Chautauqua. Large and small steamers stopped there. Here a small launch has arrived and will ferry passengers to Chautauqua and Mayville. The store on the dock sold ice cream, a popular novelty at the time. In 1901, ice damaged the dock, and part of the store was hanging out over the lake until it was repaired.

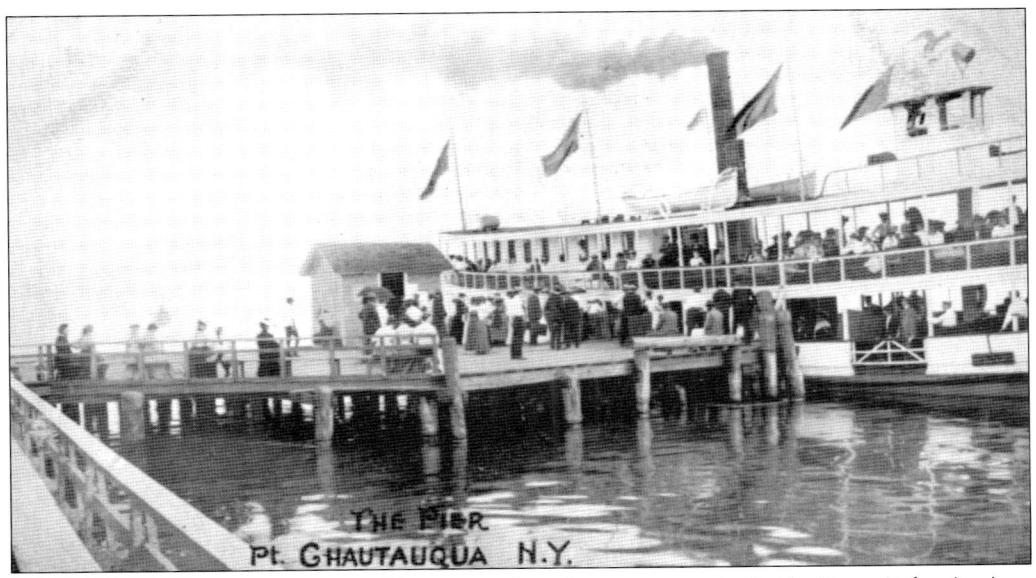

Another view of the dock at Point Chautauqua has a large steamer dockside. From its beginning, Point Chautauqua was a scheduled stop for the steamboats. Visitors at landings along the lake could catch a steamer and spend a day at Point Chautauqua strolling along the gently curving roadways, attending musical events, or even, in 1897, learning bicycle riding at Maltby's cycling academy in the former Hartson Tabernacle building.

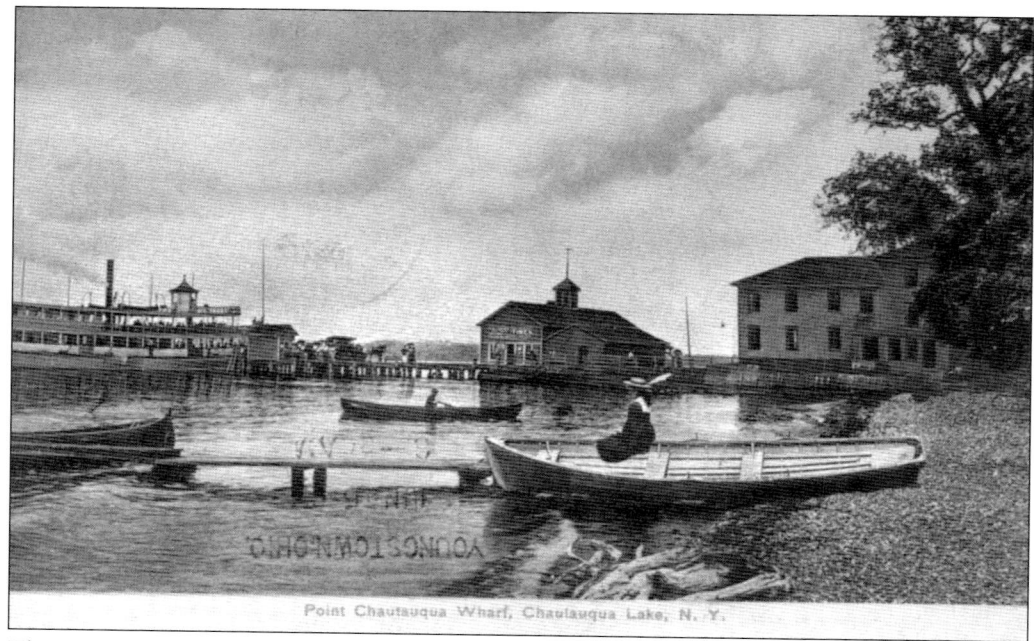

This young girl may be waiting for someone to arrive by steamboat or wistfully watching the steamers come and go. To the south of the steamboat dock was a boathouse, so she could be waiting for someone to take her out in the small boat for fishing or for a picnic.

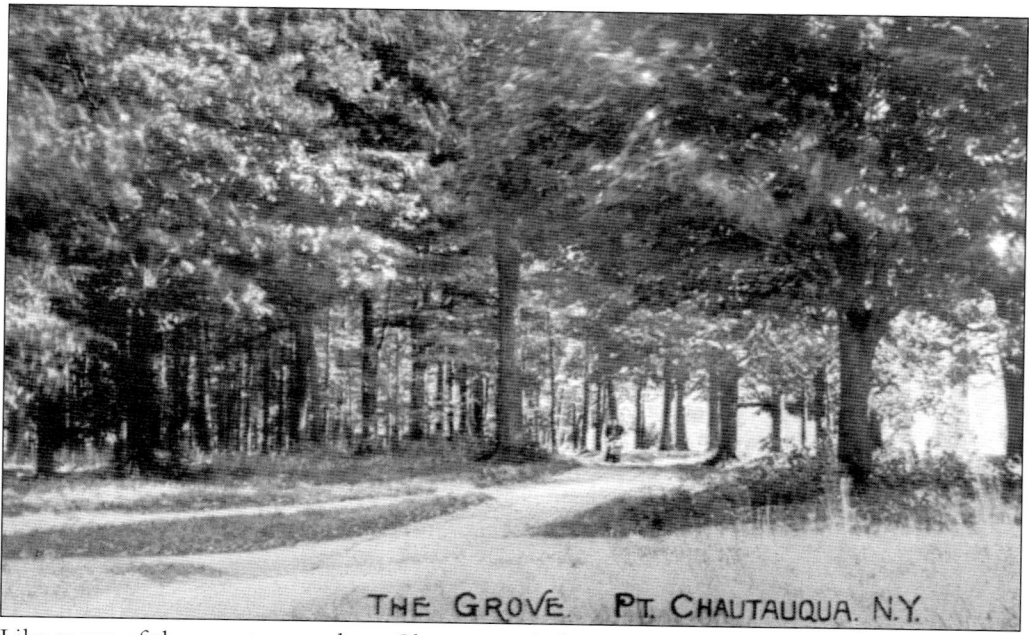

Like many of the resort areas along Chautauqua Lake, Point Chautauqua had a grove of large shade trees that provided a cool, quiet place for strolling, picnicking, or relaxing. This particular grove within Point Chautauqua is not identified; Fredrick Law Olmsted's plan called for more than one. Fountain Park, Corinthian Grove, and Sylvan Grove all appeared on his plan and remain undeveloped and natural today.

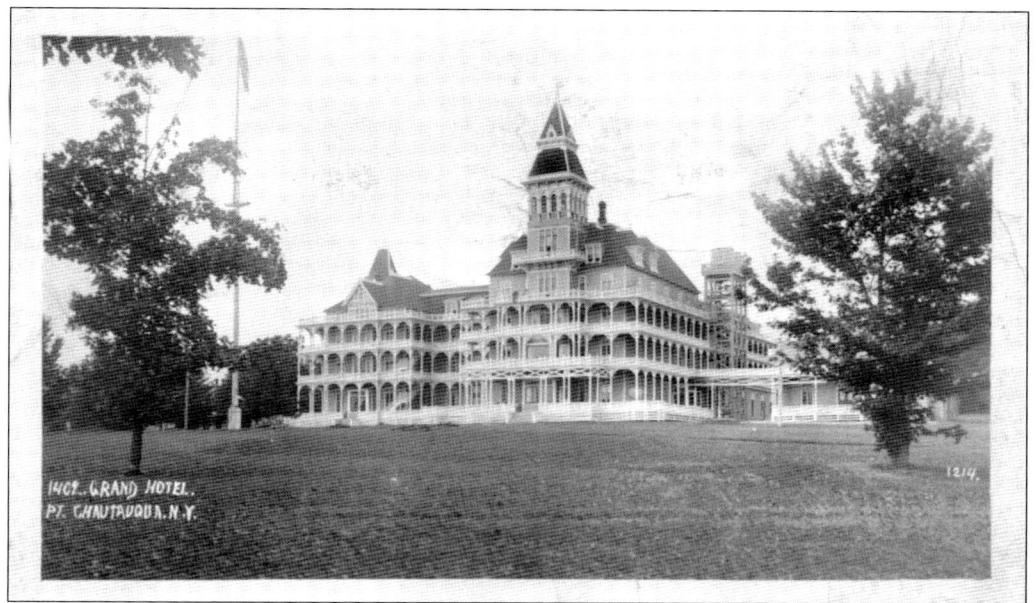

One Wednesday in June 1881, the small steamer *Griffith* carried 6,810 pounds of freight to the Grand Hotel, built in 1878 by the Point Chautauqua Association. Despite good patronage, the hotel was sold to private interests by 1888, after the association declared bankruptcy. Built on the high hill, it was seen from many places on the upper lake. The sumptuous Grand Hotel at Point Chautauqua succumbed to an arsonist in 1902.

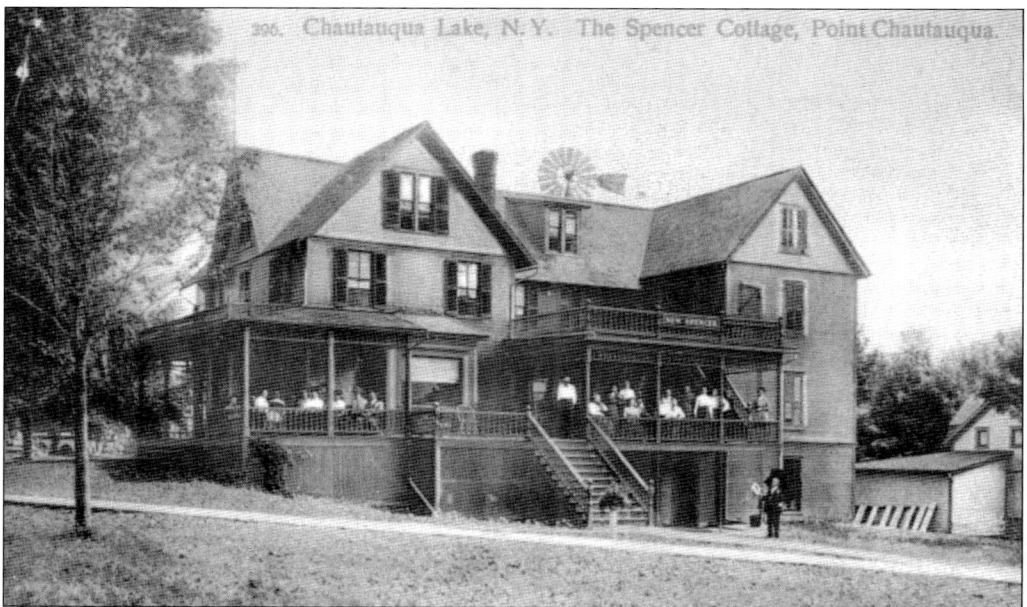

Even before the end of the Baptist Association, smaller hotels and boardinghouses began appearing. After the demise of the Grand Hotel, the smaller hotels and boardinghouses became the places for visitors to stay for a day, a week, or the entire summer. The Spencer Cottage was one such hotel. Enlarged in 1901, the dining room could then seat 100 people. The structure burned around 1909.

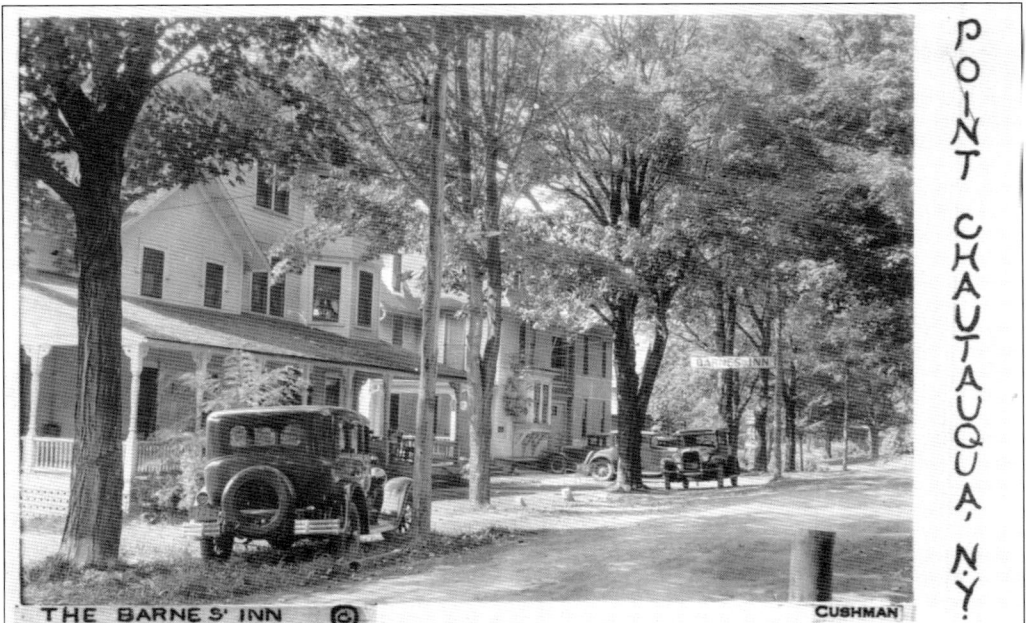

The Barnes Inn, on Floral Avenue, consisted of three adjacent buildings, the last of which was built in 1901, doubling the capacity. As can be seen in this picture, some residents had arrived by private automobile. The last of the steamboats was still plying the waters of the lake. There was trolley service, but automobiles were beginning to cause the decline and failure of both steamboats and trolleys. (Courtesy of FHC.)

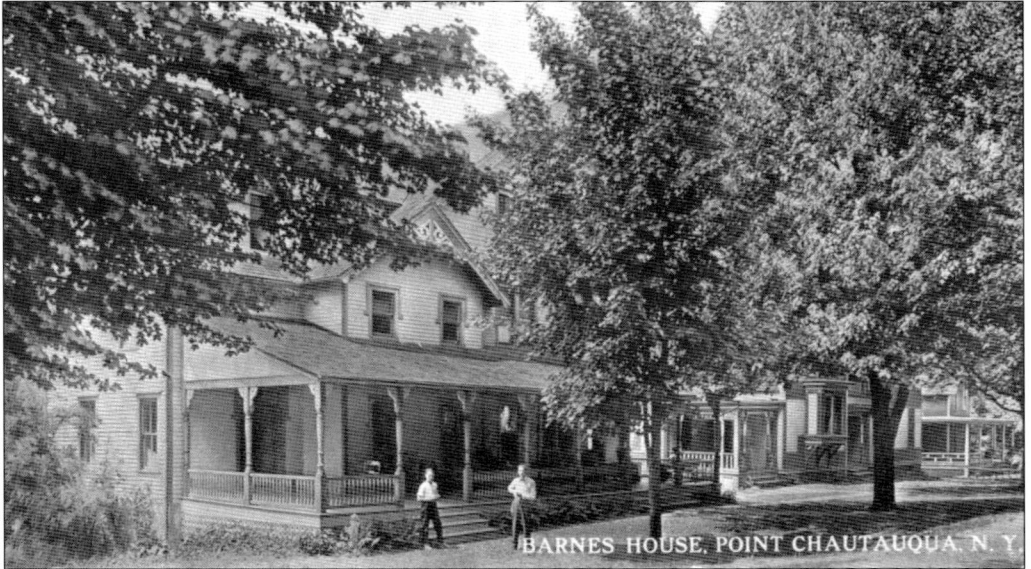

This is an earlier picture of the Barnes House, when the trees were smaller, there were no automobiles, and the fancy carpenter Gothic trim was still on the upper gables of the building. Like many of the wood-frame boardinghouses and hotels along Chautauqua Lake, the Barnes House burned around 1930 and did not see the decline in patronage the others did as the Depression worsened.

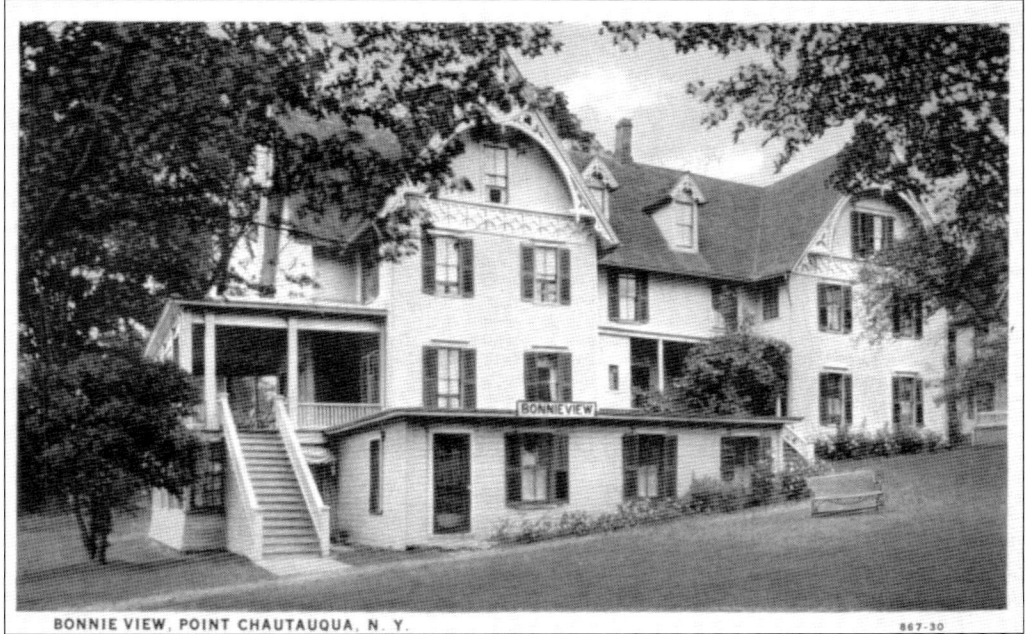

Originally built in the 1880s as Pease's Cottages, the Bonneview Lodge endured through the 1940s but was sadly deteriorating in the 1950s and was finally torn down in the 1960s. It was located at the northern end of Lake Avenue and had a great view of the lake from its upper veranda. It continued to be a favorite with residents for its dining room.

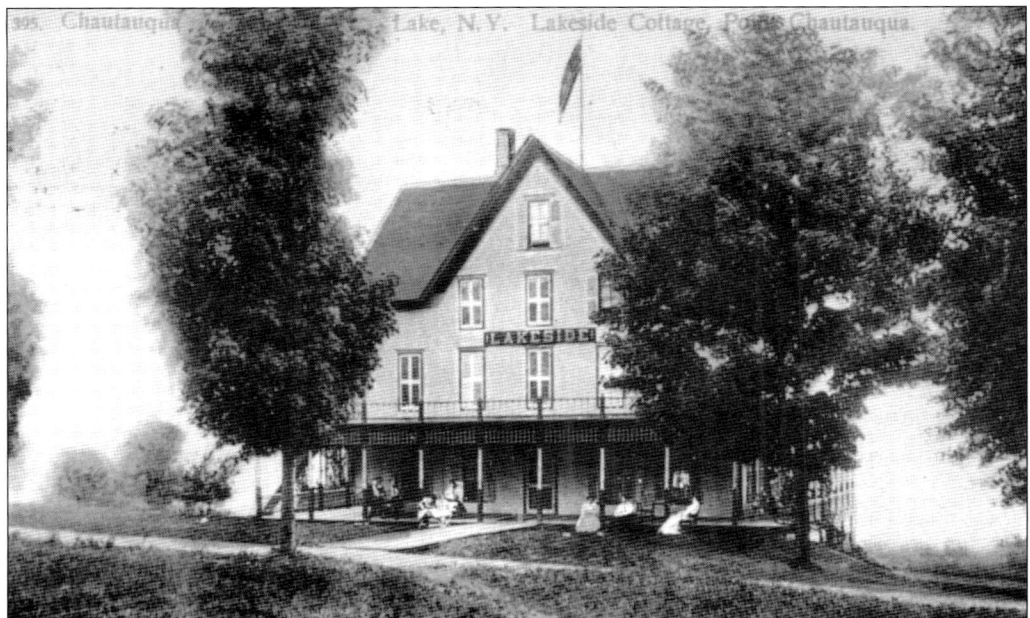

The Lakeside Hotel, known earlier as the Lake Side House, had an ideal location near the boat landing and dock house. Located on Diamond Avenue, the Lake Avenue side of the building had a wonderful view of the upper lake. This small hotel escaped a fiery end by being torn down just before World War II.

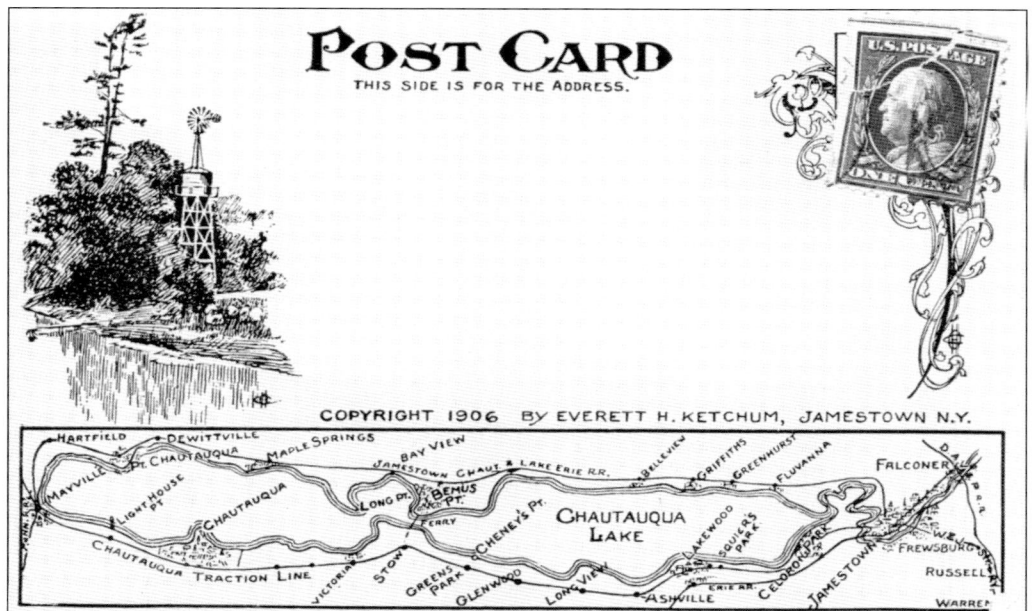

Appearing on the backs of many postcards about 1906, this map shows some of the places around the lake and the transportation system at that time. Although the back of the postcard was to be for addresses only, these ornately decorated postcards were still sent through the mail. The map was a good advertising ploy for the area resorts, trolley lines, and railroads.

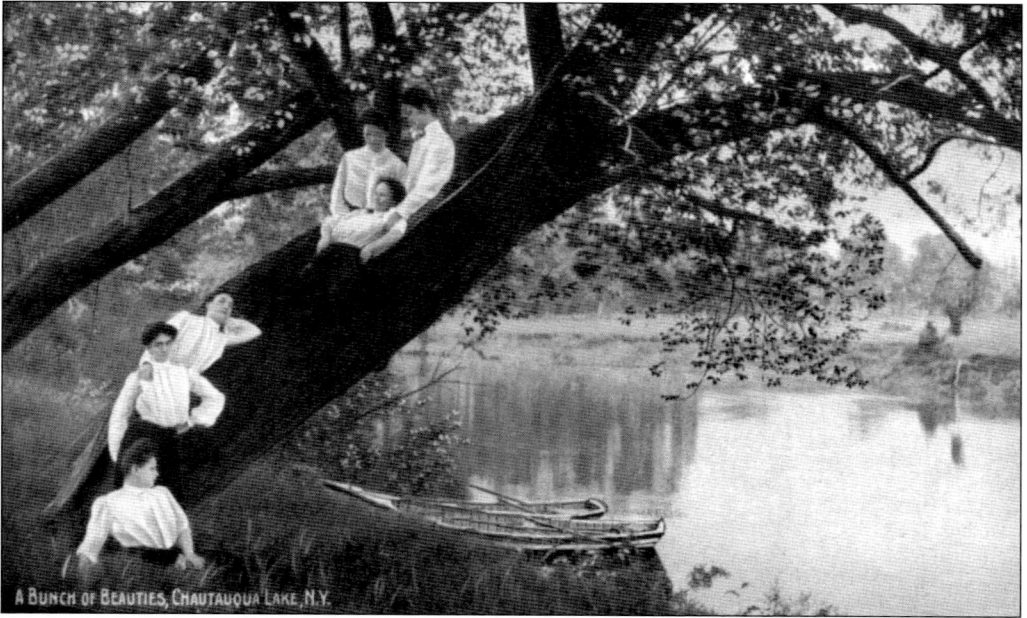

Just who these "beauties" are, where along Chautauqua Lake they are, and why they are in a tree is left up to the beholder. From the narrow body of water pictured, they have to be in one of the many inlets along the lake. The two rowboats pulled up onshore show how they arrived at this photographic setting. Hopefully the photographer and his assistant manned the oars for the trip.

Five

TOWN OF ELLERY

William Prendergast's son-in-law, William Bemus, was the early settler in what became Bemus Point along the lake. The Cheneys, Griffiths, Smileys, and other families followed and claimed land along the lake to create farms.

Bemus started the ferry, making communication with his father and the other side of the lake easier than traveling over bad roads all the way around one end of the lake or the other. The ferry still crosses the Narrows, but the bridge, finally built in 1982, gives today's automobiles and trucks the means of getting to the other side of the lake in all seasons.

The steamboat added more transportation options to the people settling in the area. More people arrived, and the settlement expanded. Small steamboats continued on the lake, and by the end of the Civil War, additional boats were plying the waters. Visitors were arriving at the small hotels that were being built. Hotels and boardinghouses became a summer industry for the lakeshore landowners.

As with the other towns along the lake, Ellery had its successes. Bemus Point developed into a resort area, with its large hotels facing the lake and smaller hotels and boardinghouses in the vicinity. The steamboat company developed picnic groves and provided the means to get to them. The railroad developed another picnic park located in Ellery. Privately developed resort areas had docks and train, then trolley, stops.

Cottages were built, and many are still there today as year-round homes, although some have been replaced by modern condominiums. Fishing prompted the state fish hatchery to operate in Ellery and eventually move across the lake to its present location. Chautauqua Lake muskellunge continues to be a much-sought-after fish.

Midway Park, developed by the rail and trolley companies, continues today as a New York state park. Long Point, the early picnic grounds that never became an amusement park and early in the 20th century became a private residence, is now a New York state park. Two state parks preserve what Chautauqua Lake visitors have known for years, even though some things have changed.

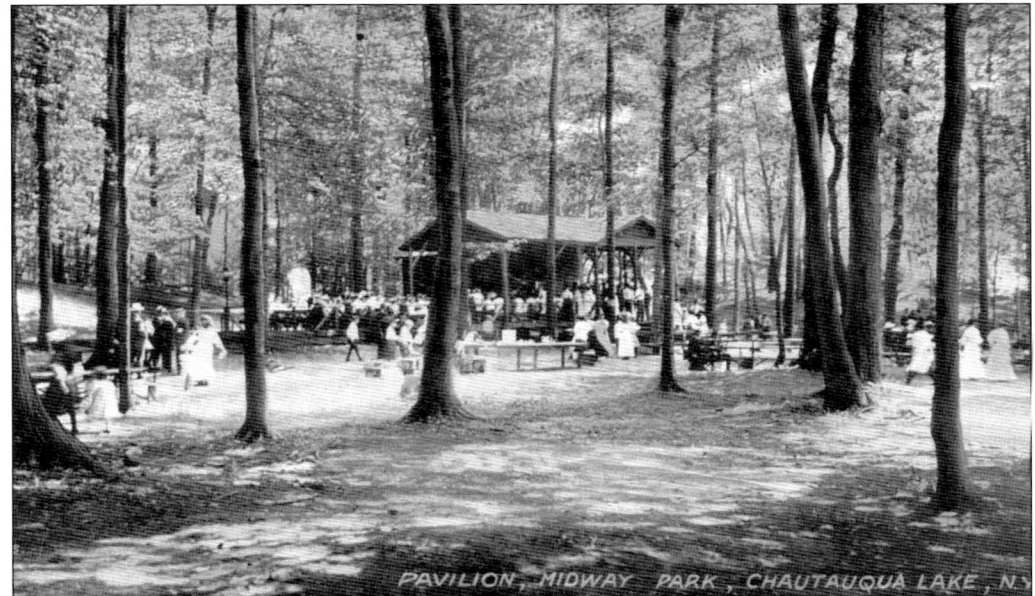

Opening in 1898, Midway Park had all the requirements of an amusement resort. The large acreage, a big grove of shade trees, and a level plot that could be transformed into a baseball field, plus a long lake frontage with a sandy bathing beach were the ingredients that have supported the park to the present day. A picnic pavilion and picnic tables greeted the picnickers arriving by steamboat or rail.

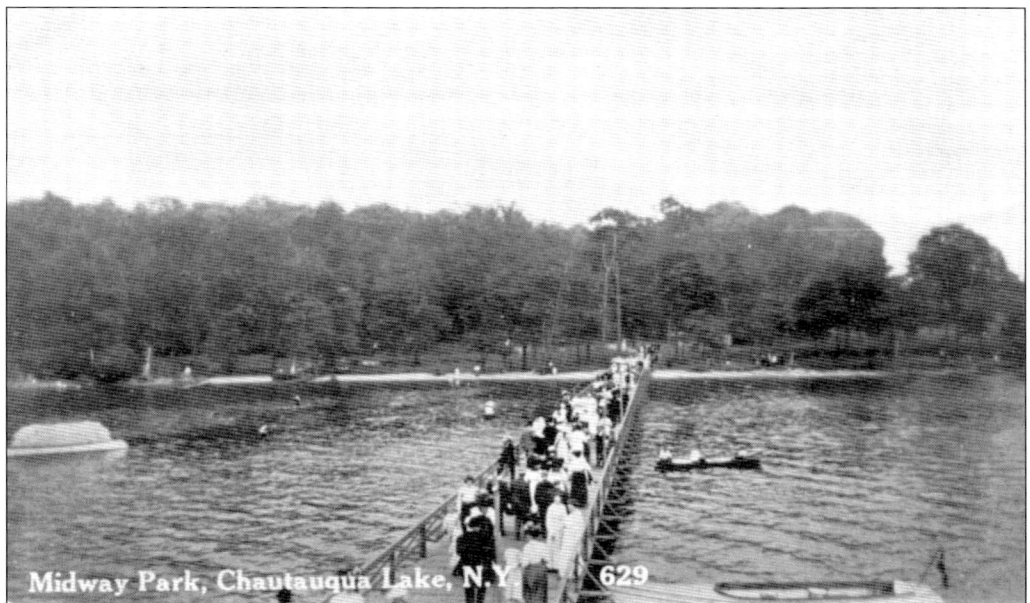

The Jamestown and Lake Erie Railway established Midway Park in 1898. When it opened, it featured baseball, lawn tennis, bathing, and boating. There was a dance pavilion, open and closed dining rooms, and tennis courts. To welcome the first guests, a first-class orchestra provided music. After 1907, steamboat passengers could disembark at Midway Park's new dock instead of walking from the pier by Maple Springs.

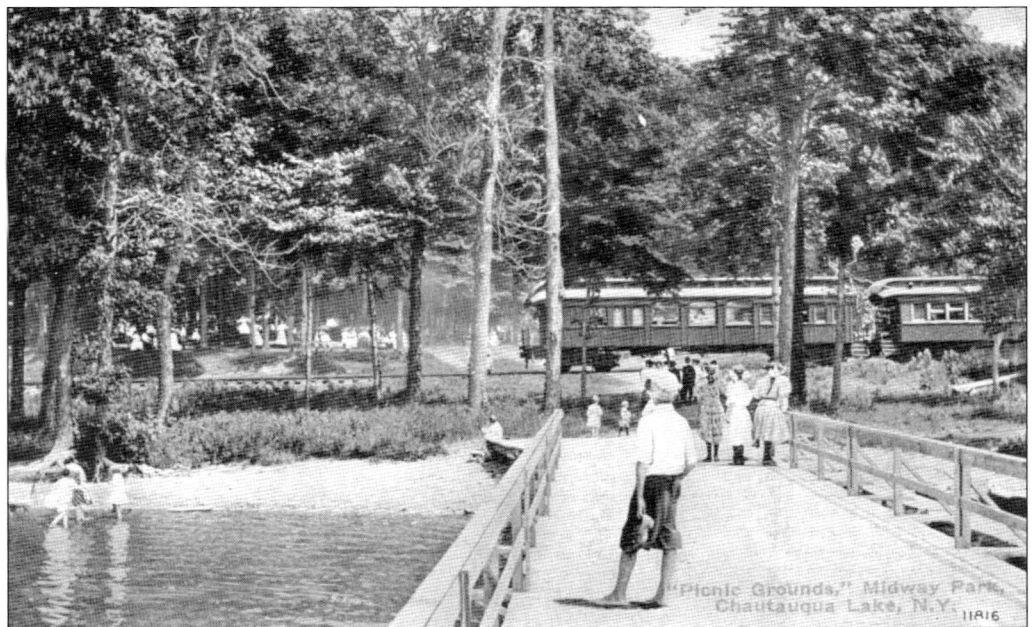

Through Midway Park, the rail line stayed close to the lakeshore, as seen here. The young boy may have arrived on the steamboat but wished he could ride the train. Barefooted, he was ready to wade in the lake, as the youngsters to the left are doing. A sandy beach was a feature of the park. The picnic grove was just beyond the train tracks.

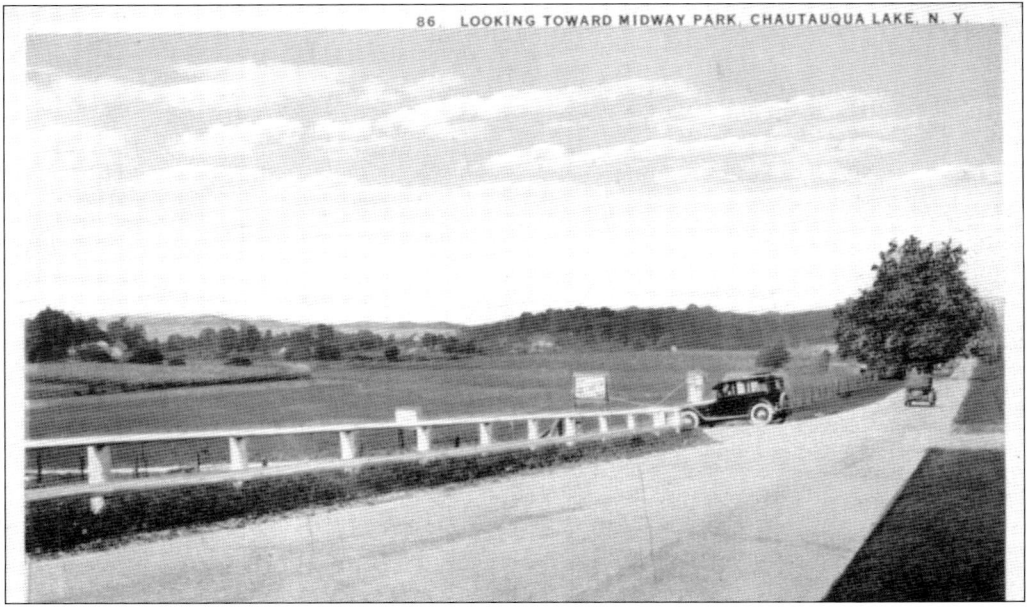

By the 1930s, automobiles provided transportation to Midway Park and other spots along the lake. Only one large steamboat was left on the lake, and the Chautauqua Traction trolleys on the west side were discontinued in 1926. The Jamestown, Westfield, and Northwestern (JW&NW) trolley line was running on the east increasingly more for freight. Midway Park continues to be a destination for automobiles.

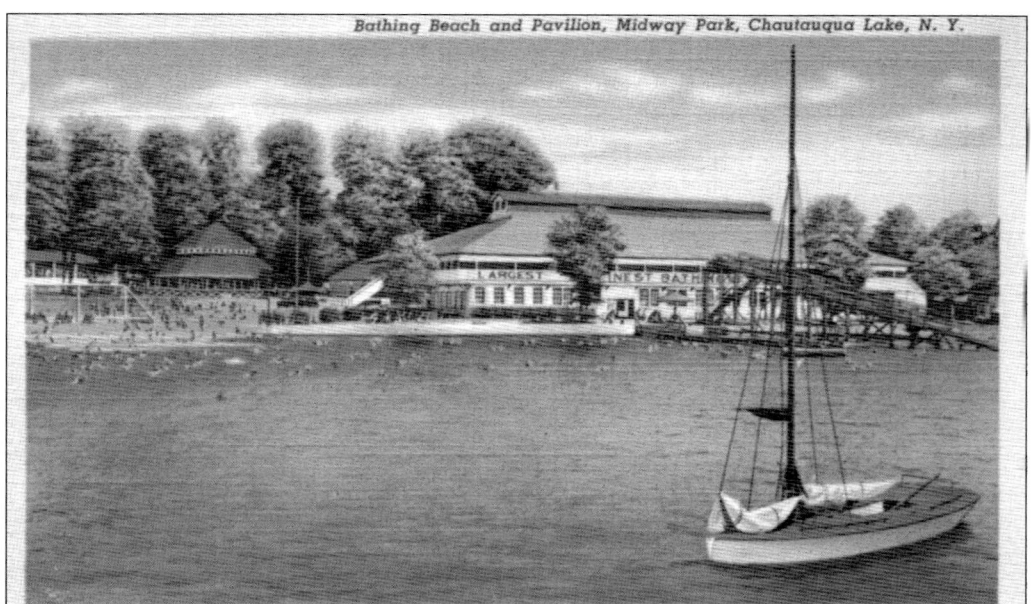

The large bathhouse and roller rink at Midway Park was built in 1915. The waterfront featured a toboggan slide and a sandy beach. The round building housed the merry-go-round, and other rides and amusements were spread out through the park. Picnics sponsored by companies or organizations were constant events at the park. Trolleys and steamboats scheduled specifically for these crowds were filled as families headed for the park.

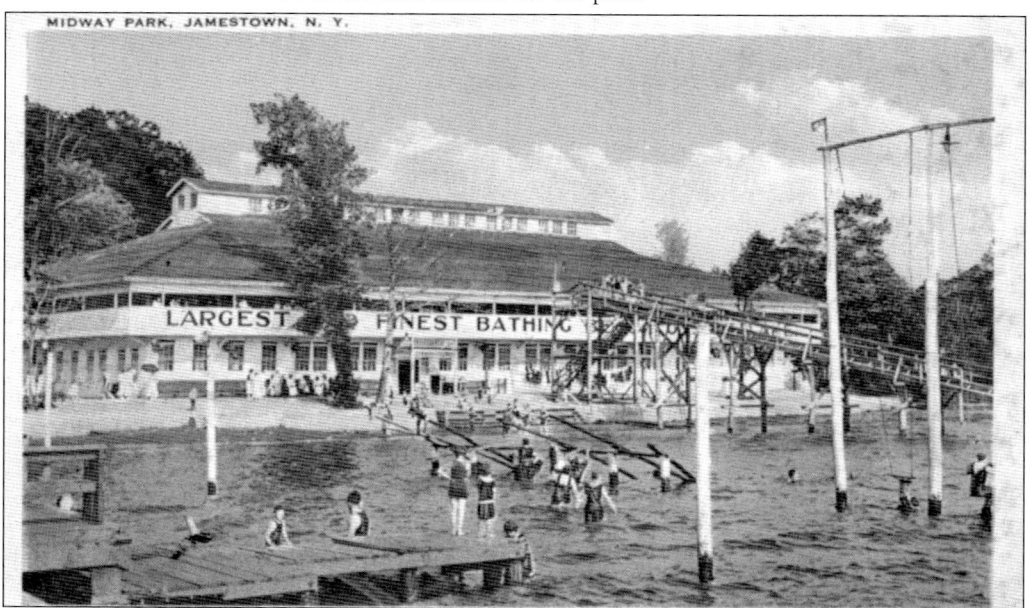

The waterfront was crowded with bathers all summer long. The toboggan slide and the swing provided thrills for the adventurous. The bathhouse's second floor contained the roller rink and a dance floor. The first floor had dressing rooms, a dining room and kitchen, a shooting gallery, and concessions. Roller-skating became a popular pastime, and many married couples can trace their courtship back to the roller rink.

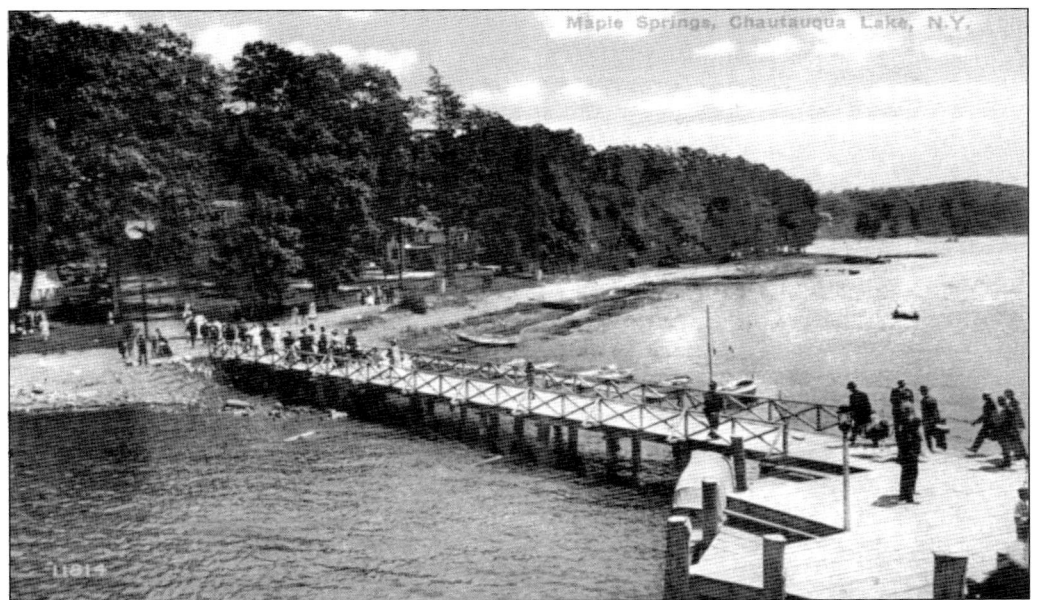

The Whiteside Hotel, built in 1879, and the Maple Springs Inn each had a steamboat dock until one pier between them was constructed in 1894 and named Midway. When the railroad created Midway Park, the name "Midway" moved to that pier, and the hotel area, with a post office, became Maple Springs. This steel pier, built in 1906 straight out from Point Whiteside, replaced the hotels' earlier "Midway" pier.

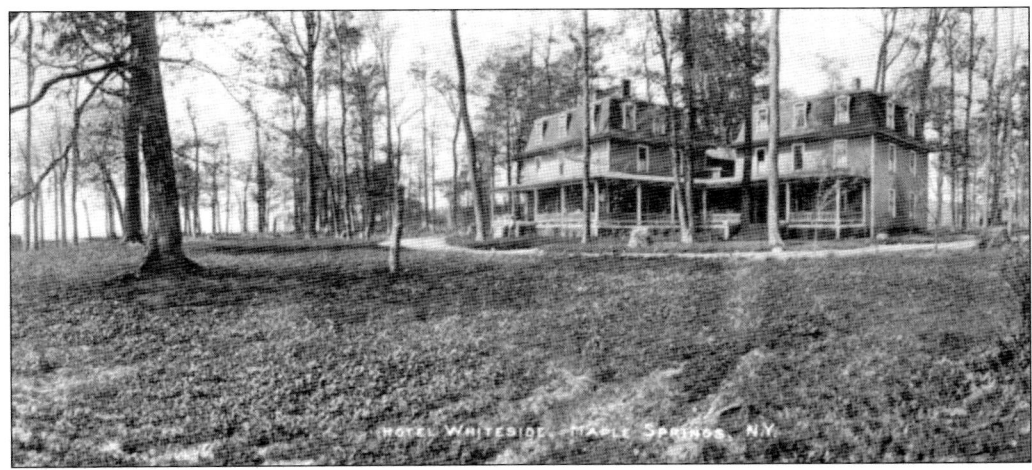

Hotel Whiteside, built by W. P. Whiteside, continued until 1984, when it was razed, leaving a site for condominiums. It was expanded numerous times, and after Whiteside died, the area was divided into lots, and development of the site began in 1906. In early 1898, Rutherford P. Hayes, son of Pres. Rutherford B. Hayes, inquired about summer accommodations. There was no report found that he and his family came that summer.

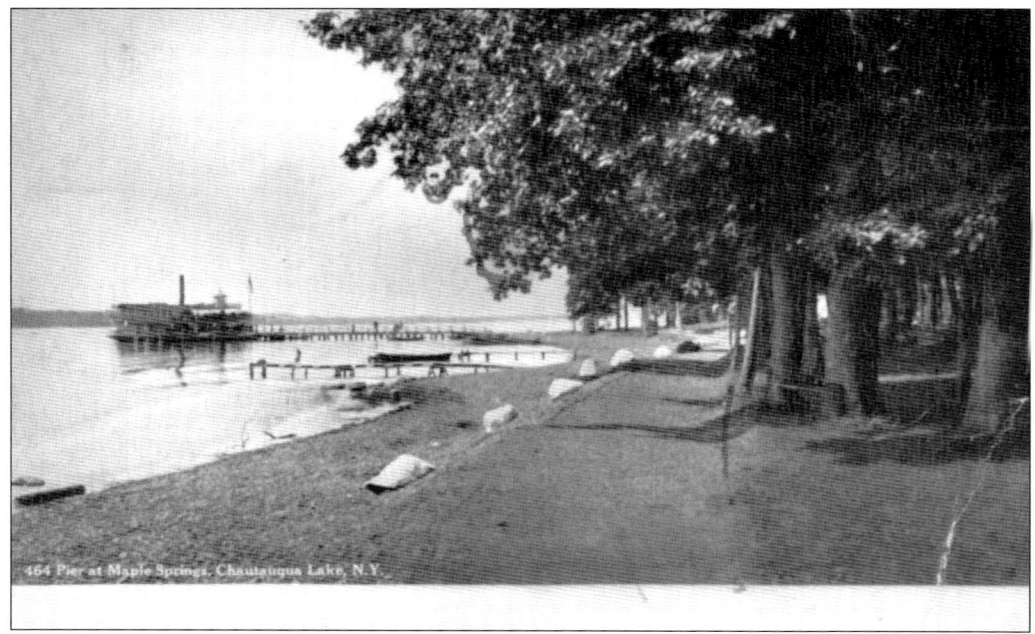

The large steamer *W. B. Shattuc* left the boat landing in late April 1882 with a large load of dressed lumber and towing a barge full of lumber totaling about 20,000 feet. This was for Perry Barnes's new boardinghouse, being built in Maple Springs. The site was just south of Hotel Whiteside. Eventually a post office was established here in 1892, and the name Maple Springs was chosen for it.

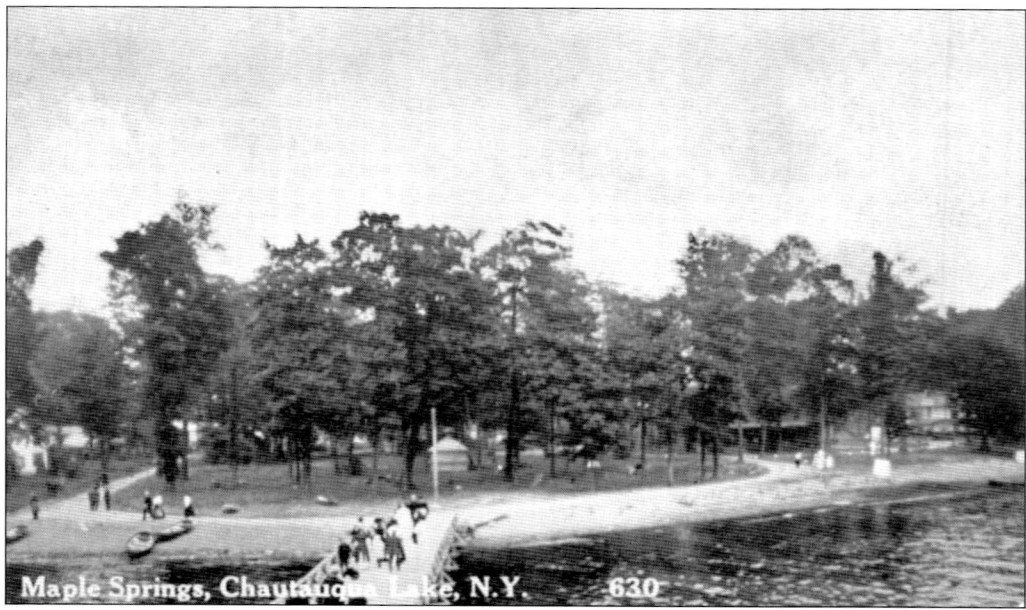

A view from a steamboat at the dock at Maple Springs shows the cottages, hotels, and other structures that can be seen through the trees. The trees, or grove, offered a park for enjoying the cooling lake breezes in the summer. The beach could be used for bathing or wading, and boats were available. (Courtesy of FHC.)

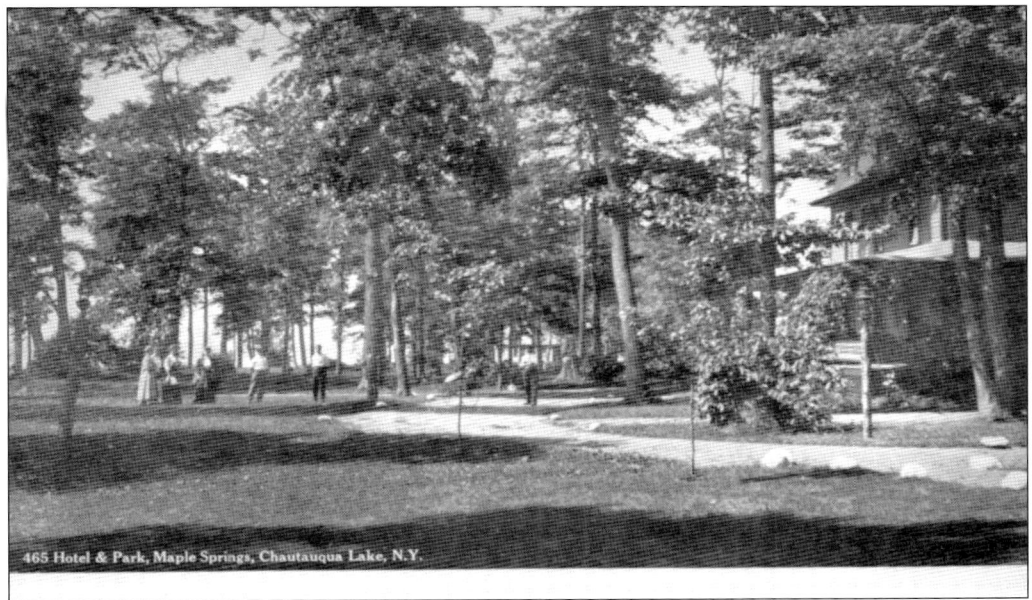

What the sender wrote on the back of this card in 1919 just about sums it up: "Doesn't this look like a pleasant place." The large trees provided shade, the level ground allowed easy leisurely walks, and the lawn was available for lawn games. With the nearby lake, Maple Springs was indeed a pleasant place for rest and relaxation.

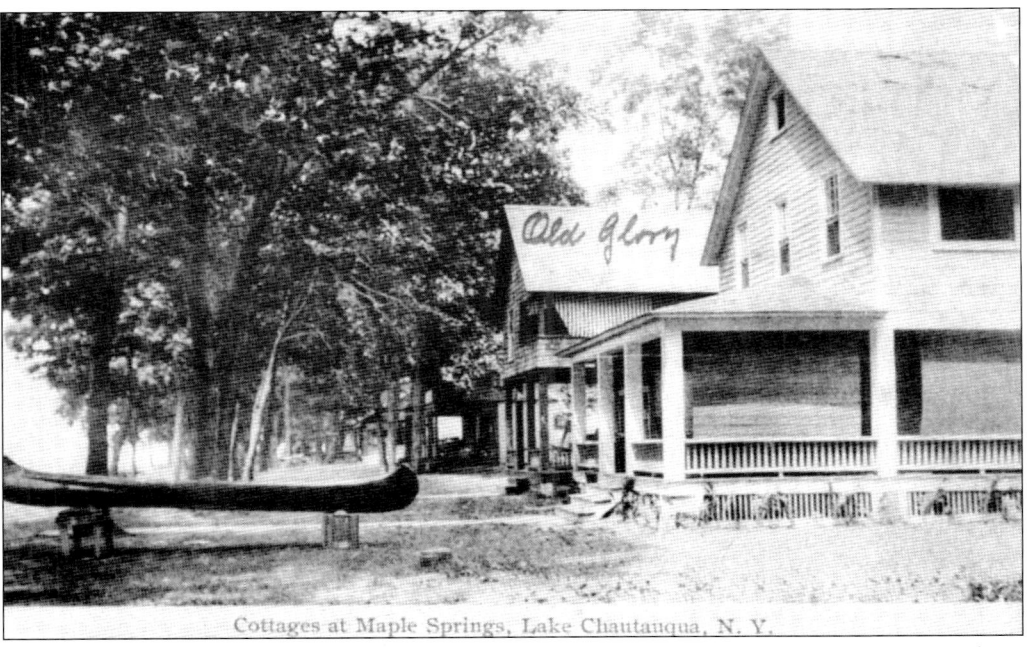

These cottages at Maple Springs were typical of cottages at the many places developing along Chautauqua Lake. If not right on the lake, they were not far from the lake, so the canoe was easily carried to the water. Often the area provided a dock for common use. Many cottages still ring the lake, and many have been turned into year-round homes. (Courtesy of FHC.)

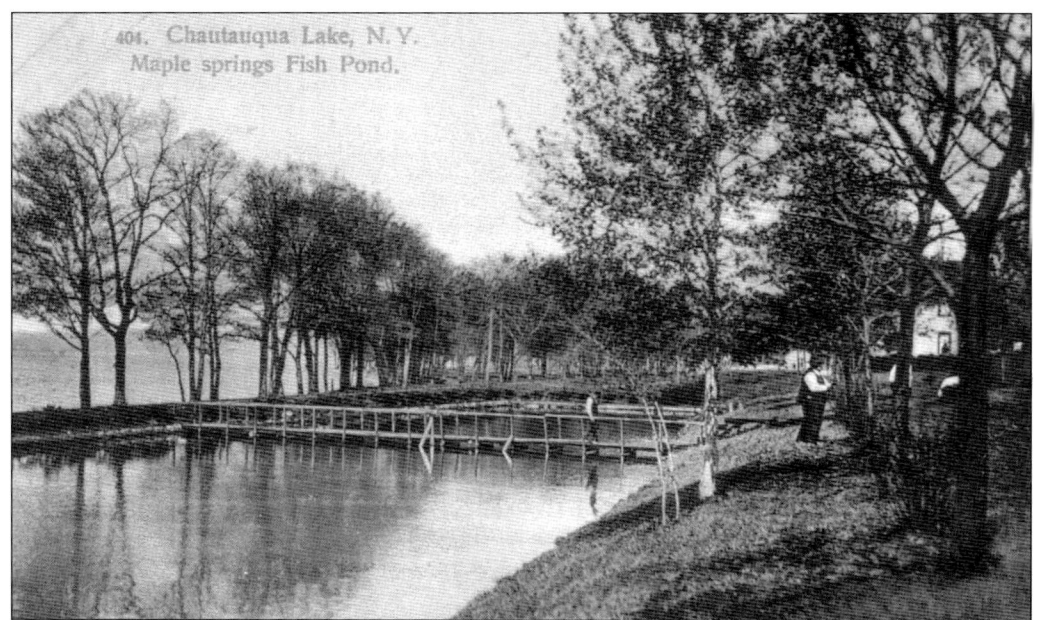

In 1878, James Campbell completed three fishponds for Perry Barnes at his Maple Springs location. These ponds were 64-by-8 feet and were 4 feet deep. They were stocked with salmon and brook trout. How long these fishponds remained at Maple Springs is unknown, but this postcard, sent in 1912, shows a different-sized fishpond. (Courtesy of FHC.)

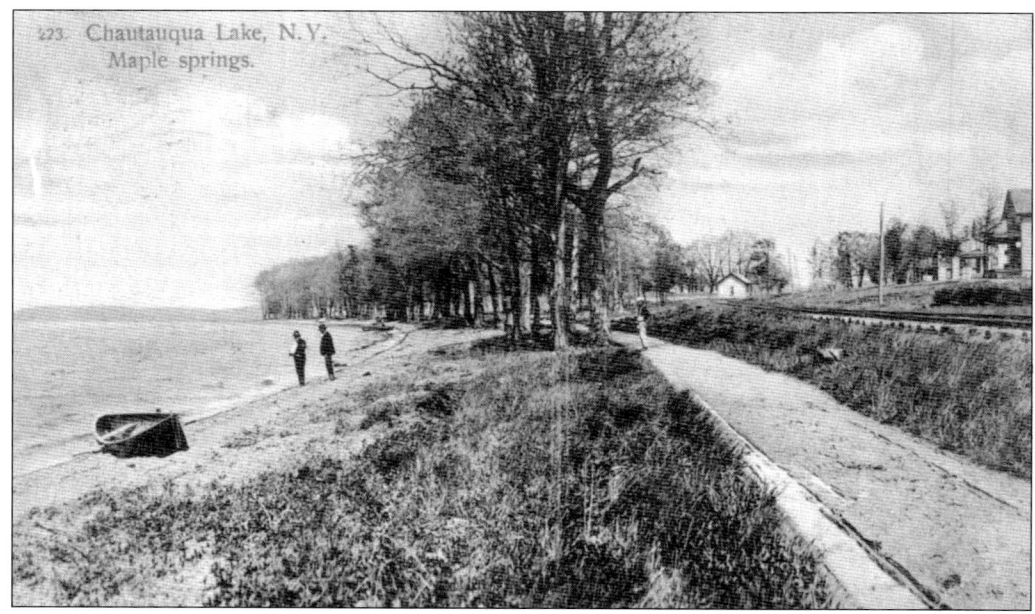

Maple Springs stretches along the Chautauqua Lake shoreline. Pictured here are the lakeshore, the train tracks, and a row of cottages. This photograph was taken either in the spring or fall, without many people or leaves on the trees. (Courtesy of FHC.)

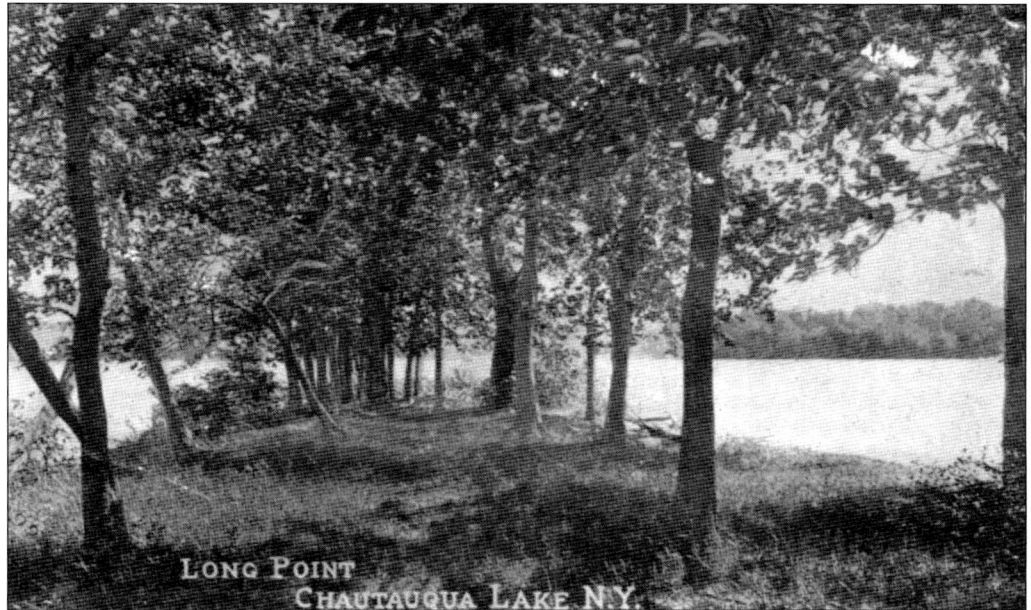

Long Point, extending 1 mile into Chautauqua Lake, has seen its share of picnics during its long history. Before Perry Barnes purchased the point and cleared some land for picnic parties in 1869, hunters had had great success bagging hundreds of waterfowl each fall and spring. Barnes erected a dock, a two-story picnic shelter, and a bandstand, and laid out croquet grounds.

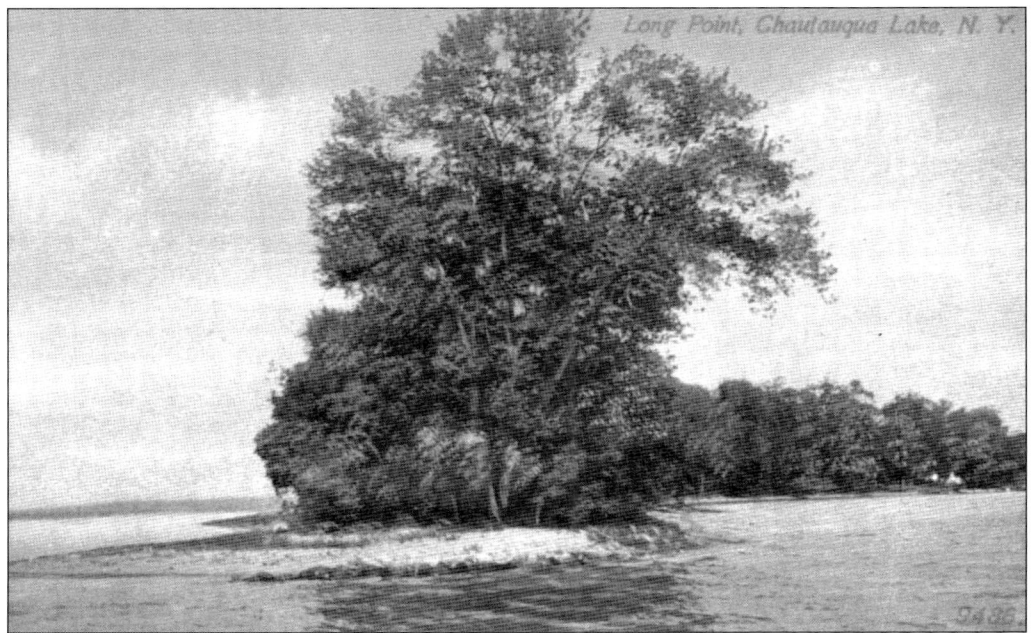

After Barnes made a few improvements, a group from Titusville, Pennsylvania, purchased Long Point. Picnicking continued, and in 1878, when Henry Harley owned the land, the newspaper reported that it was in excellent order and was almost the only place on the lake that was not taken up by hotels and cottages, which would have made it undesirable for picnics.

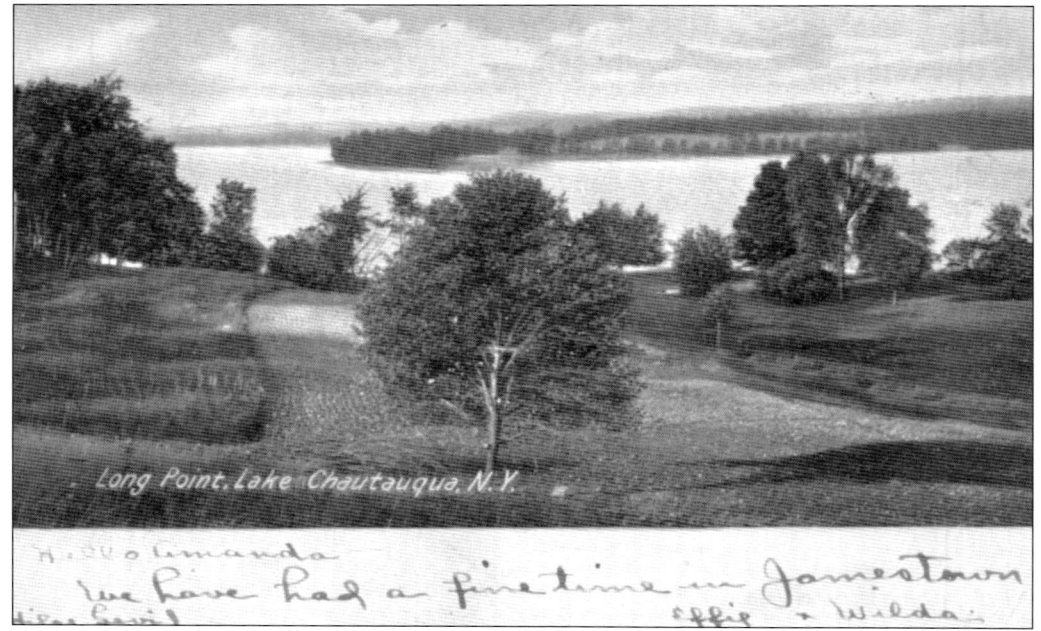

Long Point on the east side is almost opposite Tom's Point on the west side. These two points caused steamers to maneuver around each after going through the Narrows at Bemus Point on the way up the lake. From a place around Tom's Point, this picture shows tree-covered Long Point extending into the lake. Just off Long Point are some of the deepest areas of the lake.

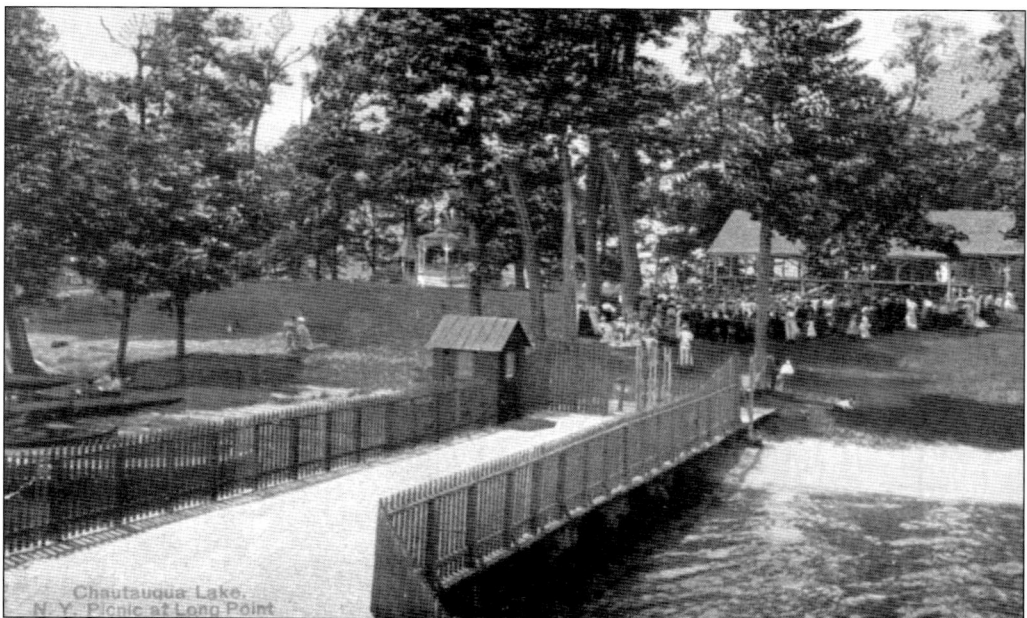

By 1880, the Chautauqua Navigation Company had made Long Point one of the loveliest resorts on the lake. There was to be dancing in the pavilion, and flannel suits were offered at the bathhouses at no extra charge. Entertainment was planned, and the cost for the day was 25¢. The next year found at least 6,000 people there for the Fourth of July.

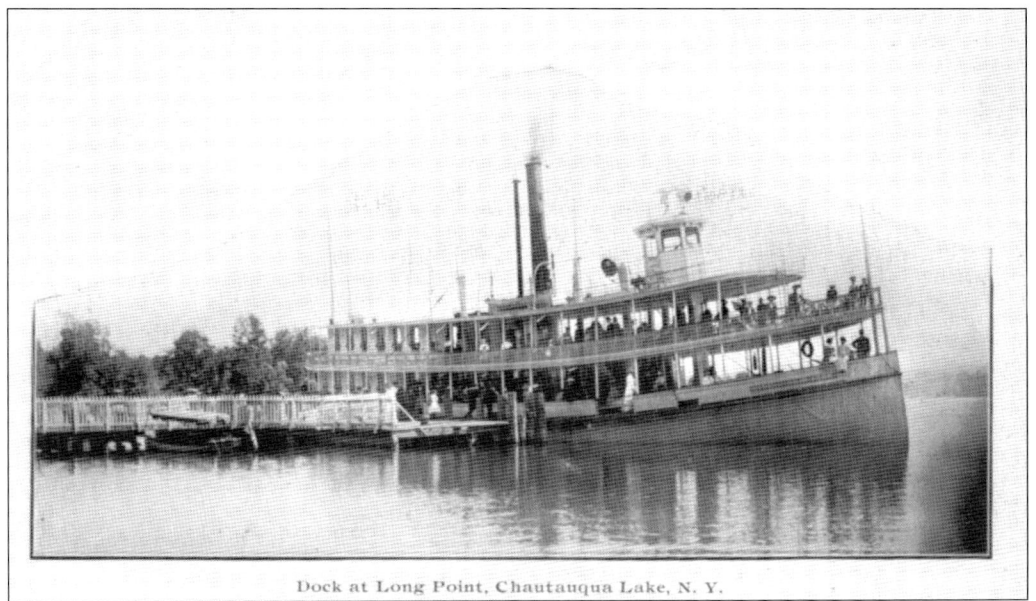

Dock at Long Point, Chautauqua Lake, N. Y.

Different entities leased Long Point. In 1885, the Burroughs brothers secured a beer license for Long Point. In 1887, A. E. Allen was superintendent of the zoological gardens with cages of various animals, including Tip the elephant, who escaped and was not captured until he got to Fluvanna. More than 10,000 people were present for the Fourth of July celebration in 1893. (Courtesy of MC.)

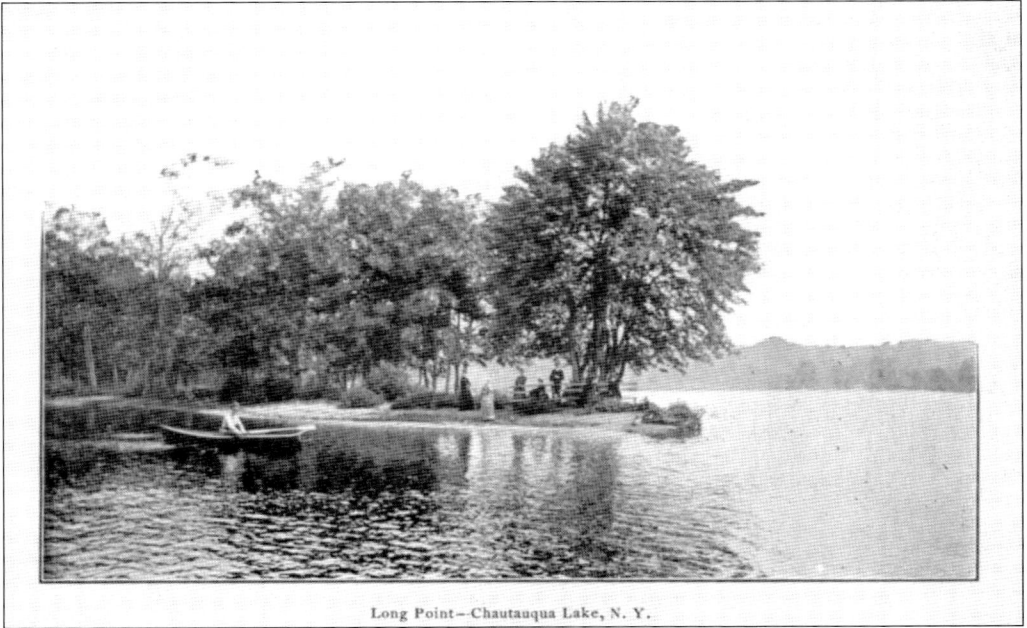

Long Point—Chautauqua Lake, N. Y.

Train service reached Long Point in 1888 and brought picnickers, as did the steamers. The people continued to picnic at Long Point, but by 1898, another picnic ground was being developed by the railroad company at Midway. Long Point did not open as a picnic ground in 1907. It became a private residence until 1954, when it was donated to New York State for a park.

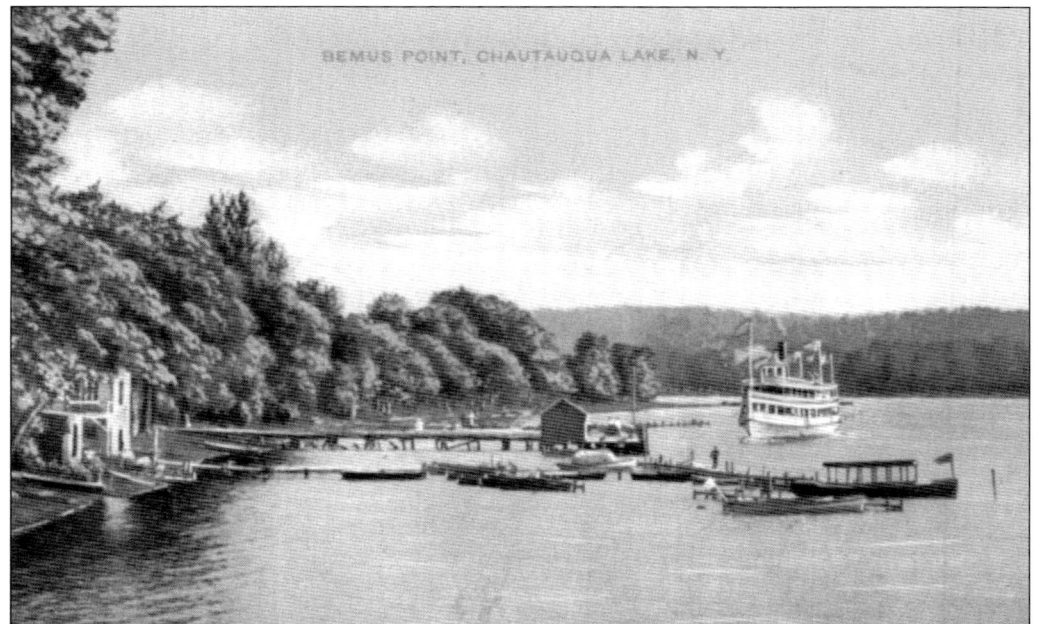

Bemus Point, located at the Narrows, has been and continues to be a resort area. Steamboats, following a narrow channel, could land at the short dock and deposit passengers close to the business section and the hotels in Bemus. The steamer is on its way up the lake.

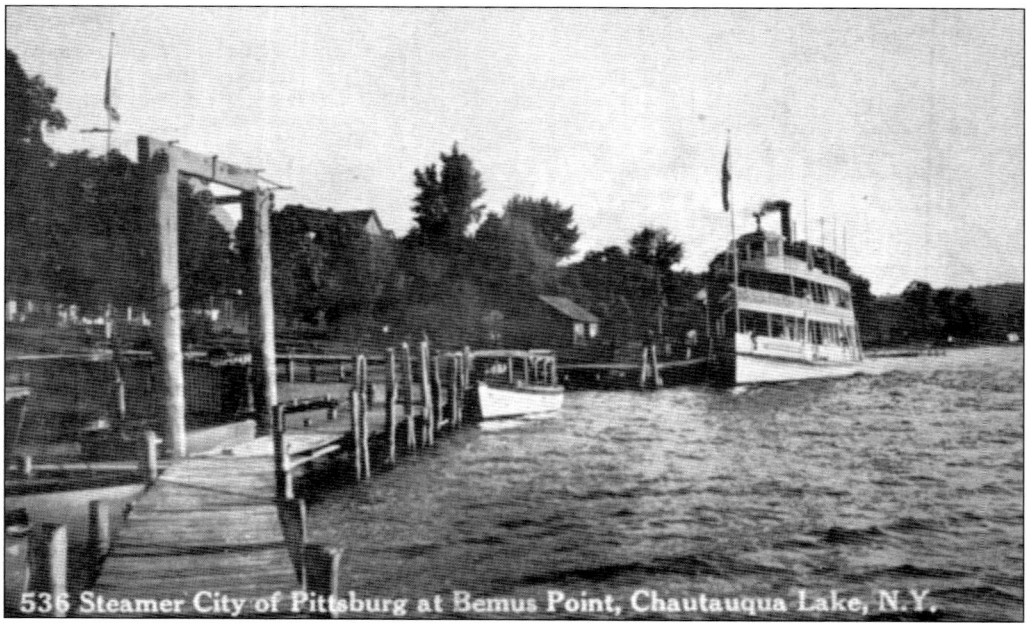

The steamboat is moored along the Bemus Point dock. In the foreground is the dock of a boat livery that rents pleasure boats to visitors. In the background, just left of the center, the tall feature is the peak of the Columbian Hotel roof along the road that led to the ferry to Stow. The hotel's dining rooms and dancing enticed visitors from other hotels along the lake.

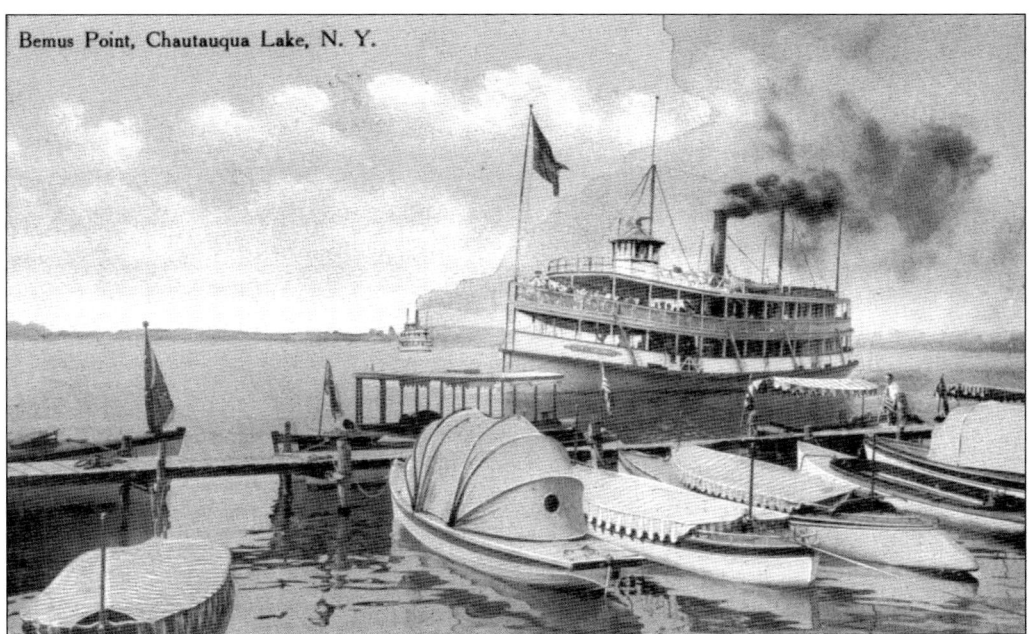

A steamer on the way down the lake with another one close behind is coming into the dock, passing the boat livery docks where many pleasure boats were available for rent. Fishing was popular off Bemus Point but so was rowing along the lakeshore. Note the covers on the boats; some to keep water out and some to shade passengers.

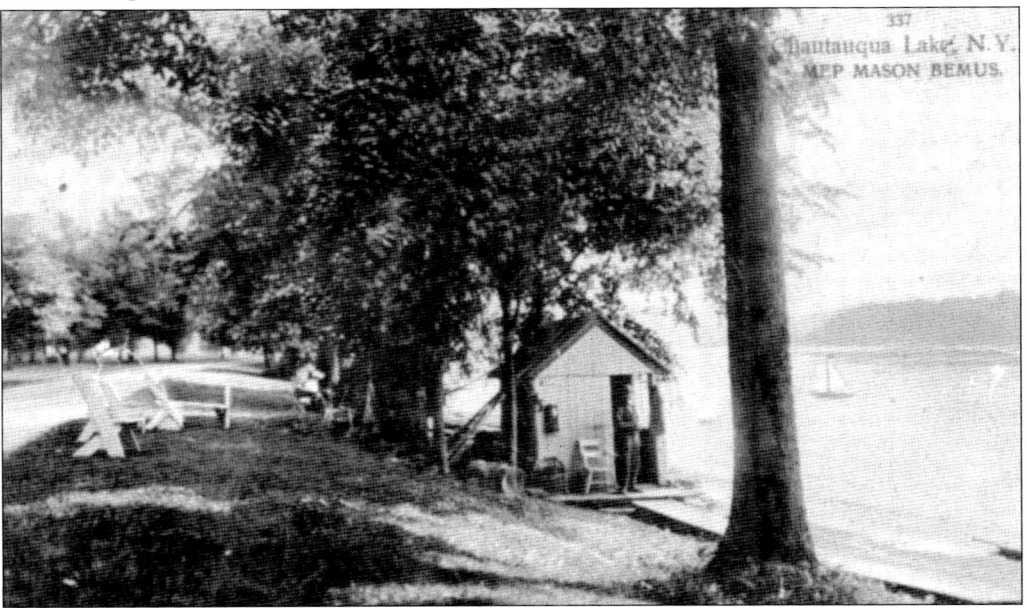

Along the shore by the hotels was Mep Mason's boat rental shack. Mep Mason's family operated Mason's Hotel, which later became the Browning Hotel, located between the Columbian Hotel and the Hotel Lenhart. Besides operating the hotel and boat business, Mep was a well-known old-time fiddler who played for years at the many dances held in the Bemus Point area. (Courtesy of FHC.)

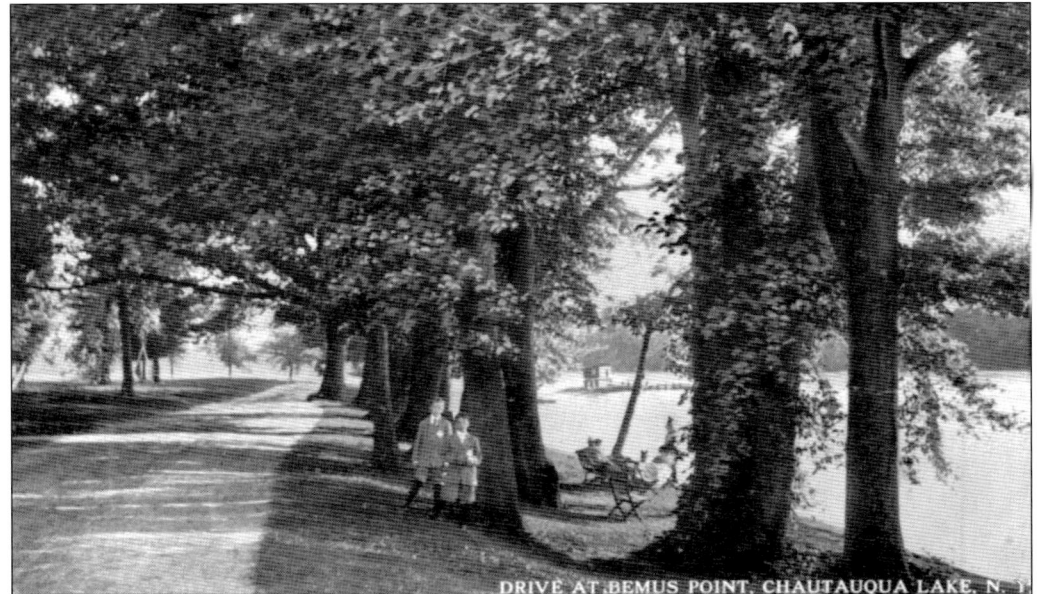

These young boys are posing for the camera along the road fronting the lake and in front of the hotels. Visitors have brought some chairs down to the lakeshore, where they can watch the activities on the lake while enjoying the sunshine. The area was, and still is, the place to watch the spectacular sunsets over the lake. (Courtesy of FHC.)

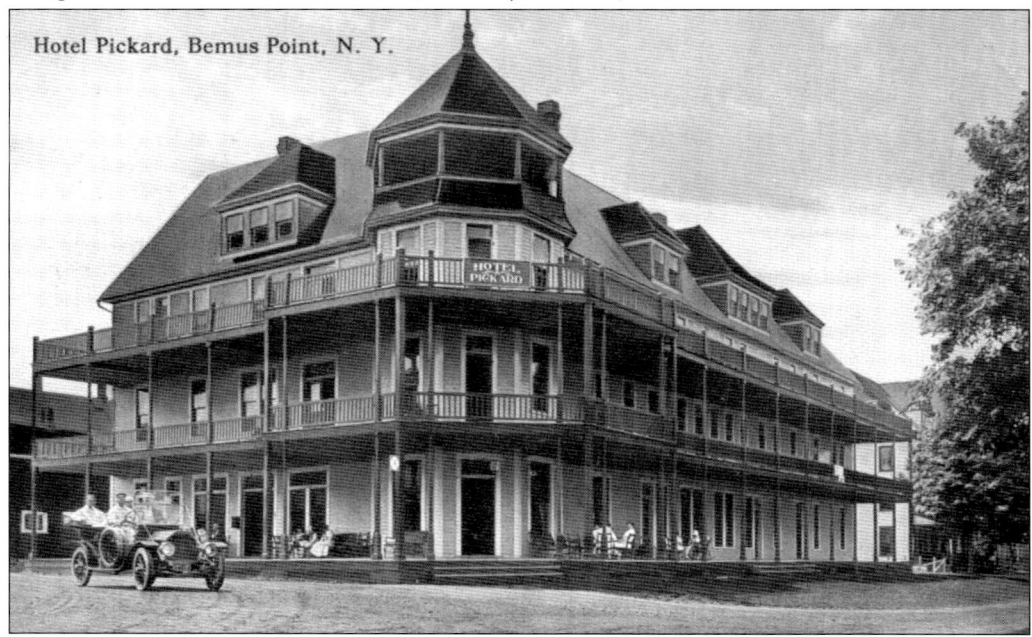

Hotel Pickard occupied the corner of Lakeshore Drive and Main Street in Bemus Point, anchoring the row of hotels facing the lake. A. J. Pickard built his hotel in 1889, replacing the earlier hotel that burned. Pickard even added a dining room and playroom for children and their nurses. In the 1920s, combined with the Columbian Hotel, it became the Bemus Point Hotel. It was razed in 1930.

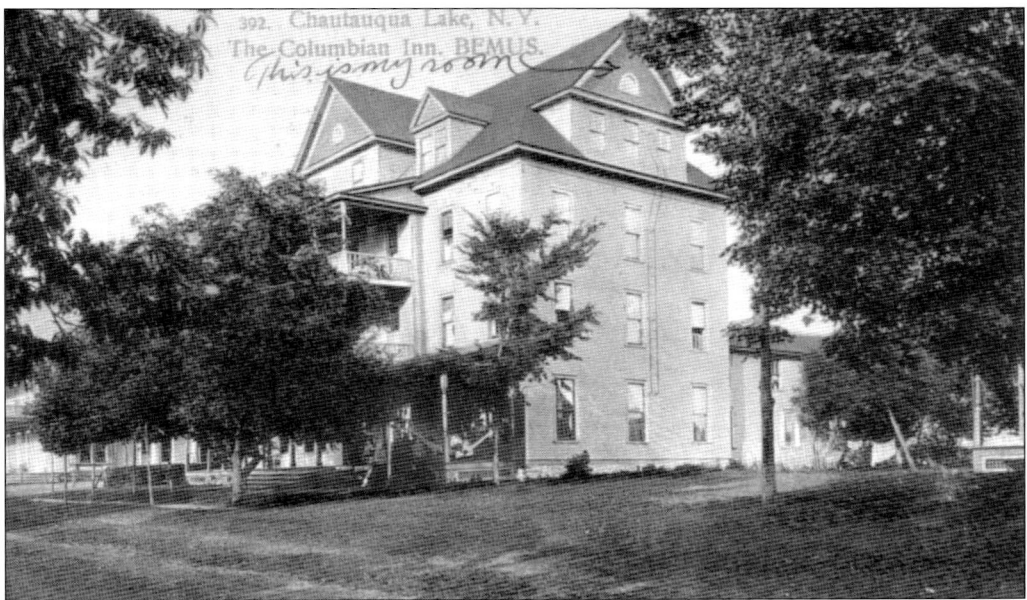

Next in line was the Columbian Hotel, built in 1893 by the Rappole family. An earlier hotel was moved back and served as a wing to the new structure. Electricity was added in 1906, and the business furnished electricity for the first street lighting in Bemus. The dining room was popular with visitors and local residents alike. (Courtesy of MC.)

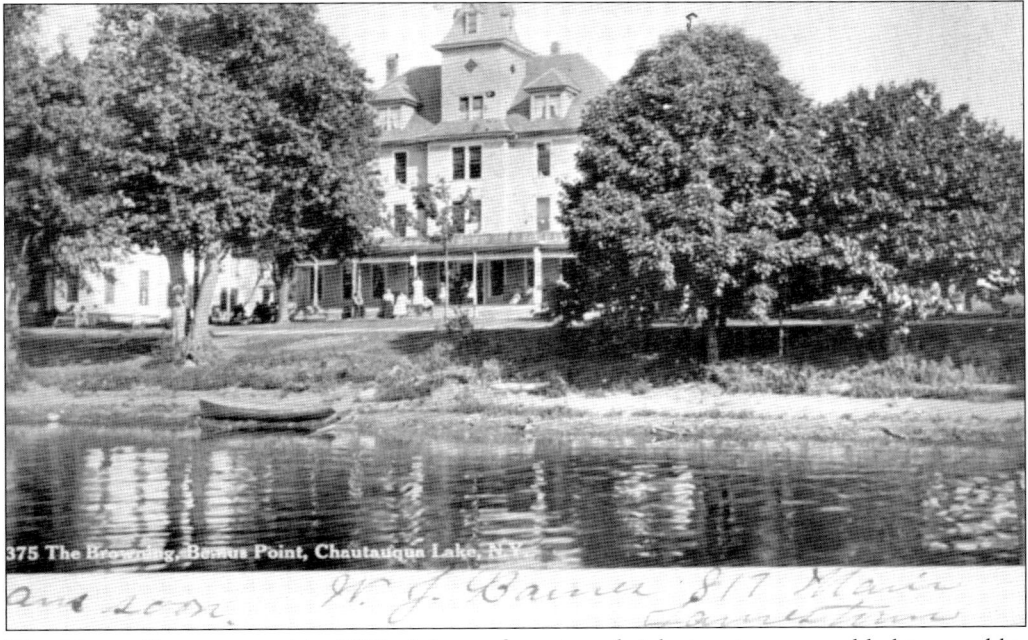

The Mason House opened in 1893. A large, four-story brick structure was added to an older house that had been moved back. In the early 1900s, Perry Brown purchased the hotel, changing the name to Hotel Browning. Part of the property was purchased in 1930 for village development, but the hotel survived the fate of its neighbors to the west and operated until a possible arson fire in 1941. (Courtesy of MC.)

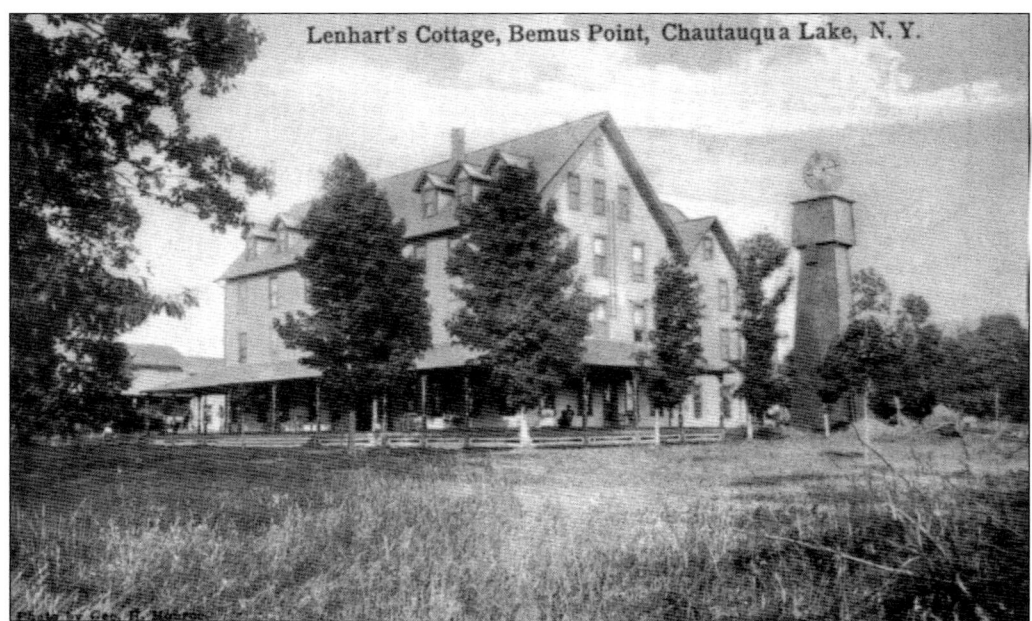

The Lenhart Hotel, opened in 1882, was managed by the owner, Dr. J. J. Lenhart, who also continued his medical practice. A fire in October 1891 destroyed the hotel, but a new structure, twice as large, was ready for guests on June 1, 1892. The new structure is the one pictured above. This hotel was the closest one to the ferry landing. (Courtesy of MC.)

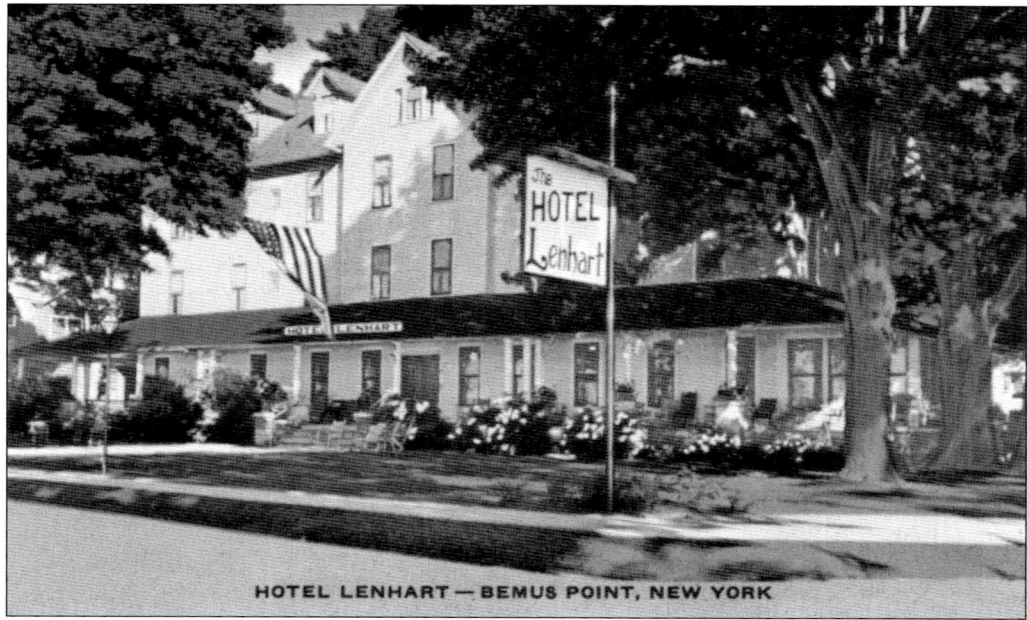

This later view of the Hotel Lenhart shows some changes. Still managed by Lenhart descendants, Hotel Lenhart is one of the two hotels surviving from the resort era along Chautauqua Lake. Both the Hotel Lenhart and the Hotel Ahenaeum at Chautauqua Institution offer rocking chairs on their verandas that overlook the lake, and visitors can sit, rock, relax, and enjoy the sights along the lake. (Courtesy of FHC.)

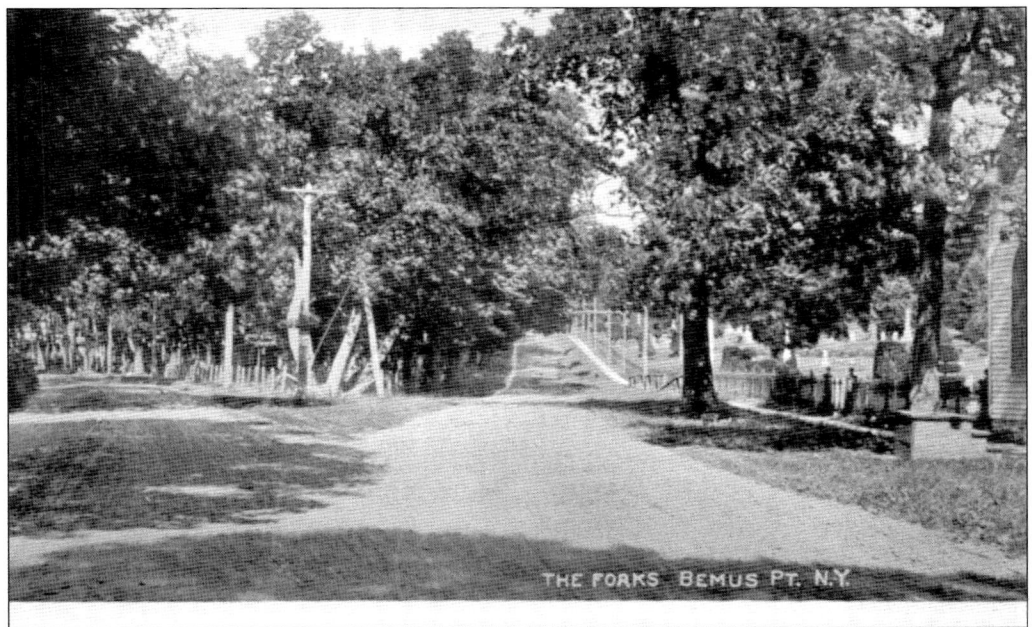

Lakeside Drive extended along the lakeshore to the west away from the business district and the large hotels. This image shows "The Forks," where the lakeside road continued along the lake and another road led away from the lake to join the road that bypassed the village of Bemus Point. The Bemus Point Cemetery can be seen at right.

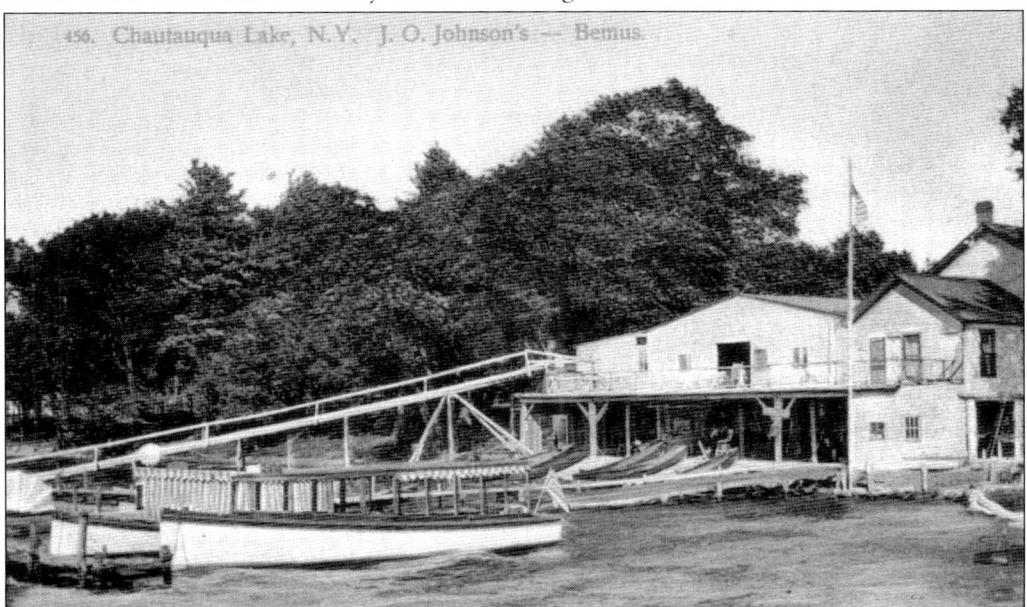

To the west of the large hotels was John O. Johnson's boatyard. Building, repairing, and renting boats kept this boatyard busy for many years. The Lawson family purchased the business after Johnson's death in 1918 and continues selling boats and supplies today. Across the street is the Hare 'n Hounds restaurant. Built in 1921 as an inn, it is now a fine dining restaurant. (Courtesy of FHC.)

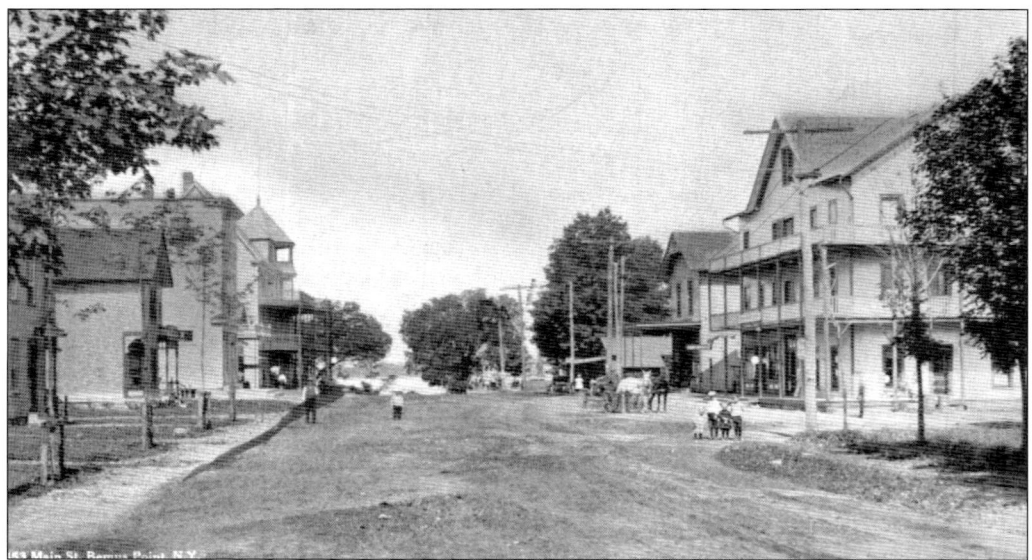

Bemus Point's business district, around the beginning of the 20th century, has dirt streets and no sidewalks. The pointed tower on Pickard's Hotel can be seen on the left. The steamer dock is at the end of the street. The three-story building with verandas on the right was a hotel. Today it is the See-Zuhr House, a popular restaurant. Bemus Point continues to be a popular summer destination. (Courtesy of FHC.)

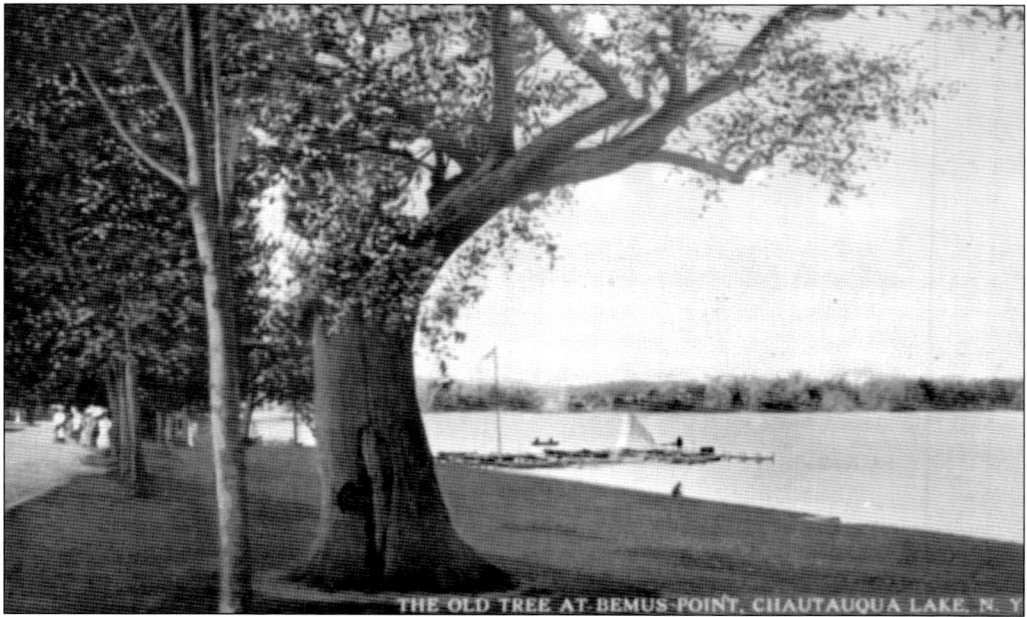

The significance of "the old tree" is lost to history. It was at the corner across from Pickard's Hotel and by the steamboat dock. It obviously lost most of its upper limbs at some time. It could have been a convenient meeting place—"Meet you at the old tree." One storm in 1883 damaged Pickard's earlier hotel and uprooted trees in Bemus Point and Long Point.

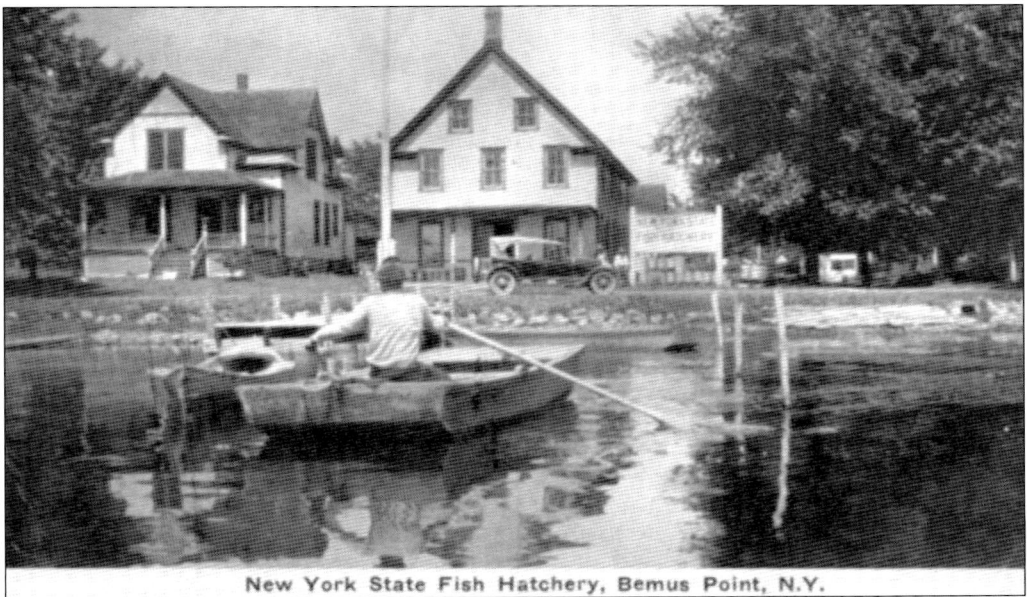

First at Greenhurst, the New York State Fish Hatchery was closed for lack of funds in 1891. Frank Cheney raised funds and continued raising muskellunge fry for the lake. A few years later, the Bemus Point hatchery opened. The ponds alongside the building drew visitors during the spring activity. Chautauqua Lake muskellunge hatchlings are still raised at Prendergast Point, south of the Chautauqua Institution. (Courtesy of FHC.)

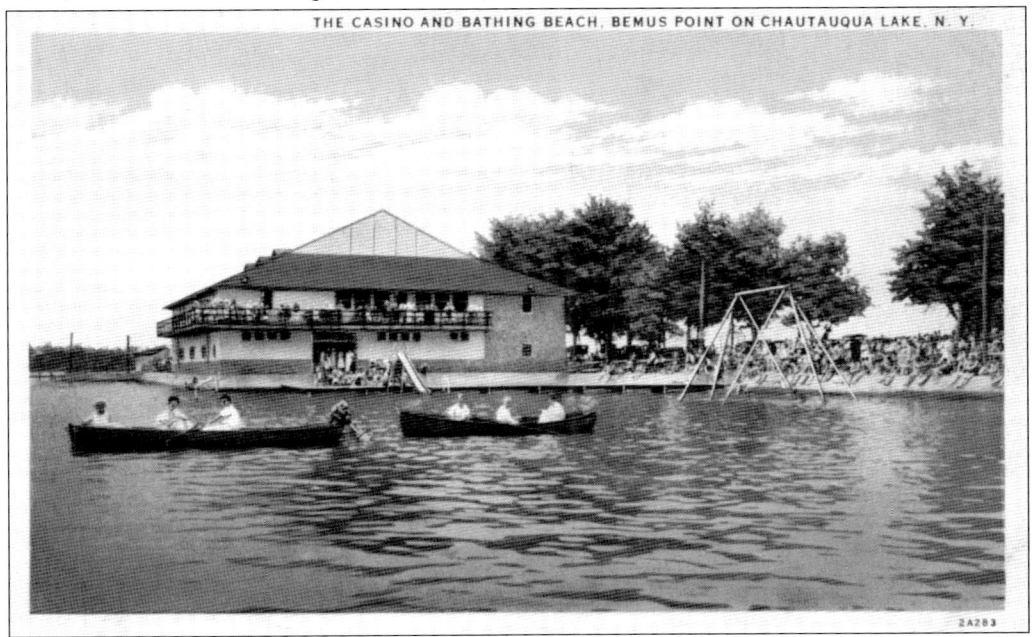

The Casino, built in 1930, is at the lake's edge by the ferry landing. During the 1930s and 1940s, the big bands of the era played the Casino and the Pier Ballroom at Celoron. Today it is a restaurant with a large hall on the second floor for dances and other parties. (Courtesy of MC.)

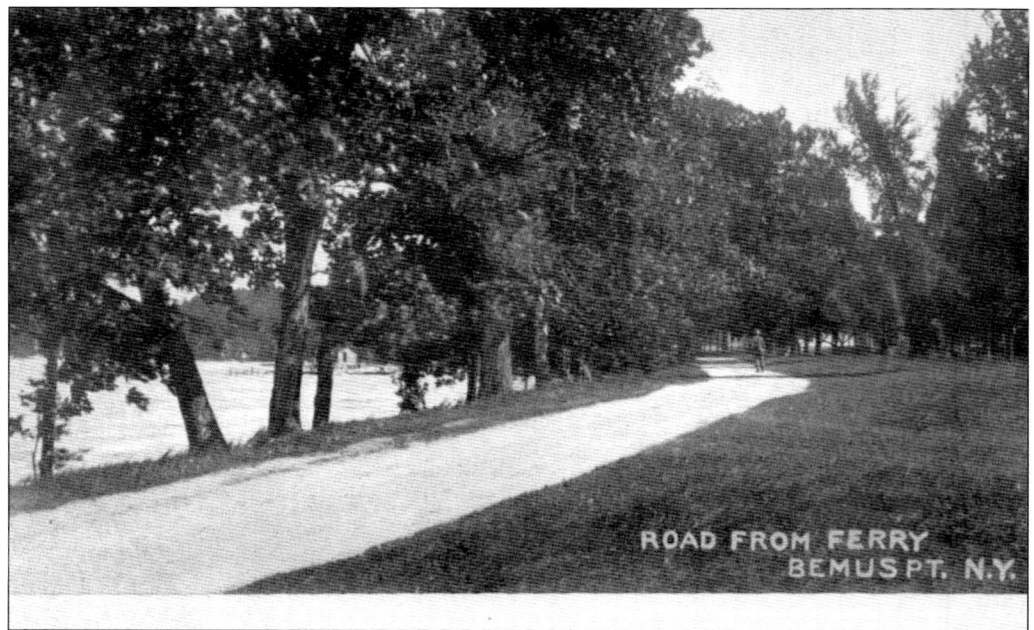

This is Lakeshore Drive coming from the ferry landing toward the business district and past the large hotels. Across the road was a common lawn, with trees and a view of the lake, for all to enjoy. It is still a favored spot for watching sunsets on warm summer evenings. Some of the boat docks are visible through the trees.

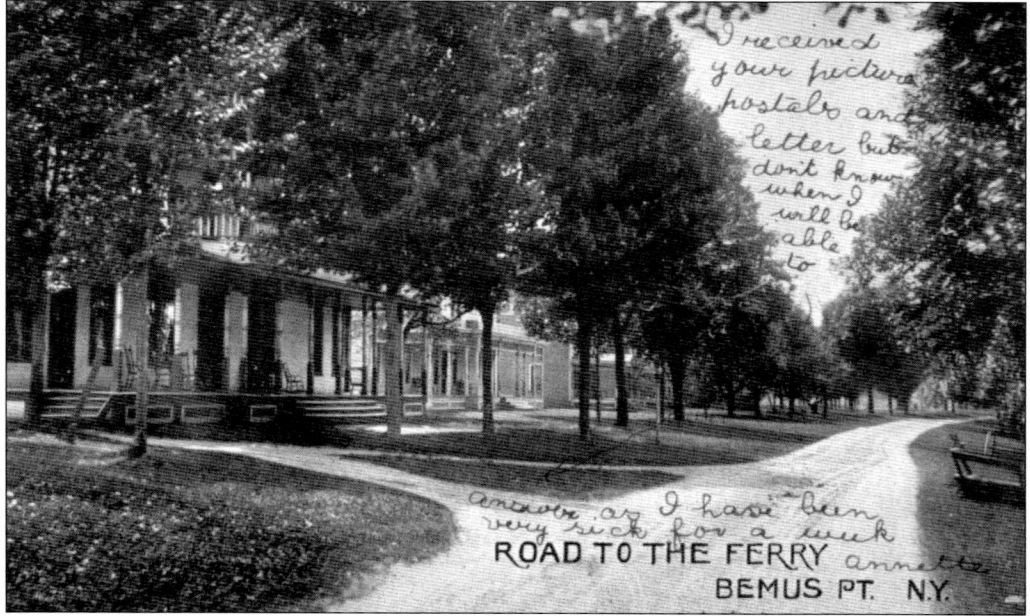

Another image of Lakeshore Drive is seen here, only looking toward the ferry landing instead. Verandas of the hotels, complete with rocking chairs, can be seen. Rocking chairs are still a fixture at Hotel Lenhart and Hotel Athenaeum. With the lake across the road from the hotels, a short walk could take visitors to the water's edge.

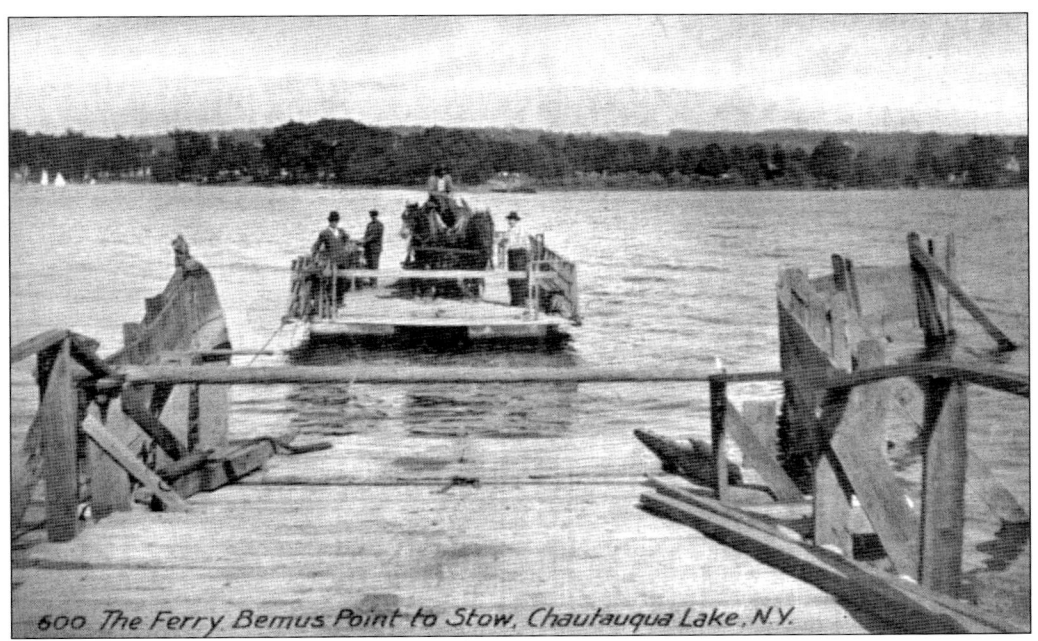

The Bemus Point–Stow Ferry had its beginning in 1811, when Thomas Bemus received a license to operate a ferry. His ferry was a crude log raft, which was pulled by hand from one side of the lake to the other. This saved a lengthy walk or ride around one end of the lake or the other. This is a later version of the ferry, still transporting horses and people.

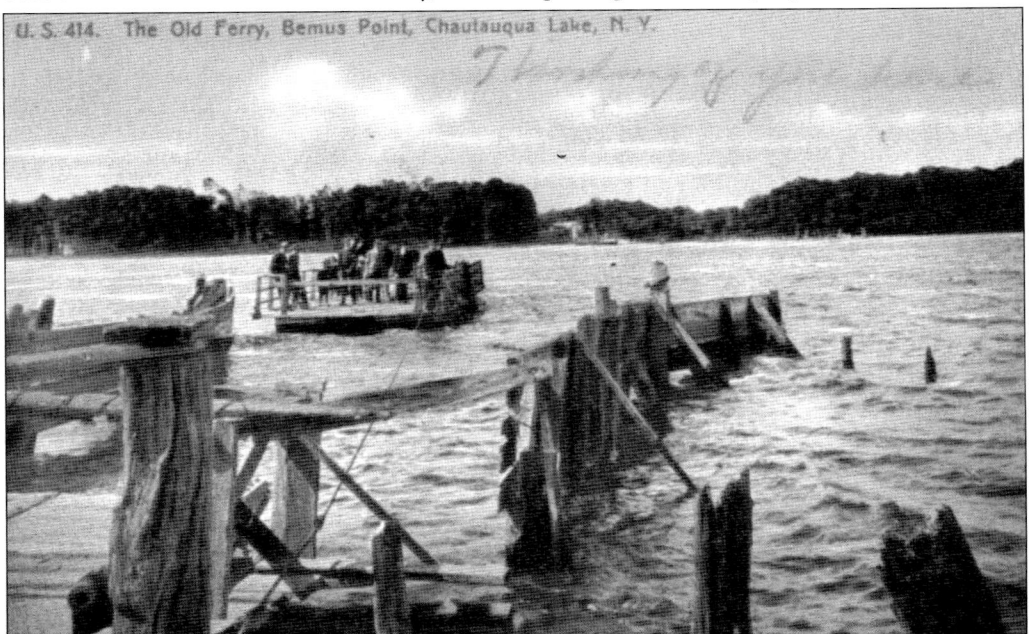

The ferry changed over the years. From hand pulling to using a hand crank to propel the ferry, the ferry continued to be hard work until 1898. Then it was reported that F. G. Ball expected to put a small engine on the ferry and run it by steam. What season that happened is not recorded, but by 1908, a steam engine was replaced by a gasoline engine.

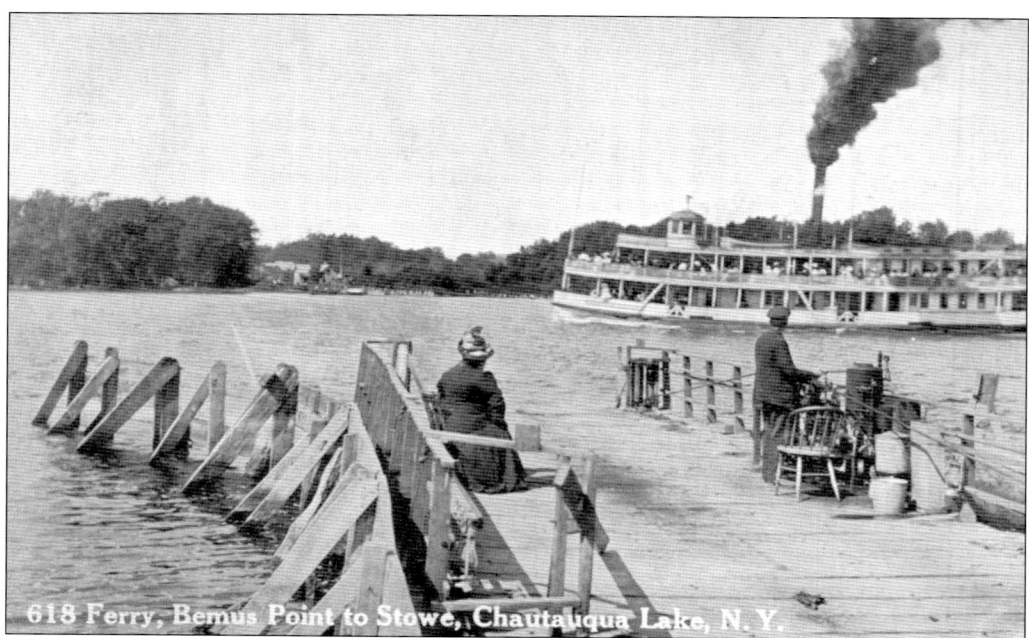

Here the ferry is waiting for the steamer to pass before attempting the crossing. In 1882, steamer *W. B. Shattuc*'s wheel became entangled with the ferry rope, severing it. Earlier a similar incident had happened with the small steamer *Waukeegan*. Both times a new rope was needed. In 1887, the rope was changed to a steel cable.

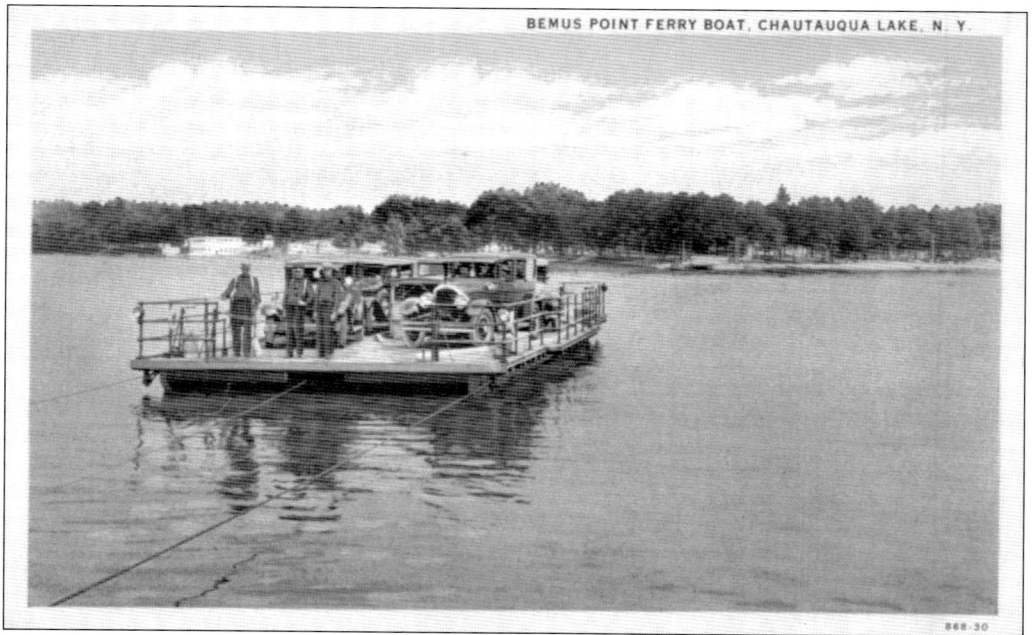

Before 1928, the ferry could transport only three cars in a single-file row. This version can take more than three cars and is wide enough for more than a single-file row. Running from the day the ice melted until it formed again, local residents and summer visitors depended on the ferry to save many miles. (Courtesy of FHC.)

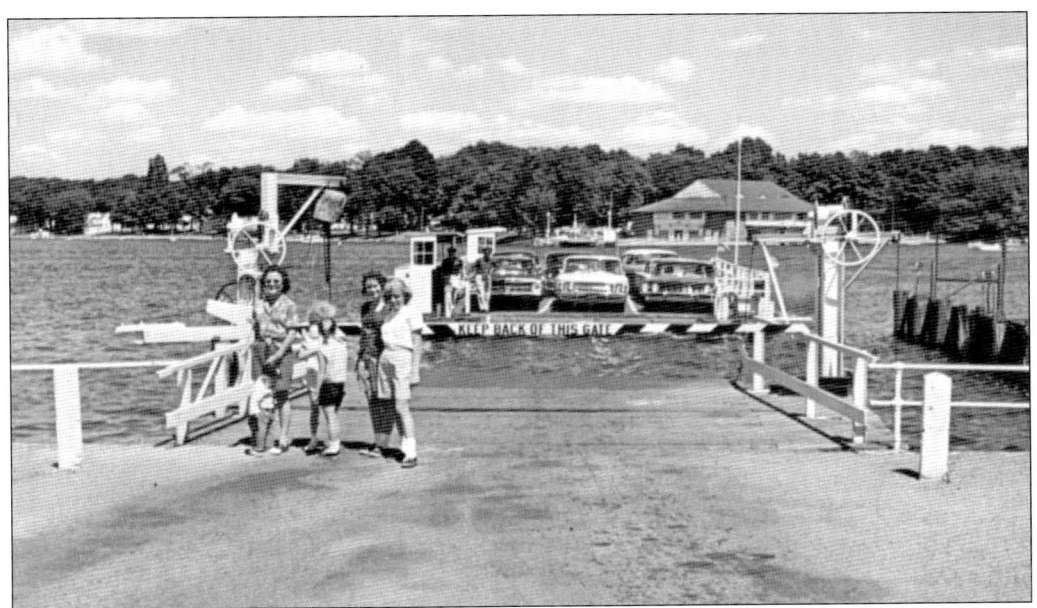

The ferry continues to run during the summer months, much to the delight of summer visitors and nostalgic local residents. In 1901 and 1923, attempts to have a bridge built across the Narrows were made. Finally built and opened in 1982, the bridge now carries Interstate 86. Today the ferry is diesel-powered and the cables are guides, but boats must slow down and watch for the cables when passing the ferry.

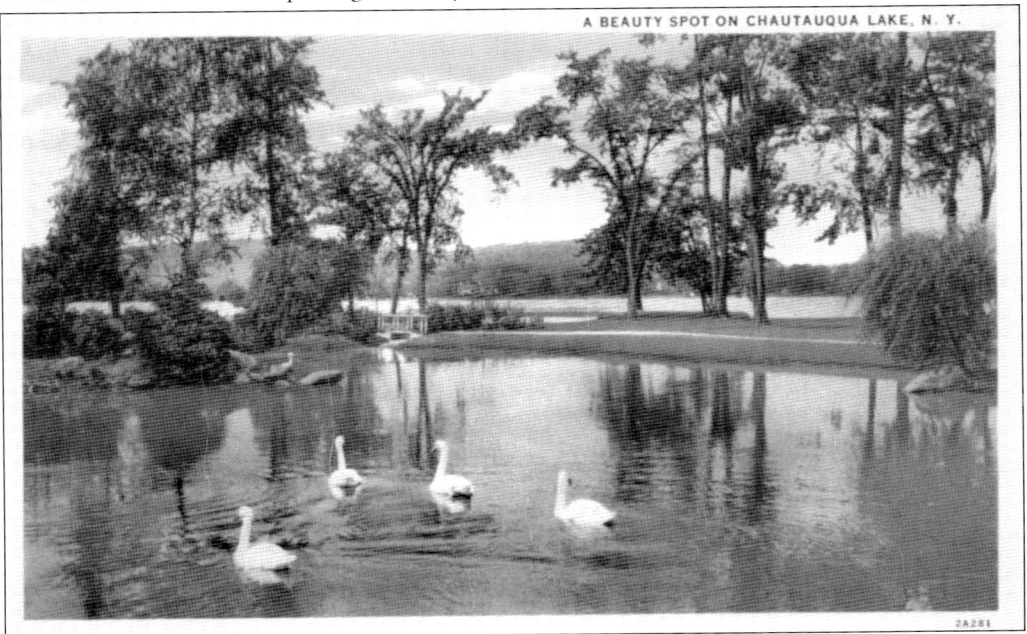

Only the photographer knows this location. One spot that may be a candidate for the location could be the fishponds at Maple Springs, which had trees growing on the shores, and swans could have been there. Regardless of where this was, the postcard was a nice marketing tool for the many other beautiful sites along the lake.

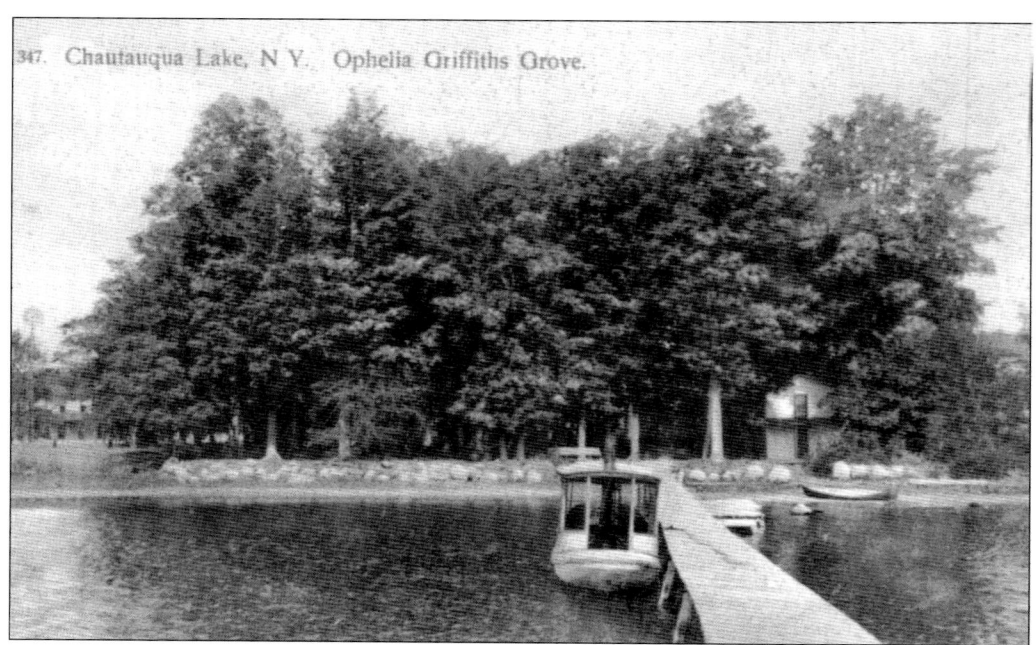

Ophelia Griffith and her sister, Martha, ran a boardinghouse on the family's homestead at Martha's Vineyard near Belleview. A bathhouse was added in 1898, and other improvements were made. The Jamestown High School senior class enjoyed a fish bake at Ophelia's on February 28, 1903, arriving by sleigh. In 1916, a reunion claimed that one lady had been spending the summer with Miss Ophelia for 40 years. (Courtesy of FHC.)

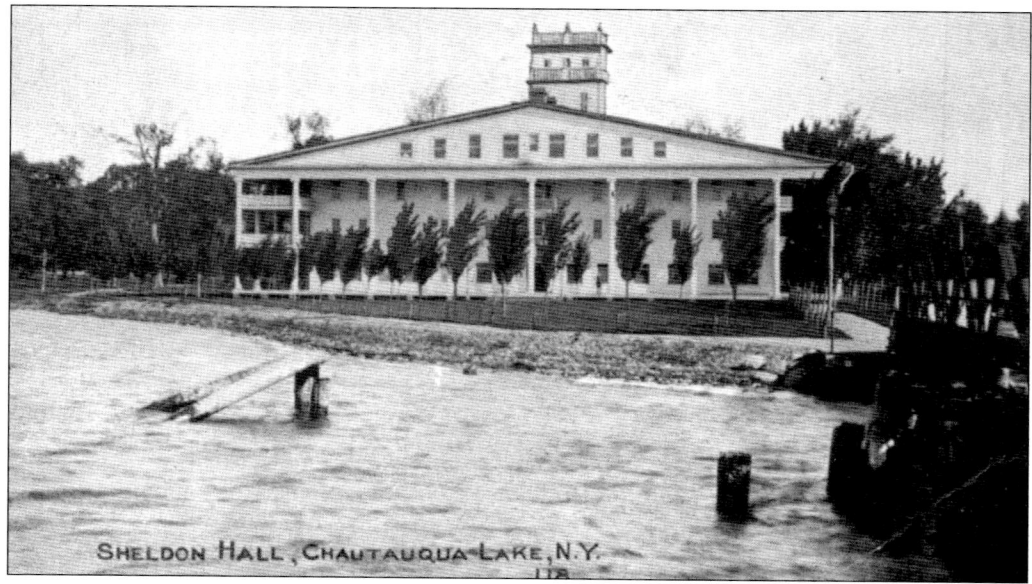

In 1900, the new pier at Sheldon Park was constructed on an iron frame and would be the most substantial one on the lake. The owner, Porter Sheldon, had razed the old Griffith House and had built a new hotel called Sheldon Hall at the resort known as Sheldon Park. It would accommodate 70 people and would be ready for occupancy in early June.

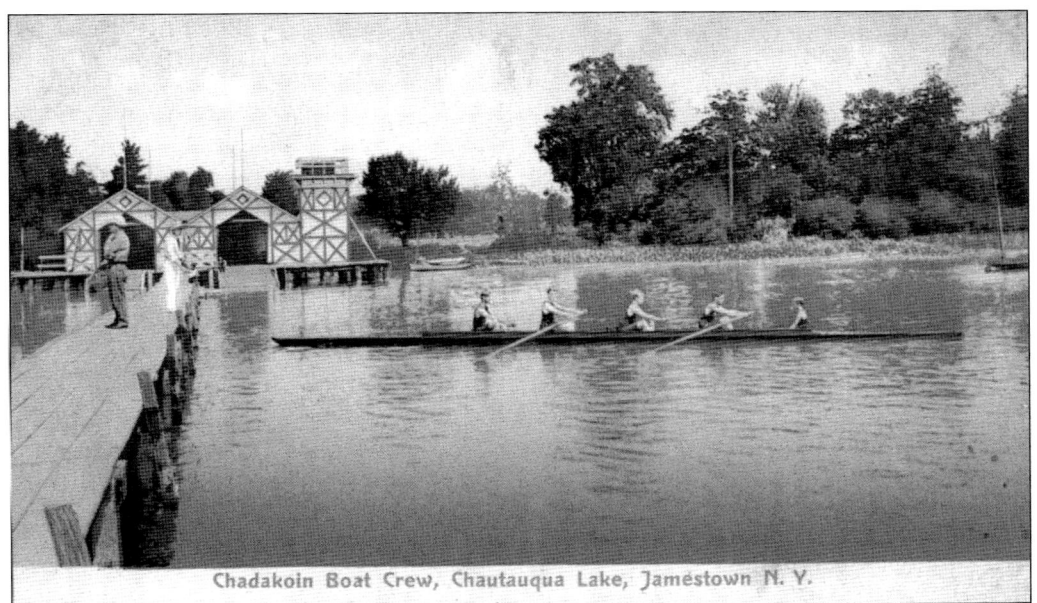

Chadakoin Boat Crew, Chautauqua Lake, Jamestown N. Y.

The Chadakoin Boat Club, organized in 1889, built a 56-by-20-foot boathouse with an ornamental tower on the lakeshore at Greenhurst. The tower eventually housed a searchlight. The boathouse was painted white with red trim, while the Greenhurst Hotel next door was first painted gray with red trim. Rowing events against Chautauqua were some of the summer activities.

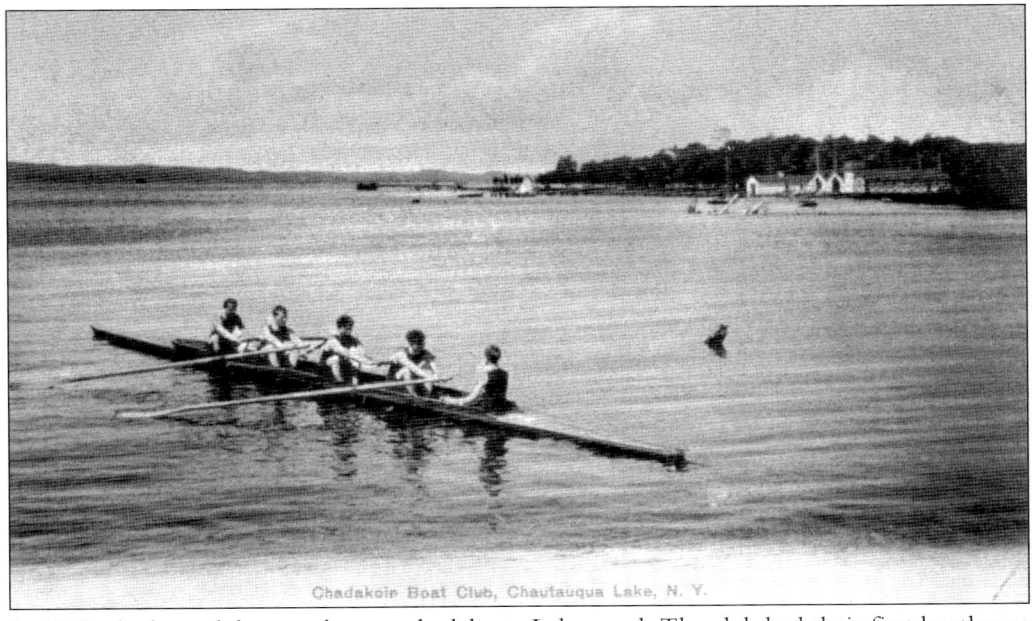

Chadakoin Boat Club, Chautauqua Lake, N. Y.

In 1908, the boat club moved across the lake to Lakewood. The club had their first boathouse torn down and had accepted Lakewood Country Club's invitation to use their new boathouse. The next season the boat club built a boathouse on land leased from the Lakewood Country Club. After 20 years, fire consumed the building, so the club purchased land and built what is now Chautauqua Lake Yacht Club's headquarters.

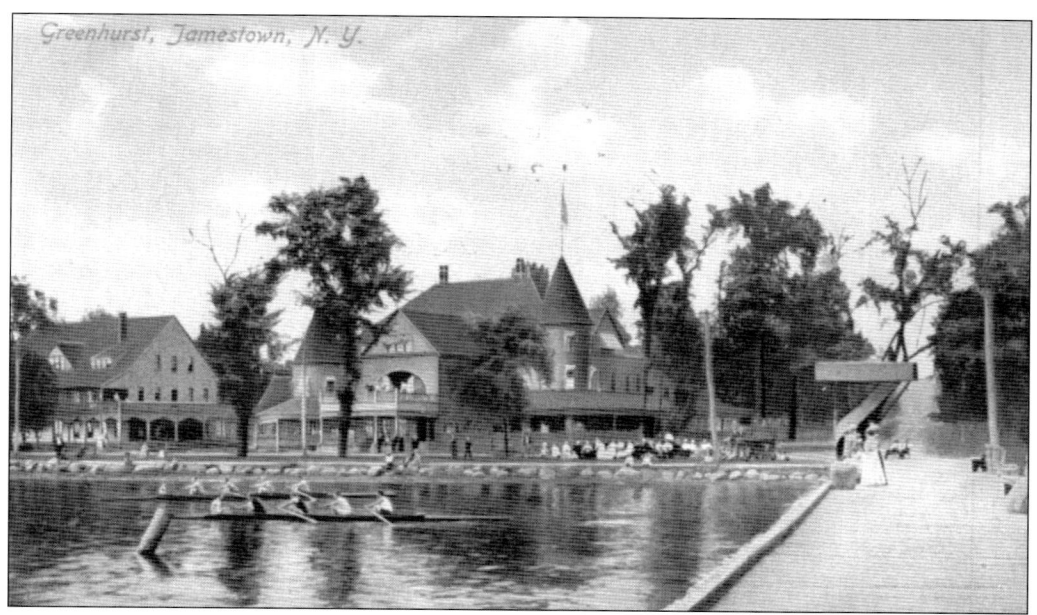

The Greenhurst Hotel, constructed in 1889, was moved the next year and became the annex to the new hotel building. It was a popular hotel for local people, being so close to Jamestown. Beginning in 1890, the Greenhurst Hotel had "swan boats" on the lake, like the ones used in New York's Central Park. One of those swans is now on exhibit at Jamestown's Fenton History Center.

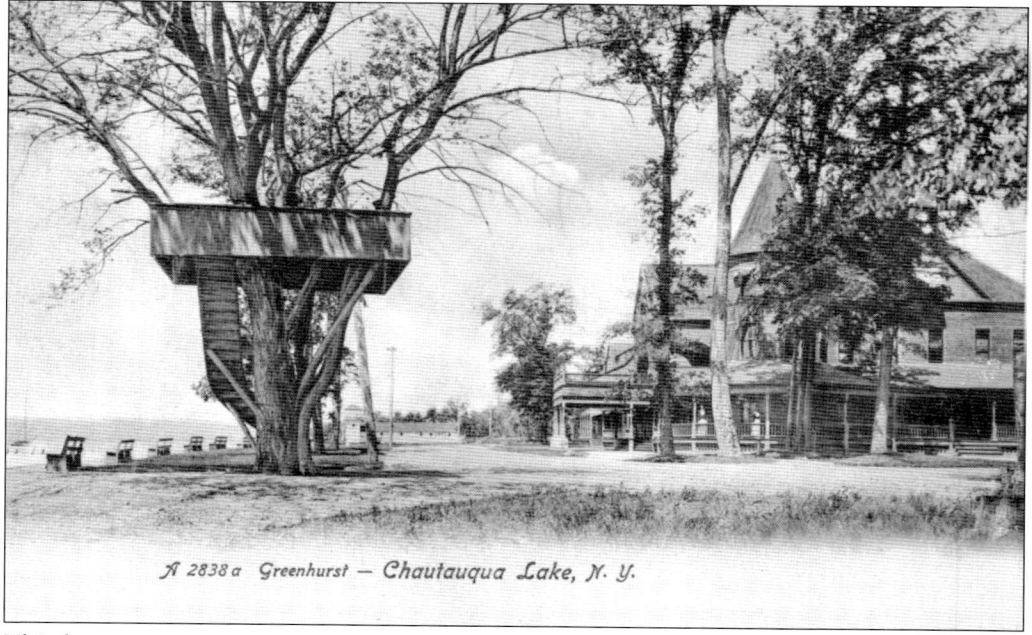

This large tree stood at the end of the steamboat dock at Greenhurst. Large enough for a bandstand, the platform was about 20 feet off the ground. It offered a most excellent view of the lake, and one could enjoy the cooling lake breezes after climbing the spiral stairs. This large tree was snapped off near the ground in a severe storm in June 1905. (Courtesy of FHC.)

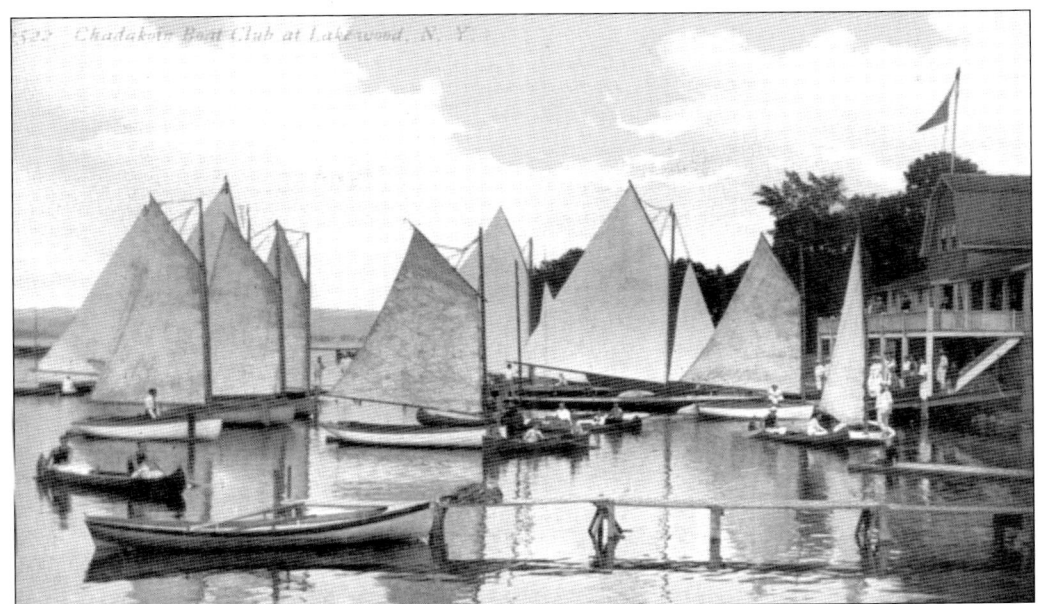

The Chadakoin Boat Club, which was started in Greenhurst, eventually was moved across the lake to Lakewood. Pictured are a number of sailboats that were at the boathouse built in Lakewood near the Lakewood Country Club. The boat club eventually became the Chautauqua Lake Yacht Club and remains in Lakewood today. The club began with rowing but gave way to sailing. Rowing is making a comeback today.

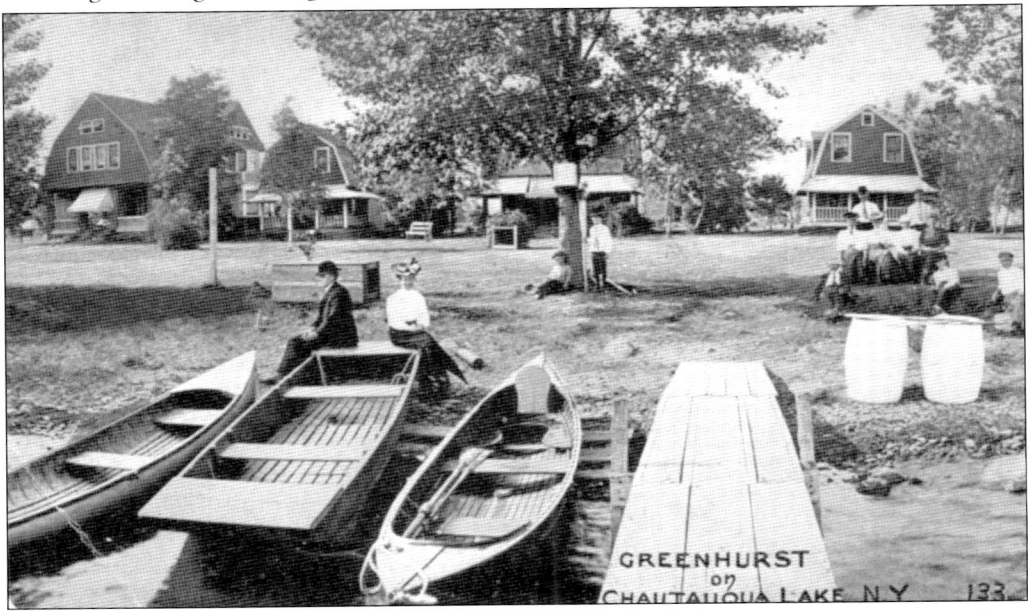

This picture shows the results of the 1889 report that the Green and Brown Tract, later Greenhurst, had been laid out in building lots, parks, and playgrounds. Lakefront lots allowed residents to have rowboats and enjoy the cooling lake breezes in the summer. The 1889 plans called for a depot for the Chautauqua Lake Railway. The state fish hatchery building had been constructed. (Courtesy of FHC.)

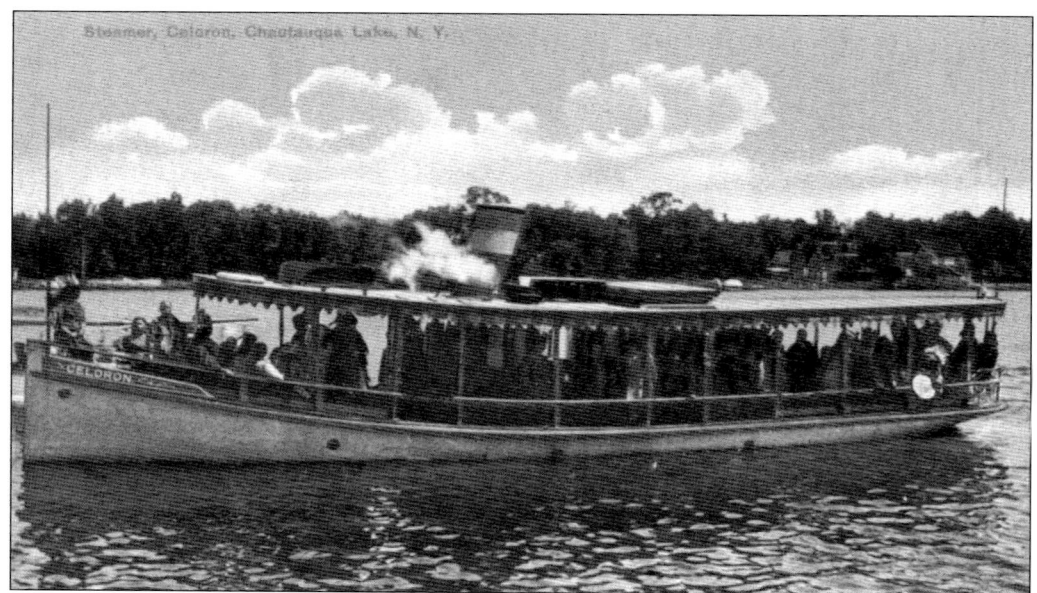

The *Celoron* and her sister ship *Greenhurst* were two small steamers purchased from the Chicago World's Fair by the Broadheads. Used for excursion parties on Lake Michigan during the World's Fair, on Chautauqua Lake the ships ferried passengers between Greenhurst, Celoron, and Lakewood from 1895 to 1912. One story about the *Greenhurst* says it was purchased by Henry Ford for his museum, trucked there, and never seen again! (Courtesy of MC.)

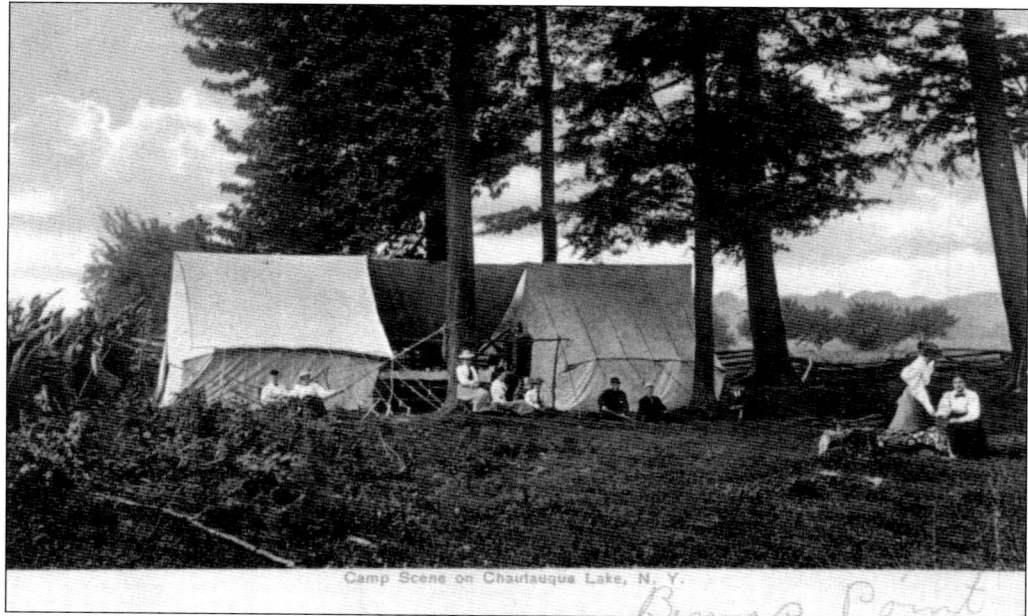

This is a generic camping scene that could have been taken in many places along the lake's shoreline. Apparently the sender wrote "Bemus Point" on the front. Camping was a way for families and friends to enjoy the healthful air of the countryside and a few days of relaxation. Camping probably appealed to those who did not want the formality of hotels and boardinghouses or their expense. (Courtesy of FHC.)

Six

Town of Ellicott and Jamestown

The Fluvanna area was the site of the first hotel on the lake, the Fluvanna House. Established in 1836, it later expanded and continued in business until the 1890s, when it became a private residence. It was the only hotel along the lake until the 1860s. The cholera epidemic in Buffalo in 1849 induced two families to spend the summer in the isolated Chautauqua Lake region at the Fluvanna House, which had catered to hunters and fishermen in the past. However, more families came to know the Fluvanna House. It operated on temperance principles.

Fluvanna was also the site of another early lake hotel that began as a temperance hotel in 1872. But the owners added a dance hall, changed management, and became a "notorious resort." A murder-suicide in 1892 and a stabbing in 1895 were two events that contributed to that reputation. Another name and management change continued a more savory business until it burned in 1918.

After Fluvanna, the outlet begins taking the waters of the lake toward the south. The Chadakoin River, whose rapids gave life to the industries of Jamestown, continued through the business district to a second area of industry before it left the city. Falconer and Kennedy were both early sawmill sites along the river as it left the city and flowed toward the Mississippi River.

One early business was the lumber industry. The hills around Chautauqua Lake had forests of large trees. The lumber industry used the streams and lake to float logs to sawmills. Lumber was then made into immense rafts and floated down the river system to southern markets. Hardwoods supplied the local furniture factories. This continued for a number of years, and forest products are still coming out of the area's forests.

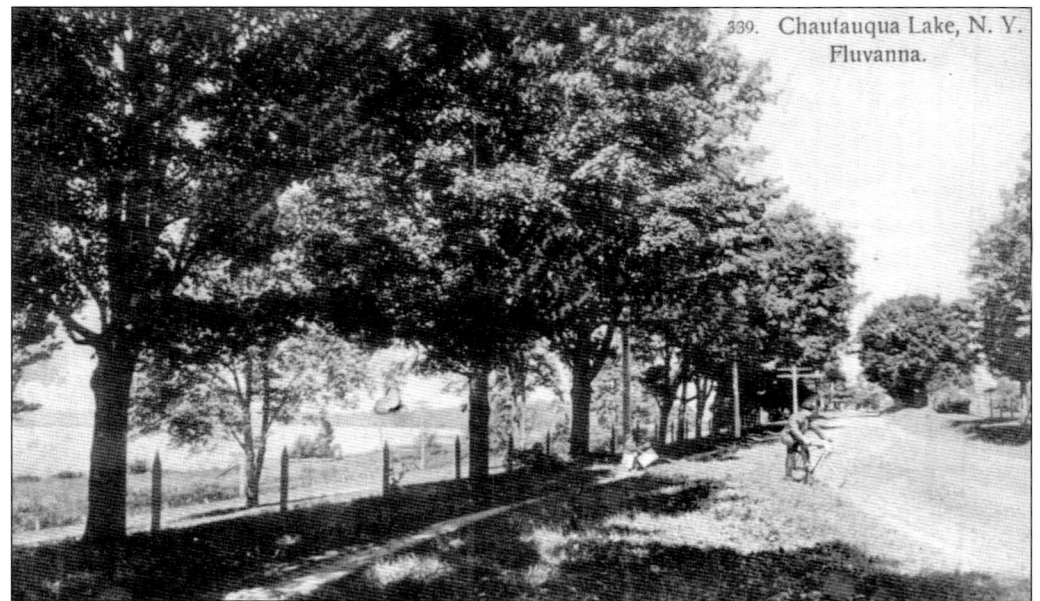

Fluvanna, on the lake's east side, is just above the outlet. The lake's earliest hotel was built here in 1836 by Samuel Whittemore, enticing big city dwellers to enjoy the healthful air at the higher altitude and setting the stage for tourism for two centuries. Fluvanna had large icehouses used to store quantities of lake ice harvested for the markets in large cities connected by rail and for local consumption.

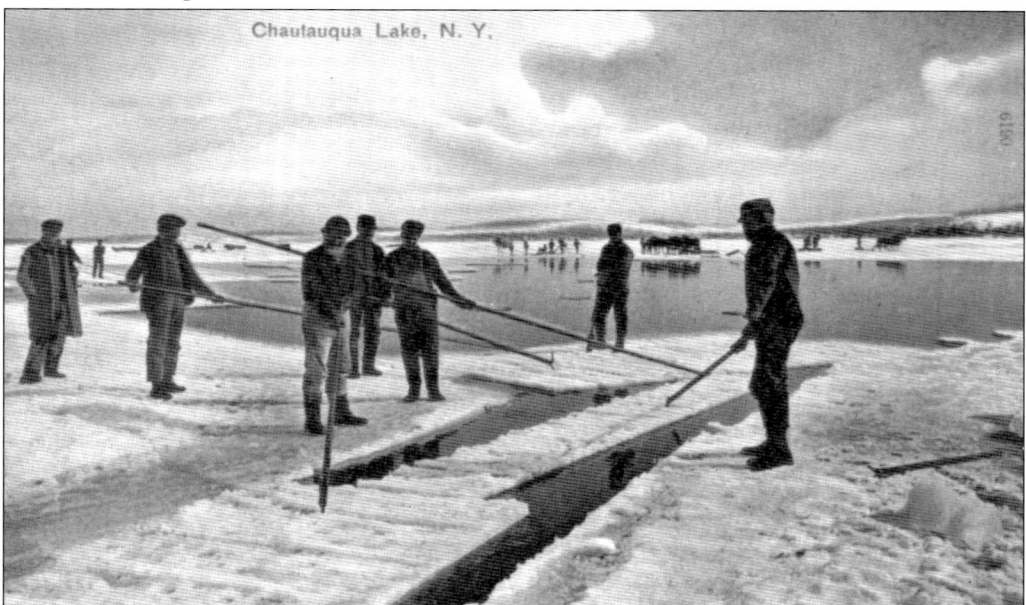

Activities on the lake continued during the winter. Ice-skating, ice-fishing, and ice-boating kept people busy as soon as the ice was thick enough. One day in 1899, more than 656 ice-fishing huts were counted on the lake. Pure Chautauqua Lake ice was in high demand during the late 1800s. Many icehouses stood along the lakeshore where ice harvesting employed hundreds supplying ice to large cities and railroads.

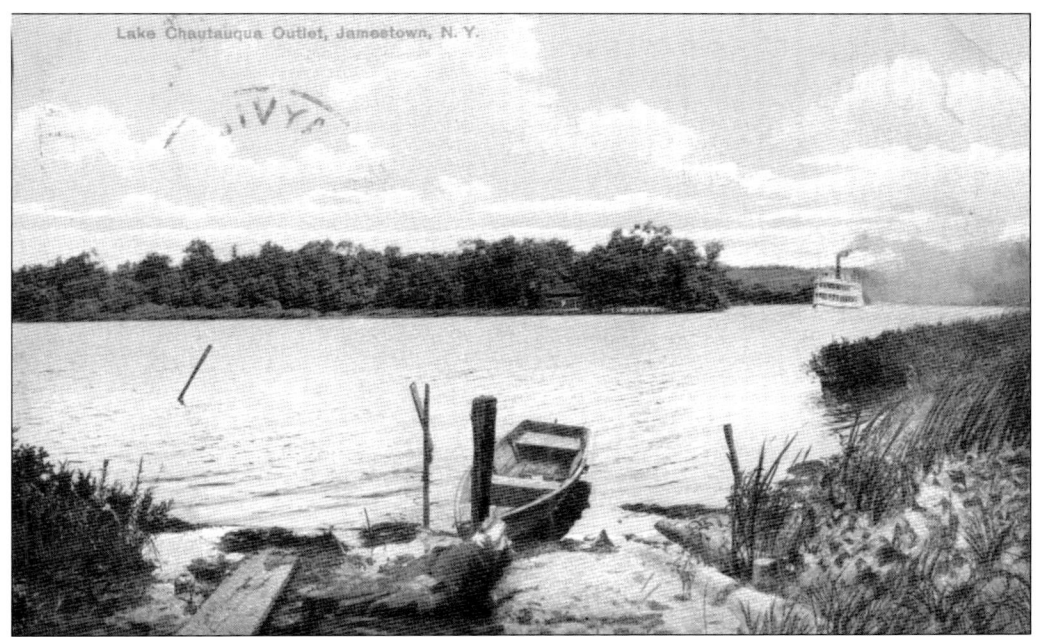

The outlet meanders for about 3 miles to the boat landing and continues through the city of Jamestown and town of Ellicott. For most of the trip to the boat landing, the shoreline has remained undeveloped and is a haven for wildlife. The steamers slowly maneuvered the nine bends through the outlet, taking about 30 minutes to make the journey. The rowboat allowed someone to slowly explore the shoreline, being careful when a steamer came by.

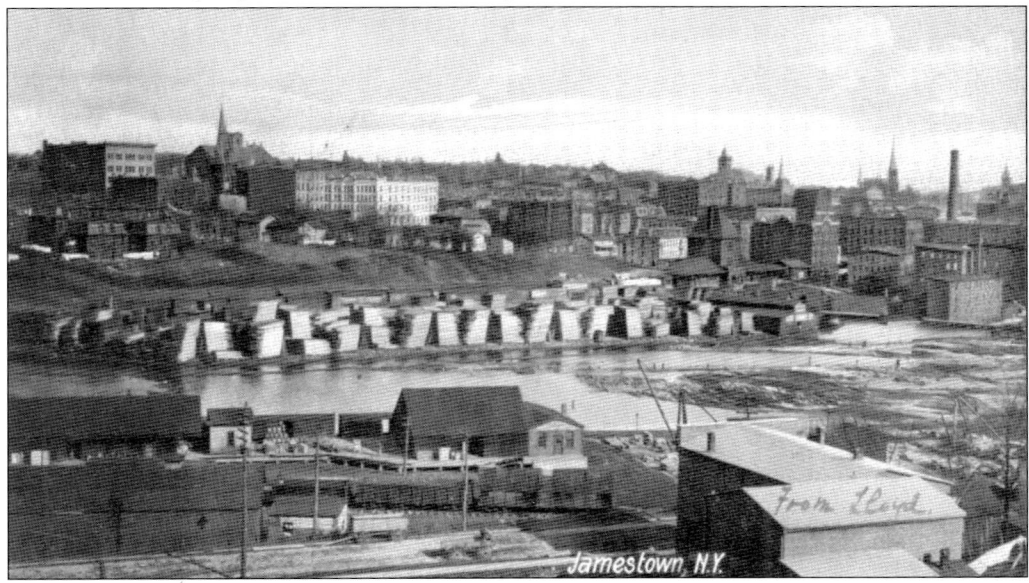

The outlet flows through the city of Jamestown, and it was a site of industrial activity in the past. This shows logs in the outlet and the sawn lumber piled along the shoreline ready to be turned into the furniture for which Jamestown became known throughout the world. Beyond the piled lumber is the railroad. Today the municipal light plant occupies the near side of the river.

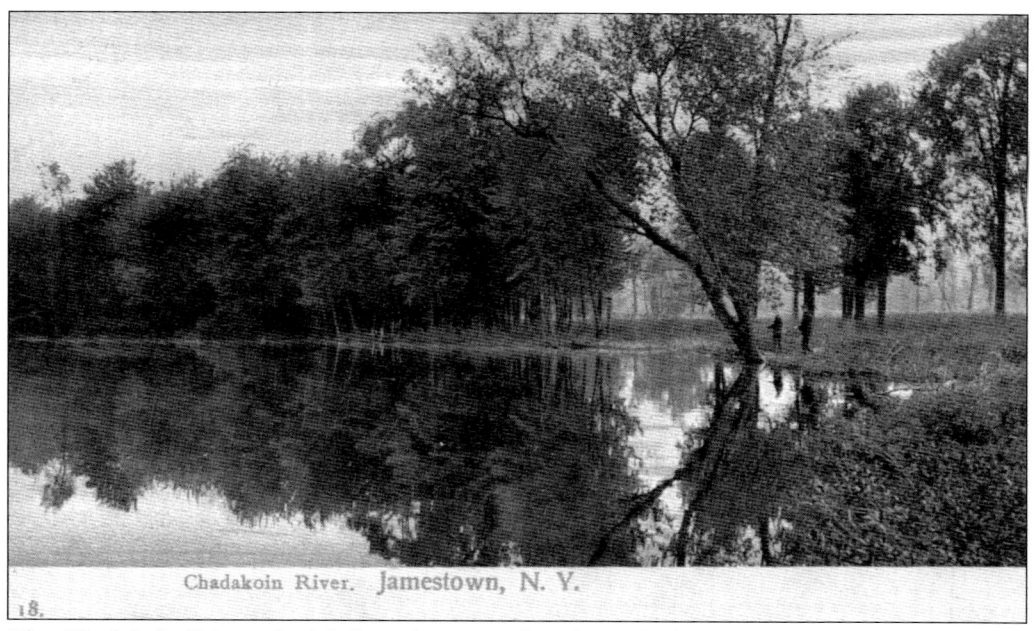

The Chadakoin River, the lake's outlet, meanders through the town of Ellicott until it joins the Cassadaga Creek as part of the Mississippi River system. The outlet divides the city of Jamestown and the town of Ellicott into two sections. To reach one section from the other, one must go through the city of Jamestown or cross the lake. The lake's elevation is 1,308 feet above sea level.

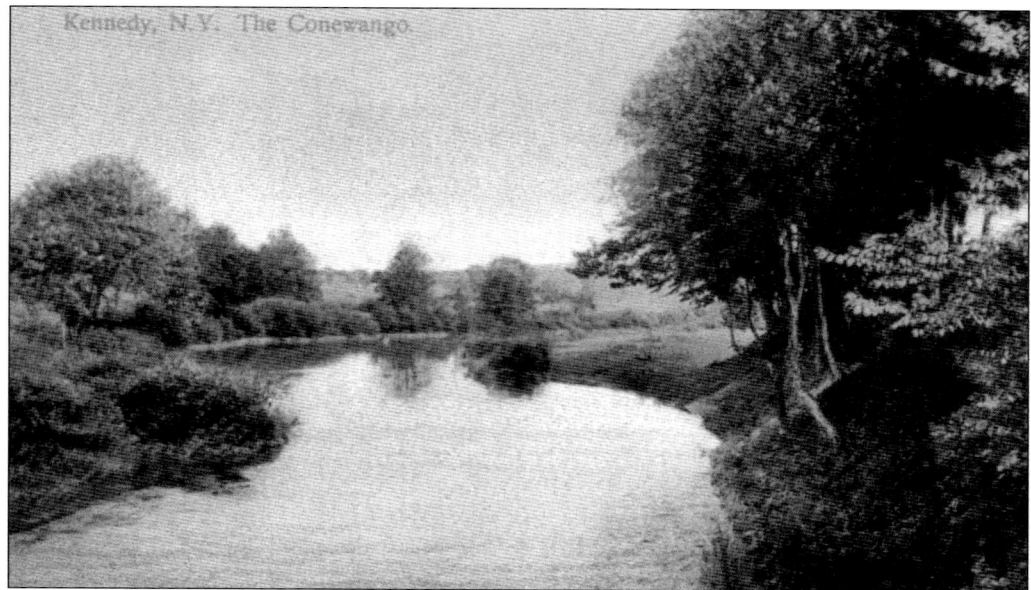

This is the Conewango Creek into which the Chadakoin River runs as it leaves the town of Ellicott. It then runs to the Allegany, Ohio, and Mississippi Rivers. This was the early route for the French to travel from their New France (Canada) settlements to their territory up river from New Orleans. With a portage from Lake Erie to the head of Chautauqua Lake, the journey could continue by water.

Seven
THE STEAMBOATS

Beginning in 1828 with the small steamer *Chautauque*, Chautauqua Lake ports and landings were visited by steamers delivering and picking up passengers and freight. The first steamboat docks were at Mayville, the county seat at the head of the lake; Jamestown, at the outlet of the lake; Fluvanna, above Jamestown on the east side of the lake; and Bemus Point, at the Narrows halfway along the lake.

Other landings developed as the large hotels and popular resort areas flourished in the late 1800s and early 1900s. Chautauqua Lake provided the water route for easy travel. Even the ice in winter was used for easier travel than the bad roads.

Some landings were scheduled stops; others were stops only if the white flag was flying. Trains arrived, bringing visitors that used the steamboats to get to their resort of choice along the lake.

Rival steamboat companies and rival captains made for a few exciting years with races to the docks to be first to pick up passengers, a few collisions with reprimands and license revocations from the Navigation Commissioners, and scheduled races to see which boat was faster. The purchase of one company by the other stopped the rivalry, and steamboat rides became calmer.

Dancing was an activity encouraged on the steamers by the addition of dance floors. The steamboat era was indeed an exciting time as passengers were moved from one resort to another along Chautauqua Lake.

Over the years, the largest steamboat was the *Nettie Fox*, which became the second *Jamestown*. It was 175 feet long with a beam of 31 feet. It was a stern-wheeler, looking much like a Mississippi River boat. Fire, which destroyed many of the steamers, claimed the *Jamestown* in 1892. The last steamer, the *City of Jamestown*, hung on until 1958, with the crew taking her out for a last run in 1959.

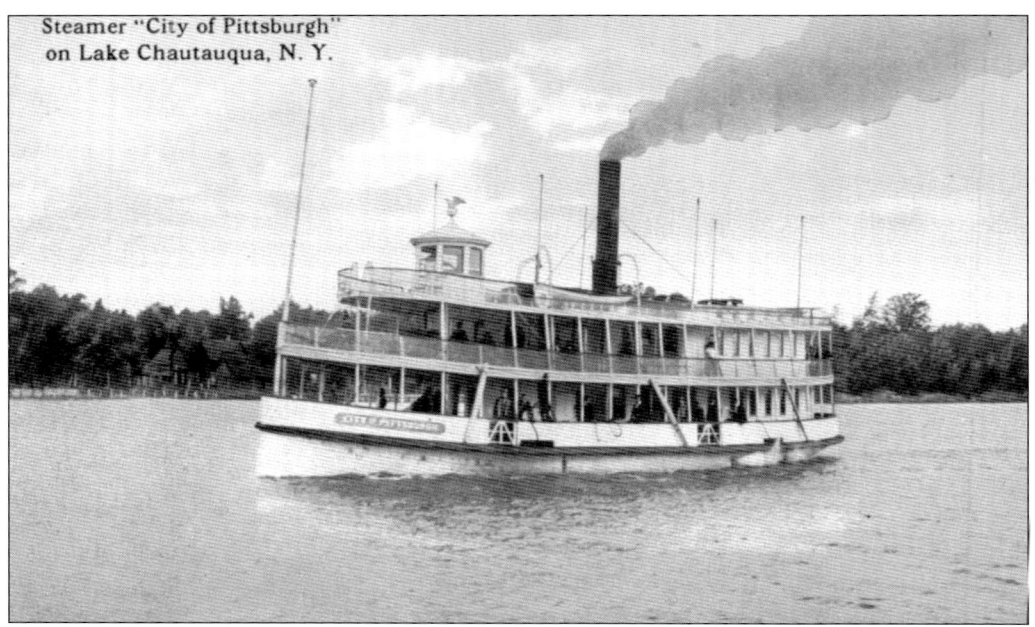

The oldest of the large "City of" steamers, the *City of Pittsburgh* began life in 1879 as the *W. B. Shattuc*. Built in Mayville, she was 100 feet long and had a beam of 19 feet. For the years 1883 to 1886, her name was *Minnehaha*. She then became the *W. B. Shattuc* again, and in 1892, her name was changed once more to the *City of Pittsburgh*, which she kept until her demise in 1929.

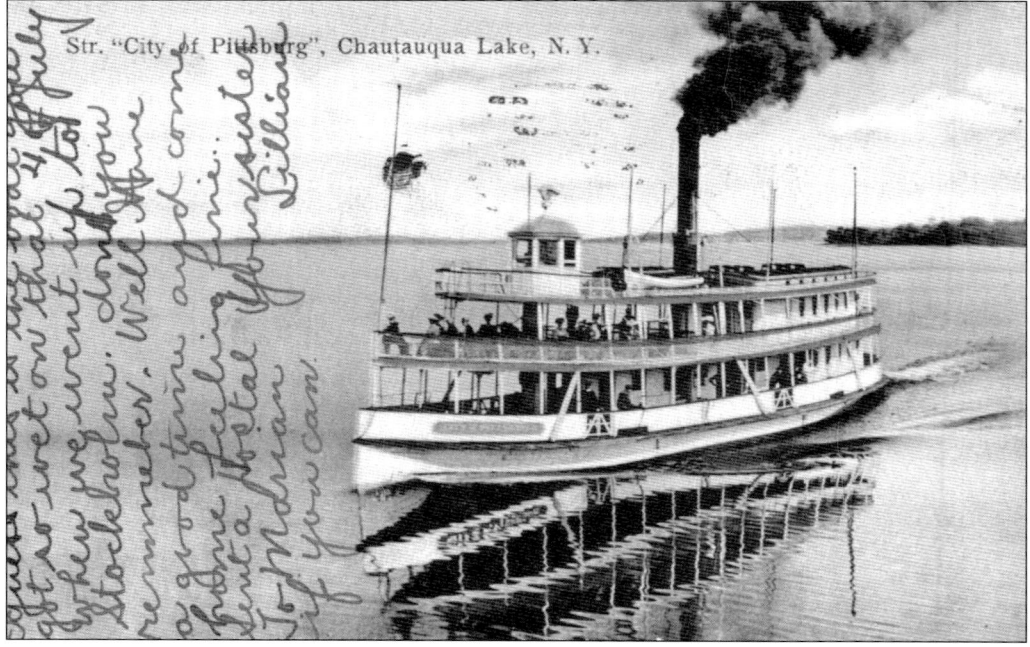

The *W. B. Shattuc*, built by Alfred Wilcox in Mayville, was run as a temperance boat for the first few years. The upper deck was clear for dancing. She sat very low in the water and was the only one of the large steamers to leave a two-wave wake. This caused small boats either a bumpy ride or an exciting time crossing the wake on purpose.

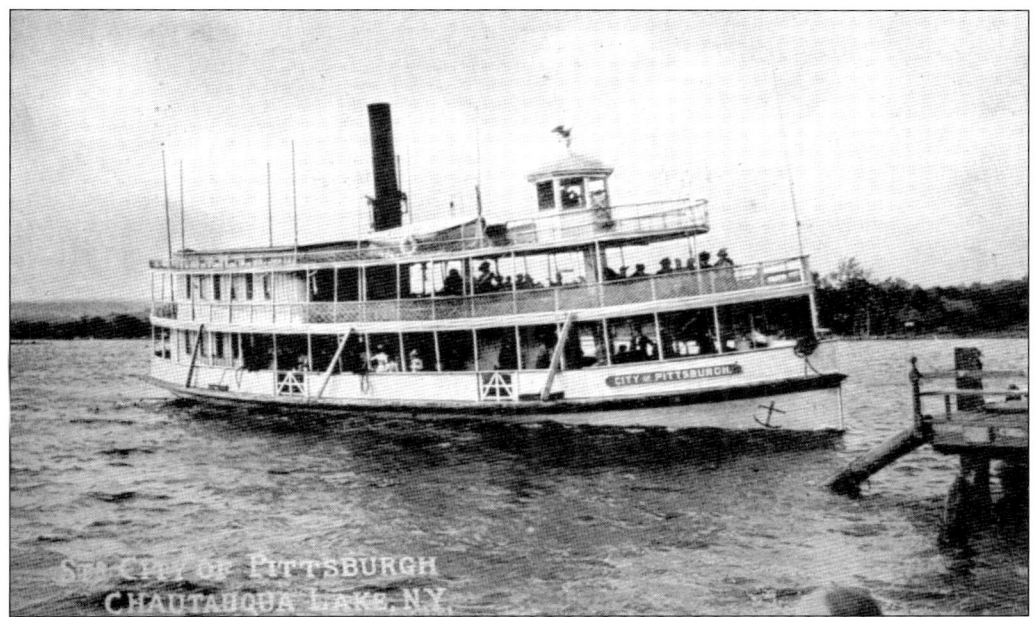

W. B. Shattuc was the season's earliest large steamer on the lake in the early 1880s. Still too cold for excursions, her trips were made to tow large rafts of logs from points along the lake to the boat landing, supplying logs to the sawmills in Jamestown. She was one of the last steamers off the lake in the fall, remaining available for excursion parties during September.

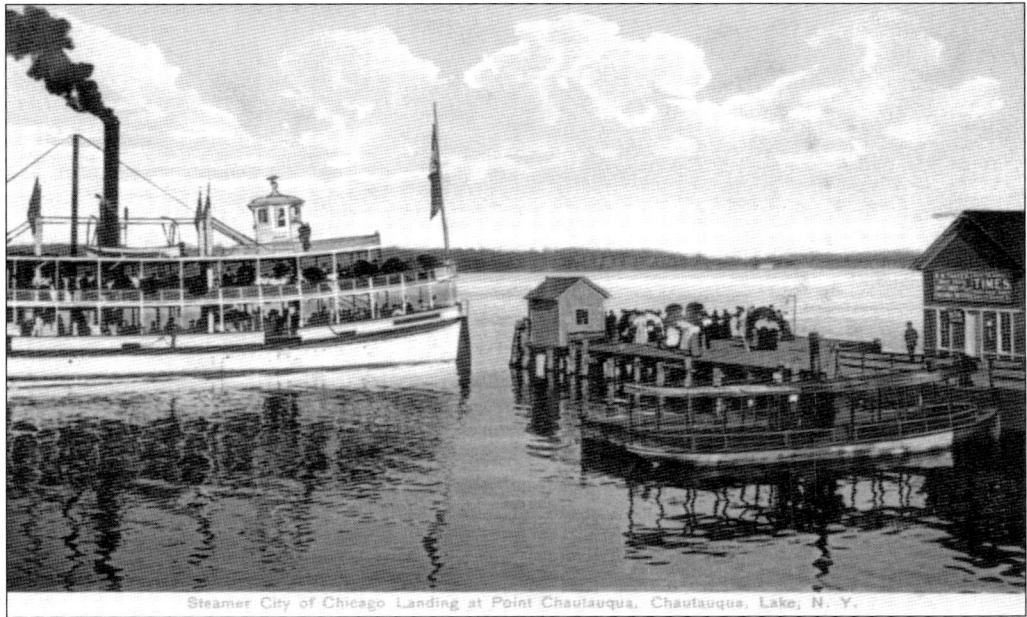

Built near Bemus Point by the Burroughs brothers of Mayville, launched in 1880 as the *J. A. Burch*, and renamed twice, the *City of Chicago* burned in November 1903 at Clifton's drydock. The cabins were fitted with costly wood and upholstered furniture, elegant carpets, plate-glass mirrors, and colored skylights. After the stern-wheeler *Jamestown* burned in 1892, the *City of Chicago* was the largest boat on the lake.

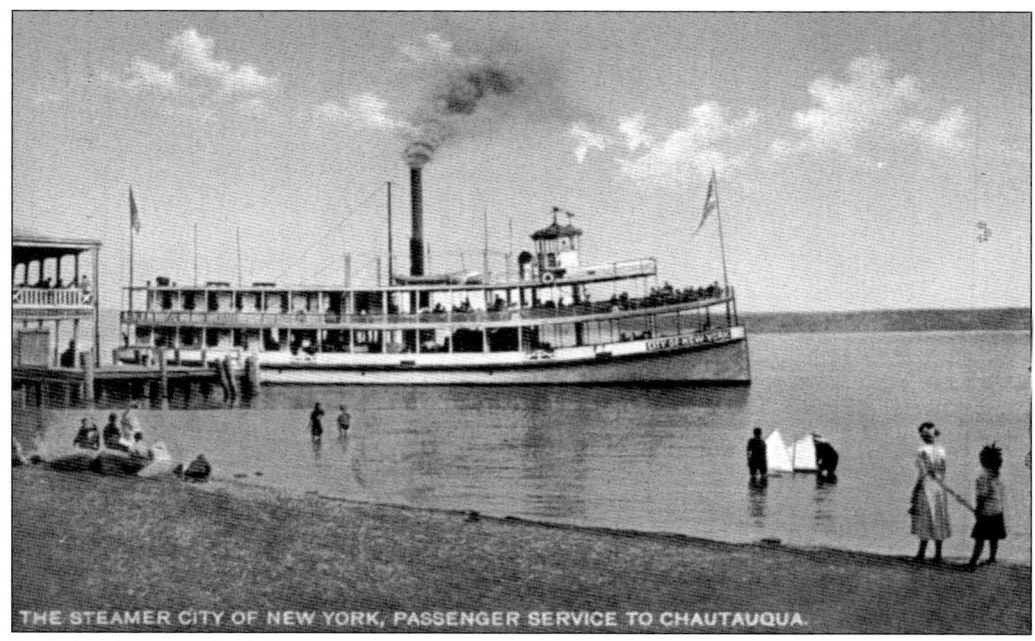

Built by the Wegefarth brothers of Mayville in 1880, the *City of New York* began as the *John F. Moulton*. She was renamed *Nightengale* in 1887, *Mohawk* in 1889, and became the *City of New York* in 1892. She was 132 feet long and had a beam of 26 feet. Rebuilt three times, she was the largest boat on the lake after the *City of Chicago* burned in 1903.

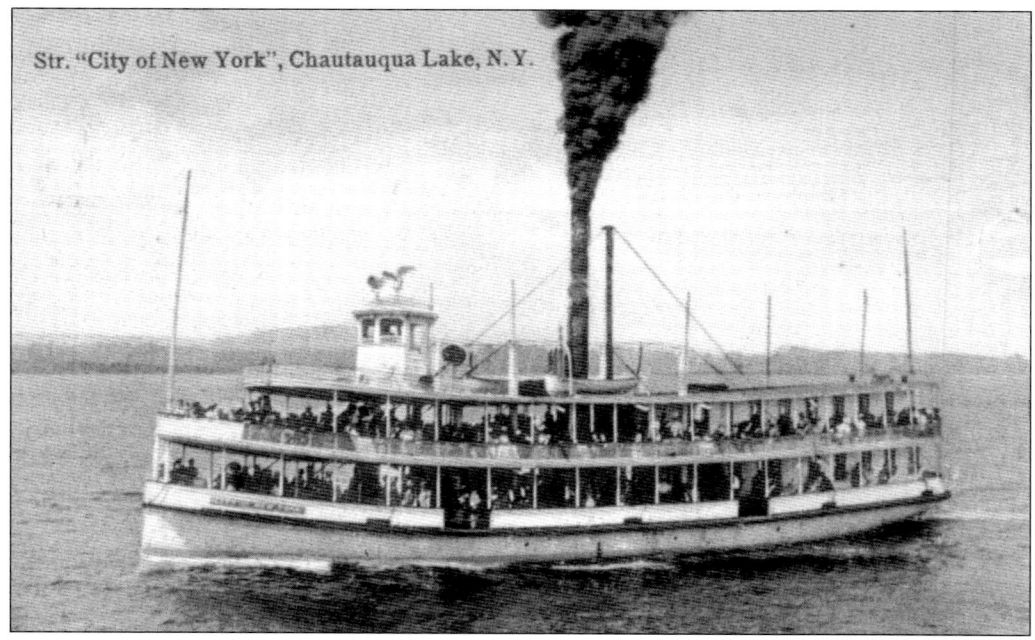

Because she was the largest boat after 1903, the *City of New York* took over the excursion business. Known as the picnic boat, for years she took many picnickers to Midway Park. Manufacturing companies from as far away as Ohio and Pennsylvania sponsored employee picnics. The families came by train and then the picnic steamboat to enjoy a day at the park. (Courtesy of MC.)

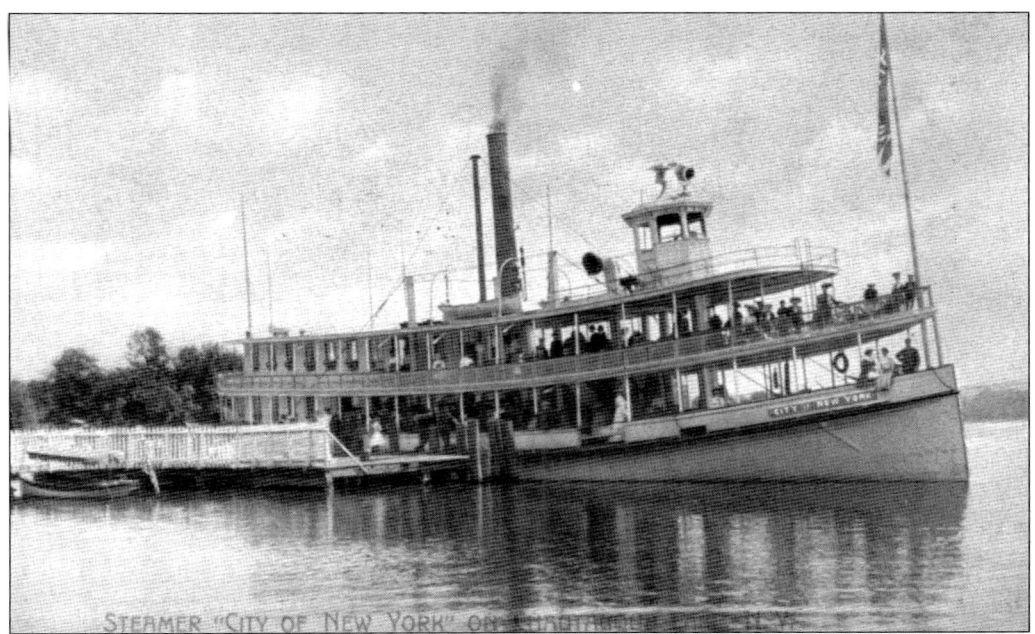

In 1904, the *City of New York* was outfitted with an electric light plant and a powerful searchlight. She was one of the last steamers to receive electric lights. The searchlight can be seen on top of the wheelhouse in front of the eagle. The searchlight is on the wheelhouse in all the *City of New York* postcards, thus they were all taken after 1904.

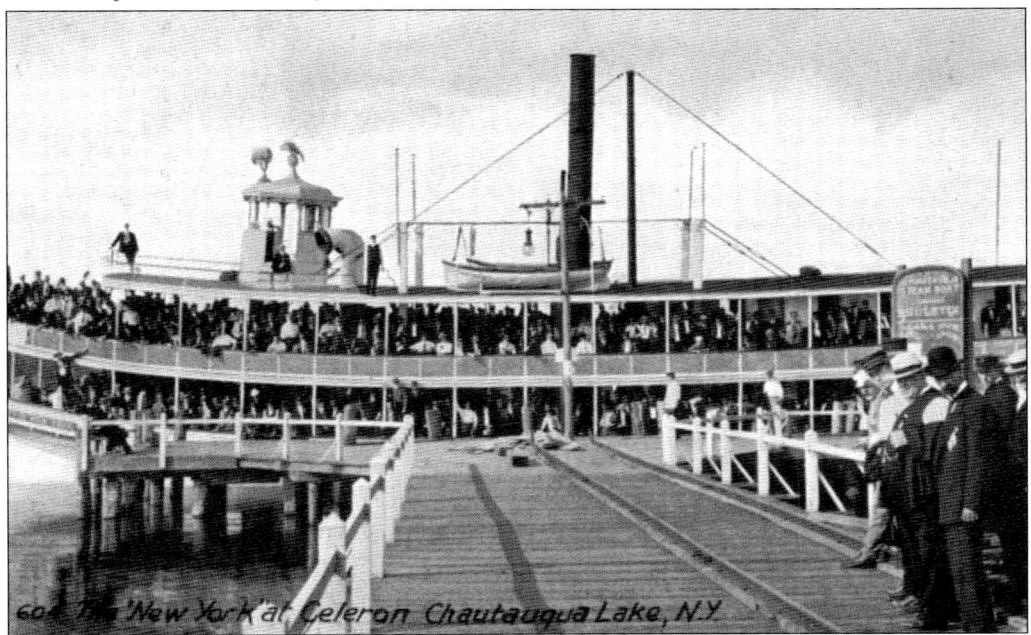

The *City of New York* was the only one of the six "City of" steamers that had a taller wheelhouse with two doors on each side. This made her very identifiable on the lake. The door on the side can be seen here as she docks at Celoron with a full load of passengers. It was at Celoron Park that she burned to the waterline on August 29, 1926.

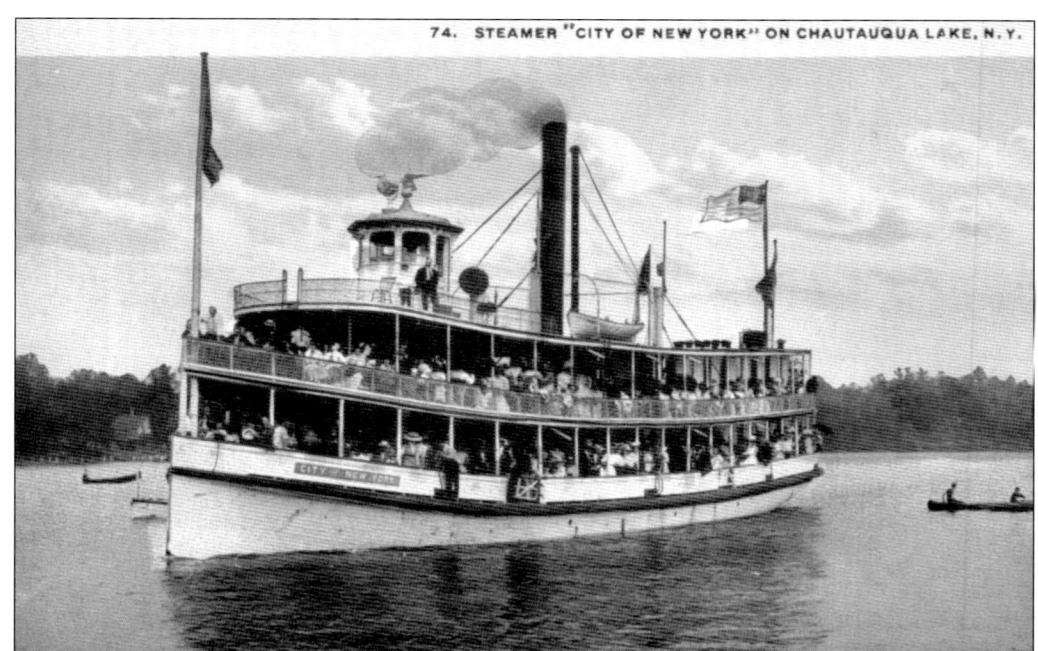

Known at the time as the steamer *John F. Moulton*, the *City of New York* struck and stunned a 35-pound pickerel with her wheel in the lake off Chautauqua. A fisherman killed the fish with his oar and earned $4 by selling it to the Chautauqua Meat Market. Steamers probably hit large fish more often, but this time a fisherman was near and the story made the local newspaper.

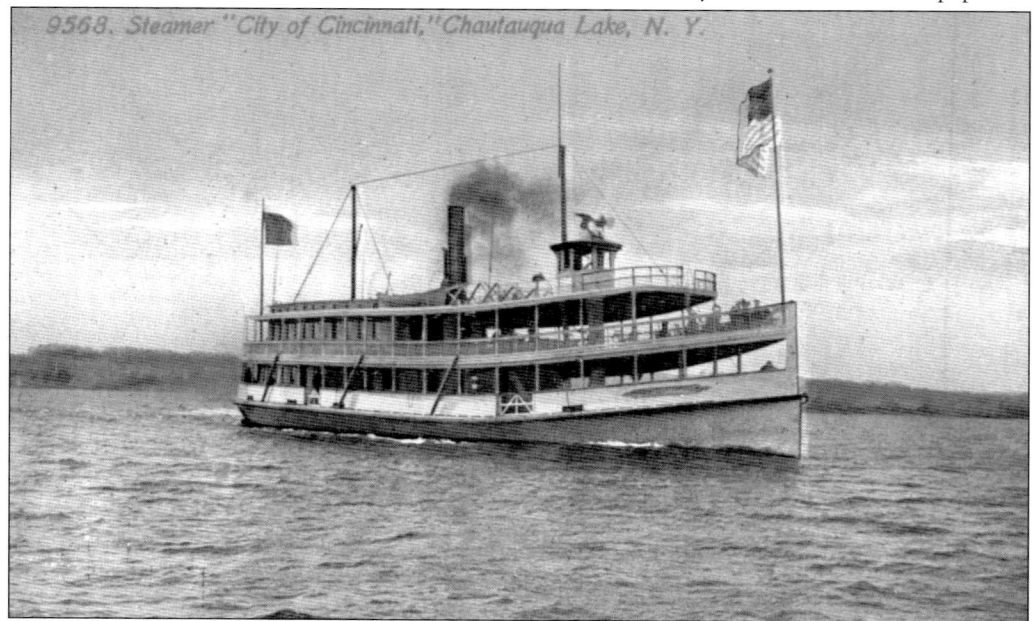

The Burroughs brothers of Mayville built the *City of Cincinnati* in 1882. She was 132 feet long with a 26-foot beam. During the 1880s, she was one the fastest ships on the lake and was involved in the rivalry with the other steamboats for position at docks and for passengers. This led to frightened passengers and reprimands by the navigation commissioners.

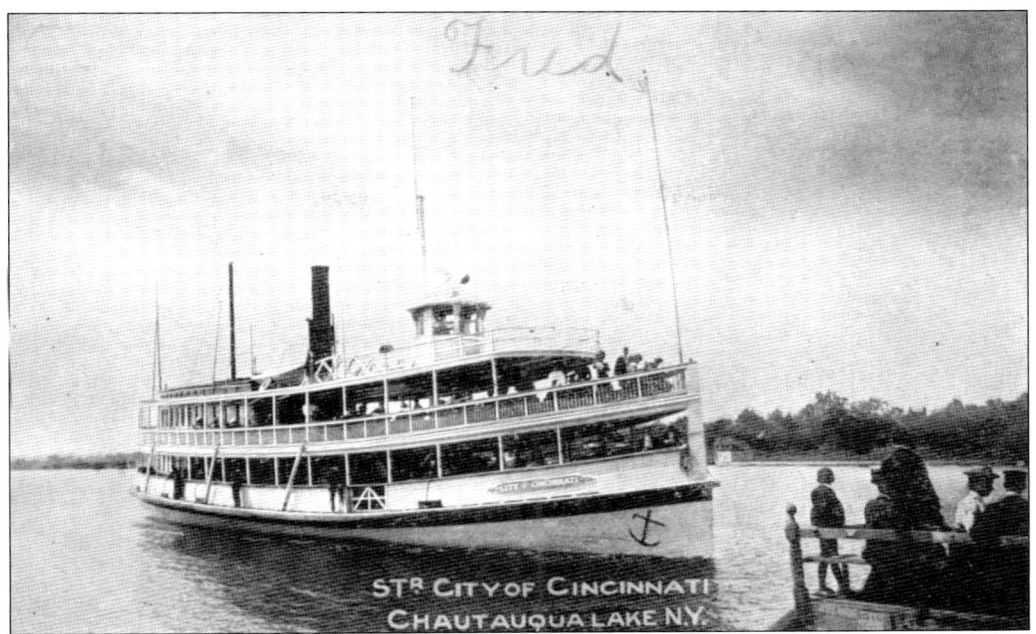

In the late 1880s, the *City of Cincinnati* was leased to the Red Stack Line and the rivalry ended. In 1890, she was once again run by the Burroughs brothers as one of the boats of the People's Line, known as the Black Stack Line. She was considered a deluxe boat and made of the best materials, just like the earlier *City of Chicago*, also built by the Burroughs brothers.

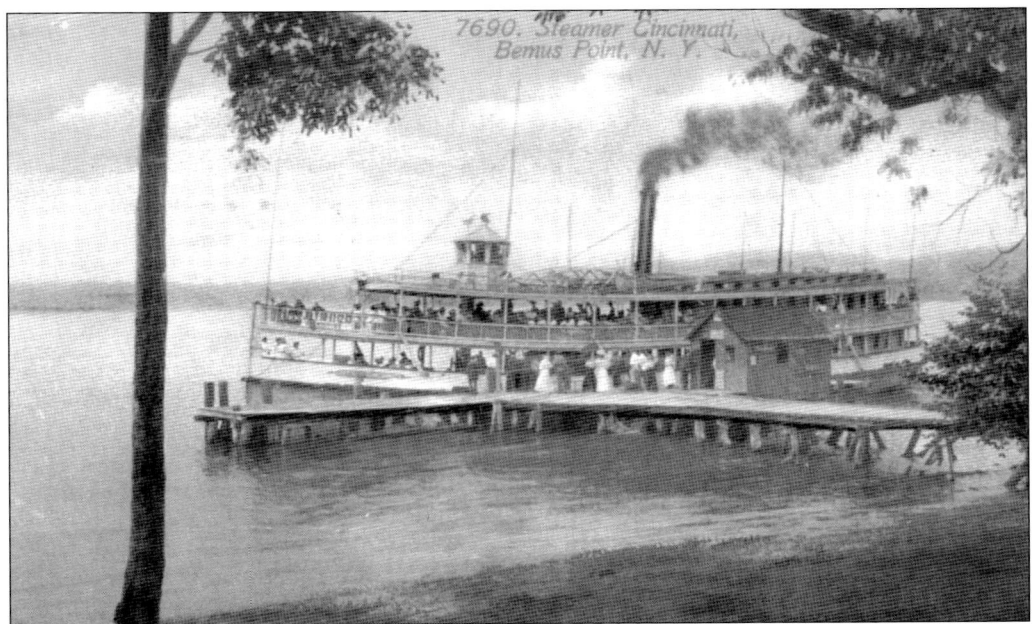

The homeport for the *City of Cincinnati* was Mayville, where she stayed the night. She made two daily runs to Celoron or Jamestown and back, plus an evening theater run to Celoron Park. After the 1927 season, she was parked in a channel off the outlet between Clifton and the boat landing. She was used as living quarters until about two years before she burned in 1938.

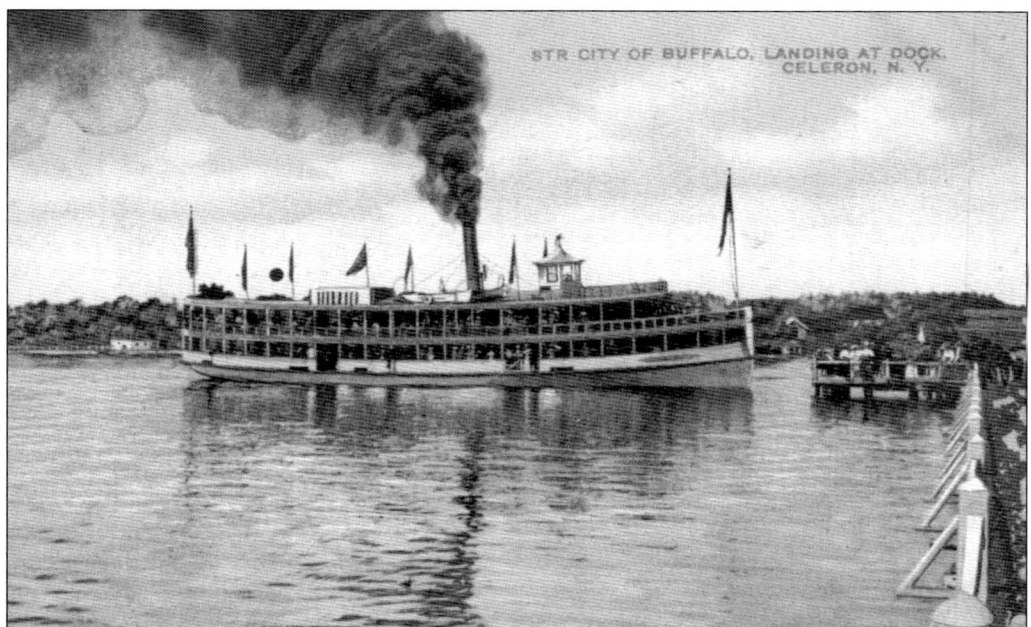

Another Burroughs brothers–built boat, the *City of Buffalo* was launched in 1890 and had no other names. The new boat was steel, with the only wood being the planking of the hull below the water's edge and the deck floors. She was the first steamboat to be lit with electric lights. In 1901, she was provided with a powerful searchlight.

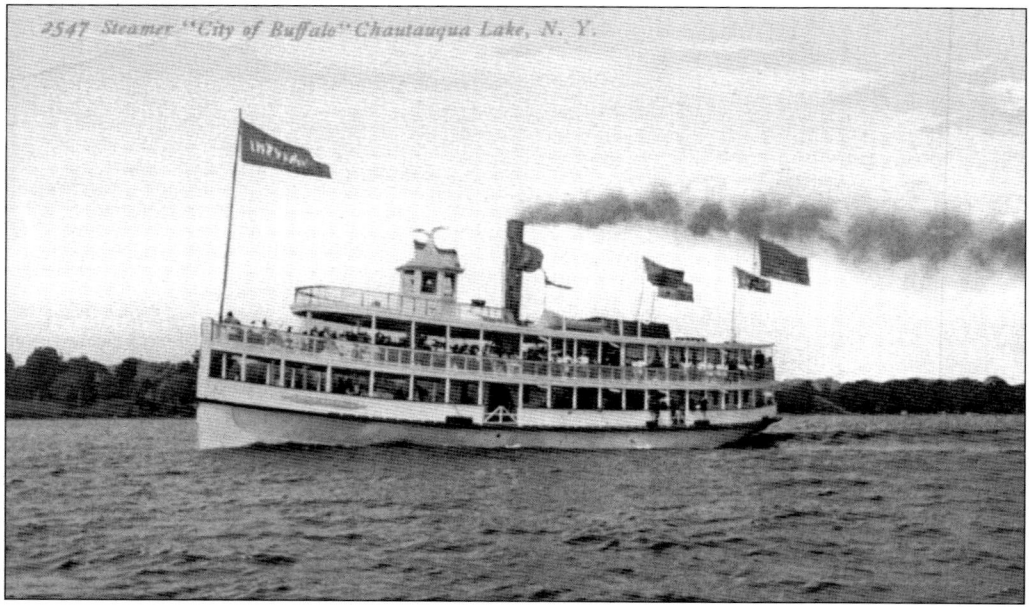

The *City of Buffalo* continued her regular schedule from Jamestown for most of the seasons through 1925. Being the next to the last steamer on the lake, she was available for excursions after the season schedule concluded on September 1927. About 25,000 people had ridden the steamer during that season. The 1928 season found a dance floor on the second deck. The steamer did not operate in 1929.

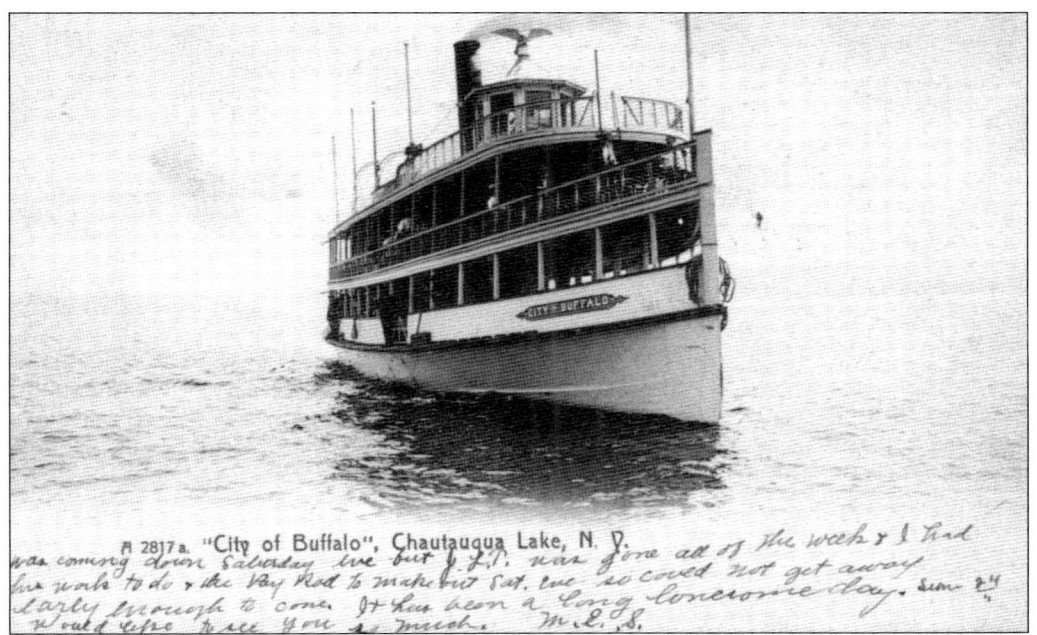

In 1900, the *City of Buffalo* was rebuilt and received a new boiler and engine. Subsequent violent shaking saw her popularity plummet. One day, as a result of the violent shaking from the engine, the eagle on the top of the wheelhouse took flight to the deck. The next year, the deck was braced and the boat ran as smoothly as before the new engine. She regained her popularity.

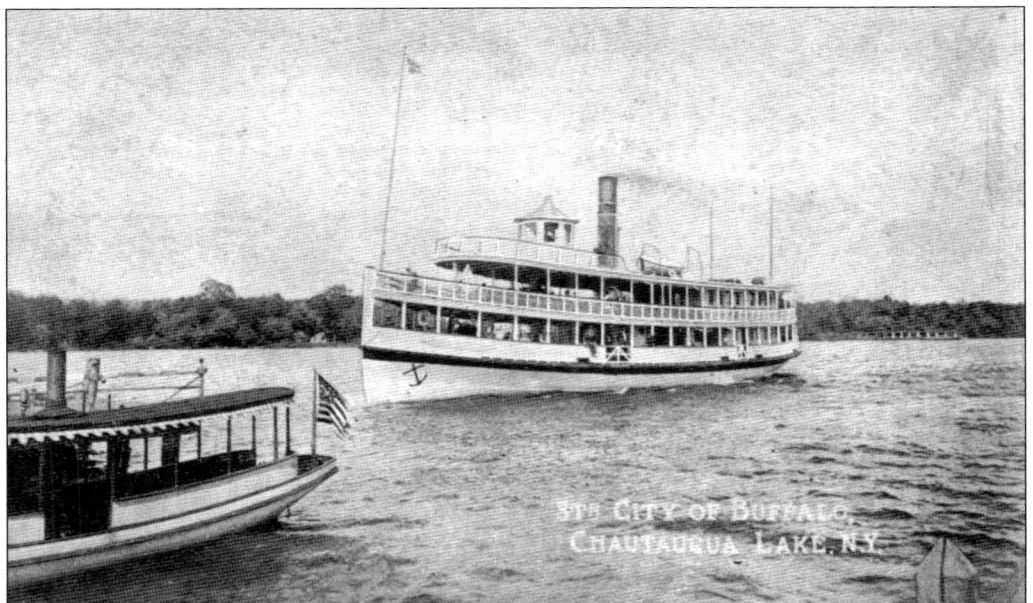

Because of low water, the towing of *City of Buffalo* to a point opposite Celoron Park was a hazardous journey up the outlet. Despite protests against the destruction of the steamer, the plans for the Labor Day burning continued. Bombs in the hold and flammable liquids saturating the decks guaranteed a fiery spectacle on Labor Day night in 1929. The hull was towed above Long Point and sunk in deep water.

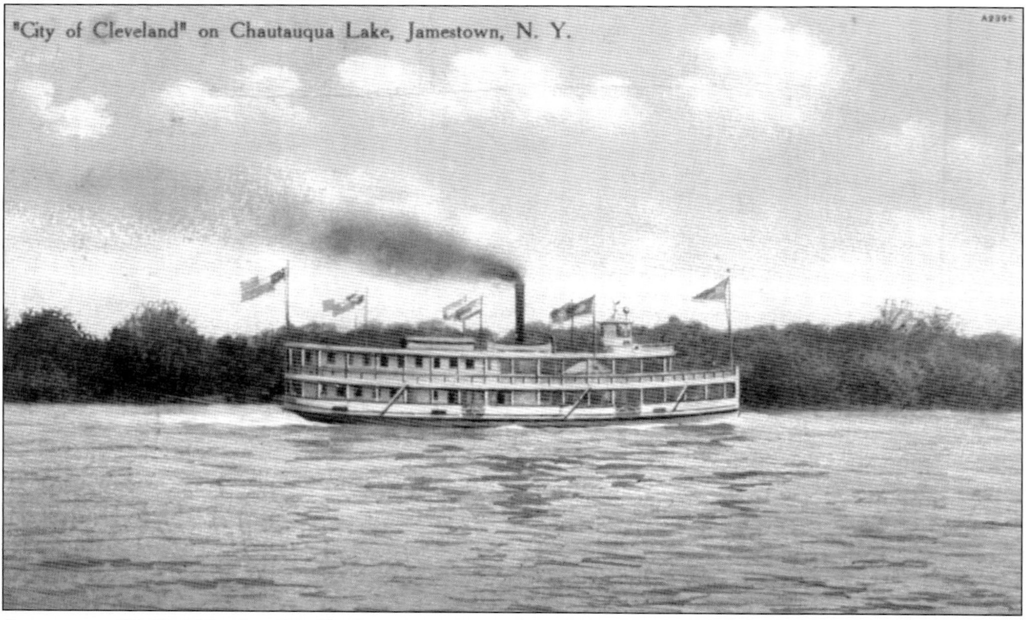

"City of Cleveland" on Chautauqua Lake, Jamestown, N. Y.

At a cost of $65,000, the *W. C. Rinearson*, a steel-hulled steamboat, was launched in June 1891. Hull sections were shipped from Buffalo and joined in Jamestown. The next year, she was renamed the *City of Cleveland*. She was the first boat on the lake and last boat off the lake each season. Her homeport was Mayville.

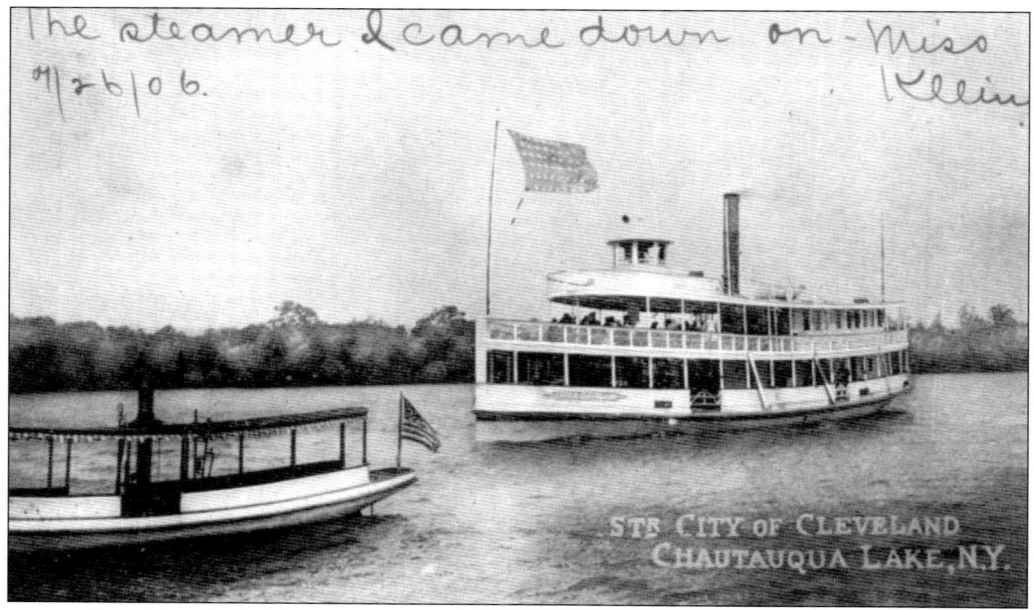

In 1901, the *City of Cleveland* was wired for electric lights. Equipped with steam heat in the pilothouse and cabin, and now lit with electricity, the *City of Cleveland* continued into November with winter work. On November 20, 1903, there was 1 foot of snow in Mayville when she arrived. That was the last ice trip made since the trolley line was operating to Mayville the next year.

www.arcadiapublishing.com

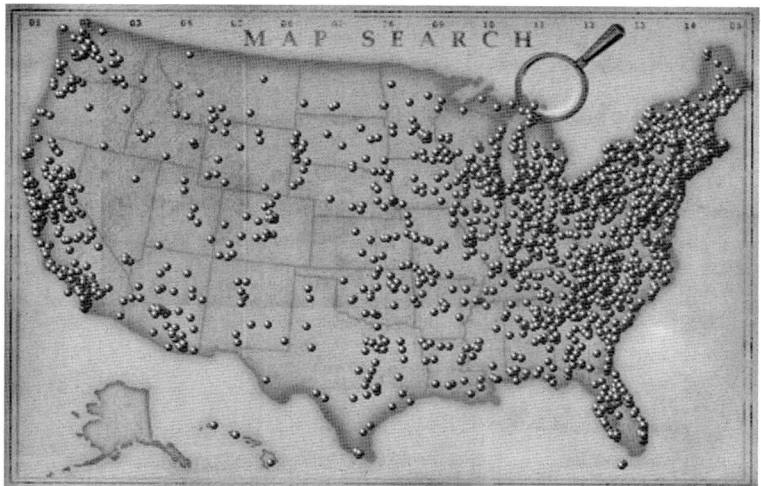

Discover books about the town where you grew up, the cities where your friends and families live, the town where your parents met, or even that retirement spot you've been dreaming about. Our Web site provides history lovers with exclusive deals, advanced notification about new titles, e-mail alerts of author events, and much more.

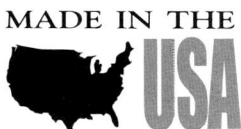

Arcadia Publishing, the leading local history publisher in the United States, is committed to making history accessible and meaningful through publishing books that celebrate and preserve the heritage of America's people and places. Consistent with our mission to preserve history on a local level, this book was printed in South Carolina on American-made paper and manufactured entirely in the United States.

This book carries the accredited Forest Stewardship Council (FSC) label and is printed on 100 percent FSC-certified paper. Products carrying the FSC label are independently certified to assure consumers that they come from forests that are managed to meet the social, economic, and ecological needs of present and future generations.

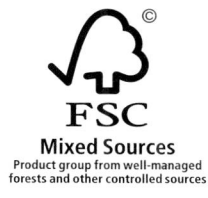

FSC
Mixed Sources
Product group from well-managed forests and other controlled sources

Cert no. SW-COC-001530
www.fsc.org
© 1996 Forest Stewardship Council

Find Your Place in History.

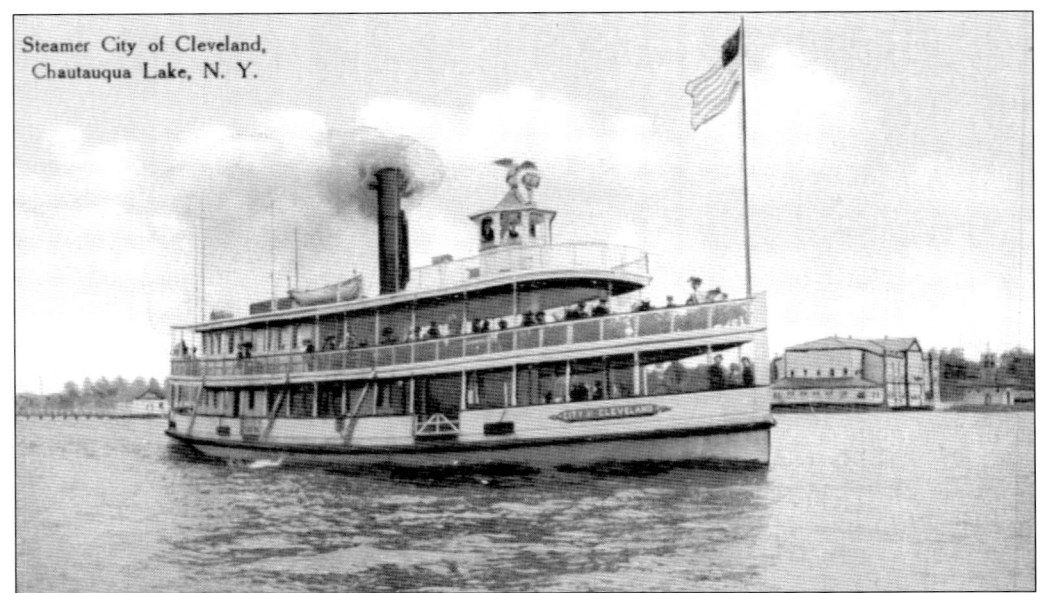

In 1931, the *City of Cleveland* underwent repairs, got a new steel hull, and was renamed the *City of Jamestown*. The last large steamer on the lake after 1928, she was used for ferry service between Chautauqua, Point Chautauqua, and Mayville until demand for charters pulled her away. The small steamer *Mayville* continued the ferry service. The *City of Jamestown* was idle in 1935 but saw some service through 1958.

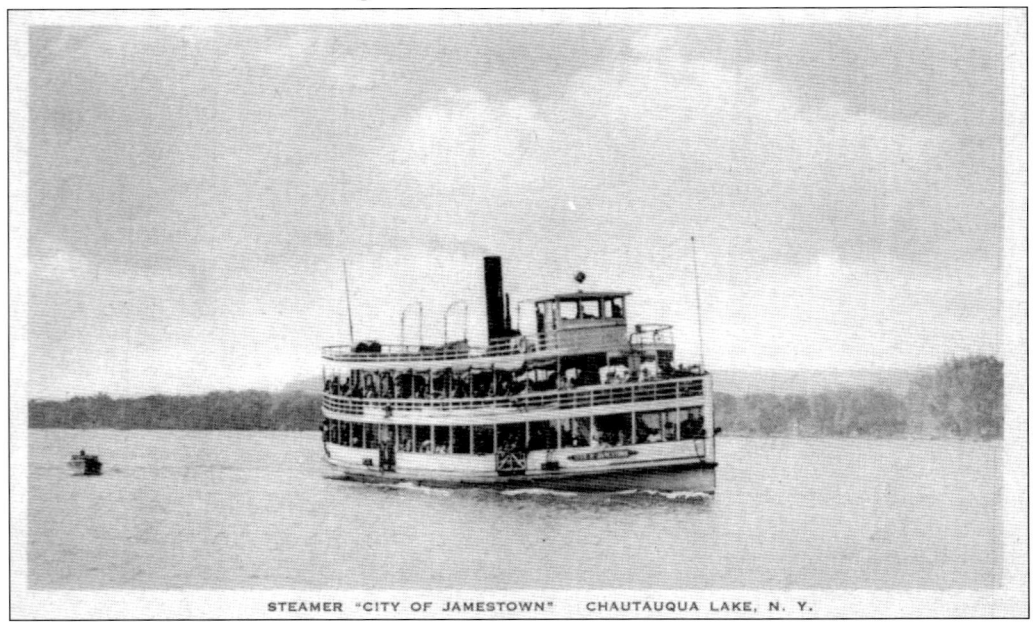

In 1950, the *City of Jamestown* navigated an ice-free Chautauqua Lake on January 30. The *Col. William Phillips* had last done that on New Years Day 1876. Gas rationing of World War II rescued the *City of Jamestown*, which continued to be used for charters through 1958. Rebuilding plans failed as she was moved about the boat landing from 1960 to 1963 and then disappeared into memories.